T0316832

Technological Retrogression

Technological Retrogression

A Schumpeterian Interpretation of Modernization in Reverse

Sylvi B. Endresen

Foreword by
Erik S. Reinert

ANTHEM PRESS

Anthem Press
An imprint of Wimbledon Publishing Company
www.anthempress.com

This edition first published in UK and USA 2021
by ANTHEM PRESS
75–76 Blackfriars Road, London SE1 8HA, UK
or PO Box 9779, London SW19 7ZG, UK
and
244 Madison Ave #116, New York, NY 10016, USA

Copyright © Sylvi B. Endresen 2021

The author asserts the moral right to be identified as the author of this work.

All rights reserved. Without limiting the rights under copyright reserved above,
no part of this publication may be reproduced, stored or introduced into
a retrieval system, or transmitted, in any form or by any means
(electronic, mechanical, photocopying, recording or otherwise),
without the prior written permission of both the copyright
owner and the above publisher of this book.

British Library Cataloguing-in-Publication Data
A catalogue record for this book is available from the British Library.

Library of Congress Control Number: 2021937605

ISBN-13: 978-1-78527-713-9 (Hbk)
ISBN-10: 1-78527-713-8 (Hbk)

Cover image: Janus (Digital Media) by Andrey Kokorin

This title is also available as an e-book.

In memory of Marius Melgård

The privileged and the needy
share a common faith
in the power of technology
to abolish misery.

Denis Goulet

CONTENTS

FIGURES

FOREWORD

Sylvi Endresen's book raises key issues that were once high on the agenda of important economists who are considered forefathers of modern theory. She shows extreme, but entirely logical, real consequences of diminishing marginal returns. Even though he did not refer to this term, diminishing returns underlies the pessimism in Reverend Malthus' 1798 book *An Essay on the Principles of Population*. Malthus argued that population grows geometrically while food production increases arithmetically, resulting in a population outgrowing its food supply. Famous for his 1817 *Principles of Economics*, David Ricardo explained that as more land is cultivated, farmers would have to start using less productive land: the geographical extension of production would cause *diminishing returns* as less productive land was put into use. Malthus and Ricardo's ideas about limited food production stem from the same diminishing returns Sylvi Endresen analyses in the present book.

In 1848 John Stuart Mill gave this same factor even more importance. Under the heading 'On the Law of the Increase of Production from Land', he discusses the 'limiting principle': that 'doubling labor does not double production'. Mill complains that this 'limiting principle' is not sufficiently considered, writing,

> I apprehend this to be not only an error, but the most serious one, to be found in the whole field of political economy. The question is more important and fundamental than any other; it involves the whole subject of the causes of poverty; […] and unless this matter be thoroughly understood, it is to no purpose proceeding any further in our inquiry.

Diminishing returns made economics into a 'dismal science'.

Endresen brings the arguments of Mill and Ricardo one important step further. In the absence of alternative labour markets, diminishing returns – for example, in fisheries – will lead not only to diminishing income to the workers but also to technological retrogression. Fishing fleets that once had used sailing boats had been motorized as the fishermen could afford outboard engines.

With fish stocks being depleted, these fishermen could no longer afford outboard engines and gasoline. Over the years the art of sailing had been unlearned, so the fishermen went from outboard engines to rowing boats. This is the kind of technological retrogression this book is about.

Almost 100 years after Malthus, Alfred Marshall – the founder of neoclassical economics – in his 1890 textbook *Principles of Economics* describes the huge impact of diminishing returns: 'This tendency to Diminishing Returns was the cause of Abraham's parting from Lot, and of most of the migrations of which history tells.' In an attempt to show us the age of this fundamental insight, Marshall refers to the Bible's Genesis 13:6: 'And the land was not able to bear them that they might dwell together; for their substance was great so they could not dwell together.'

In this sense there are biblical proportions of the poverty-producing mechanisms in this book. Endresen shows us extreme consequences of theories that have long been recognized. In fact already in 1613 Italian economist Antonio Serra built a theory of uneven development based on the dichotomy of increasing versus diminishing returns. The importance of her analysis was evident already in her 1994 PhD thesis at the University of Oslo, where I had the pleasure of being an opponent. I am now very pleased to see Sylvi's arguments fully spelled out in this book.

In its original form this phenomenon of diminishing returns is observed when one factor of production is limited by nature: in agriculture, mining and fisheries. Of course, if a factory decided not to increase its production area when demand grew, we would observe the same phenomenon. But in manufacturing and services additional space is normally available in the same quality as the space previously used. Not so when nature has limited the supply of high-quality arable land, of rich mineral ores and of fish.

The phenomenon of diminishing returns has been compared to a 'flexible wall'; you do not meet it head-on immediately but feel the effect gradually. In a diversified economy the problem tends to solve itself, high wages will make it difficult to move into diminishing returns activities because the marginal cost of the product will also tend to raise. So the problems are normally felt seriously only in situations – as in this book – when resource monoculture dominates the economy of a region or nation. In fact Australians understood very well that they had a 'comparative advantage' in rearing sheep, but they created an industrial policy because they understood that if herding sheep was their only economic activity, they would gradually be rearing sheep on more and more marginal land. One way to stop this gradual movement into more marginal land was to create an industrial sector with a relatively high level of wages. This wage level in the same national labour market would prevent sheep-rearing from being profitable on land unsuited for this activity.

Today we find industries characterized by zero marginal costs. These represent the antithesis of the diminishing returns/technological retrogression mechanisms described in this book. Microsoft's 'production costs' for adding one more customer are virtually zero. Such industries easily produce virtual monopolies.

Particularly since the 1989 Fall of the Berlin Wall the 1817 trade theory of David Ricardo has become much more influential than it ever was. By not distinguishing qualitatively between economic activities – by modelling the world on qualitatively identical labour hours as the only input – Ricardo's theory gave an illusion of a market that produced economic harmony. In 1997 this theorem saw its final ideological victory when the WTO director-general, Renato Ruggiero, declared that we should unleash '*the borderless economy's potential to equalize relations among countries and regions*' (my emphasis).

Sylvi Endresen shows us why this assertion is fundamentally flawed: specializing in the 'wrong' economic activity may mean specializing not only in being poor but also in exploiting the environment to its limits. The answers to the dilemmas in this book are found in Alfred Marshall's 1890 textbook referred to and in the Australian example referred to above: 'subsidize manufacturing industry' said Marshall, the founder of neoclassical economics. This is the same economic policy that John Stuart Mill recommended in 1848 as 'infant industry protection'. It is a protection that can be removed when the 'infant' has grown up. In a country where industry and exploitation of natural resources coexist, the sustainability problems raised in this book are much easier to overcome than if the whole country is based on exploiting resources subject to diminishing returns only – be they in agriculture, mining or fisheries.

19 April 2021
Erik S. Reinert

ACKNOWLEDGEMENTS

First and foremost, I would like to express my sincere gratitude to my mentor, Erik S. Reinert. Thank you for guided tours through many misty landscapes of economic theory. Your book *International Trade and the Economic Mechanisms of Underdevelopment* holds many of the keys to the understanding of technological retrogression.

To the fisherfolk of Sri Lanka and Malaysia, and the many interpreters of language and culture I met with, my heartfelt thanks. Without your help, there would not have been any theory of technological retrogression.

Thanks also to the funders of the empirical research in Sri Lanka and Malaysia: the Norwegian Research Council. I am also grateful to the Department of Sociology and Human Geography at the University of Oslo for funding the Russian pilot study and the preparation of the manuscript for publication.

To the editors of Anthem, especially Megan Greiving, thank you for your professional guidance and help throughout this process.

I am indebted to Olga Tkach and Elena Bogdanova; thank you both for introducing me to the context and for collecting and analysing cases of technological retrogression in post-Soviet Russia. Thanks also to Olga Papalexiou for our discussions on Russian agriculture, and the work with abbreviating the empirical chapters. Thank you Anja Sletteland for checking references and correcting mistakes. Furthermore, graphic designer Marit Heggenhougen has patiently improved my figures, and illustrator Andrey Korokin allowed the use of his drawing of Janus on the cover. Thank you so much!

Furthermore, I would like to express my thanks to anonymous reviewers of this manuscript for their mix of enthusiasm and confusion which inspired me to present the arguments more precisely.

To my family I am forever grateful for support during this seemingly endless project; thank you Torodd, Lars, Therese, Alexander, Tina and Anders. You're simply the best!

PREFACE: THE BOOK WITHIN THIS BOOK

The major purpose of this book is to formulate a theory of technological retrogression. To do so, I make use of the experiences of the fisherfolk of Malaysia and Sri Lanka during the historical periods when fisheries were modernized. The research was undertaken for the purpose of my PhD dissertation (1995). The theory of technological retrogression is thus constructed from 'scratch': primary data at micro level, collected during long fieldworks. To explain the puzzling fact that some fishermen turned their back to modern technology, the standard explanation of technological change had to be reconstructed. This demanded a new empirical approach – the work history method; a sample of fishermen's technological choices over time were noted, as were their justifications for the choices.

The reconstruction of technological change at individual and village levels uncovered technological retrogression, producers' choice of technologies which lower labour productivity. The fieldworks undertaken and minutely described, I turned to the task of explaining the findings. It brought me on a seemingly endless journey to find 'The Book' where the phenomenon of technological retrogression was spelled out. To make a long story short, in the end I had to overcome my inbuilt reverence for theory and theorists and accept that I had to formulate my own. Still, today, 'technological retrogression' is an under-researched concept, finding only 1,460 Google hits. A more generic concept, 'primitivization', gets 24,000 hits.

I identified technological retrogression in two Third World capitalist countries, late in the twentieth century. To explain the phenomenon, I analysed how major theorists at the time (and times bygone) would have explained the phenomenon of technological retrogression if they had recognized the process. I was looking for their understanding of the confusing state of technological heterogeneity, the period where old meets new. What could be learned from modernization theorists' teleological belief in an end state of modern bliss? And from neo-Marxists' and dependency theorists' quarrelsome efforts at understanding the nature of capitalism in the Third World? In a sense, I 'extrapolated' these theories. I came up with the production system approach, bridging the gap between grand theory and the empirical level. The experiences of the fisherfolk could thus be linked to general socio-economic phenomena and to Marx's idea of different modes of production.

The content so far described is *the book within this book*: my dissertation is reproduced almost unchanged in Chapters 2–5. The original empirical chapters have been abbreviated, but I have hardly touched the theoretical chapter. This means that I have not made any attempts at 'updating the dissertation', for instance, incorporating contemporary development theory into the analysis. This is a deliberate choice.

You may, rightfully so, ask why you should read these old case studies. The empirical data are decades old, and the theories of Chapter 2 too may seem unfamiliar to contemporary readers. Realities on the ground have changed, and new development theories are being published. But if you are interested in technological retrogression and looking for empirical analyses, you may find them interesting. Studies of this topic are few and far between. So, the uniqueness is one reason. One other important reason is that the insights from this study may help explain important present phenomena, for instance, why agriculture in so many African countries seems unable to become more capital intensive.

Furthermore, my case studies provide a methodology; they are examples of how you may approach the phenomenon empirically as well as theoretically. The work history method developed for the purpose was crucial in documenting the process. Likewise, the production system approach was instrumental in explaining why technological retrogression occurs in these contexts at these points in time. A second reason is thus that you may find the studies useful.

However, I do not claim that the way I interpreted the process all these years ago cannot be challenged and improved by applying contemporary theory. New theory may shed new light on the nature of capitalism in the societies studied. And the examples of technological retrogression may enrich contemporary development theory. To find out *how* is not within the scope of this book, which is to convince you that understanding technological retrogression is important, no matter where it is found or what causes or triggers it. So, for the purpose of *furthering the understanding of technological retrogression*, I cannot see how updating the case studies would be worth the effort. I find it more fruitful to focus on the formulation of a general theory of retrogression by exploring Schumpeter's theory of technological change. Whether the empirical evidence is taken from ancient Turkey or Asian countries three or four decades ago is of no significance to my arguments.

The dissertation finished, my efforts at publishing the work started. Since nobody had heard of the phenomenon of technological retrogression, publishers judged the market to be non-existing. Likewise, I got no further research funding. The theory was put on ice for a couple of decades. For how long should you knock on closed doors? I cannot say for certain why I have experienced so many shaking heads, so much resistance. But a probable hypothesis is that social scientists have not observed the phenomenon due to a *persistent belief in progress*, which is challenged when I claim that modernization reverses. I have therefore included a brief philosophical account here.

In the years following my first formulation of the theory, Erik S. Reinert encouraged me to study the works of Joseph Schumpeter. At the outset I dismissed the thought since Schumpeter was *most* optimistic regarding the power of technology to abolish misery. However, I was intrigued by the dynamics of his model: through creative destruction new opportunities of applying high-productive technology would turn economic downturns into upturns, setting cumulative spirals of economic growth into motion. 'What if', Reinert asked, 'your theory of technological retrogression is Schumpeter in reverse?' Clearly the cost of labour versus the cost of capital is a key factor in the choice of technologies. Diminishing returns seemed to create situations of low wages which – in a perfectly logical way – stood in the way of technological progress. This renewed my interest in working with the topic and resulted in one successful research project, a pilot study of Russian agriculture which is briefly treated in this volume.

Schumpeter analyses positive cumulative effects of technological modernization during economic downturns. But his model does not cater for producers who do not get the chance to surf the progressive dynamics. A handful of them jump off skyscrapers, but the vast majority manage the best they can, making use of whatever tool available, stagnating or retrogressing in terms of technology. The outcome at the societal level may be persistence of poverty and social polarization, depending on how societies cope with recessions. We should therefore incorporate negative cumulative effects of technological retrogression into Schumpeter's equation, building on his dynamics but improving the knowledge of the anatomy of economic *recessions*. In short, the model should encompass diminishing as well as increasing returns. I have made a first attempt here. I have not come far. How successful my efforts at furthering Schumpeter's analysis are, you may judge when you have read the final chapter.

Interpreting technological retrogression in Schumpeterian terms involves what human geographers like myself fear the most: building general theory. It means stripping phenomena of context and studying 'naked' economic dynamics, irrespective of the where, when and how I must spell out how poverty persists and deepens due to diminishing returns – and how diminishing returns in turn may spur technological retrogression. We could look for technological retrogression not only in twentieth-century capitalist societies: all historical epochs and societies experience upturns and downturns. Economic recessions may follow not only from the inbuilt overproduction/underconsumption crises of capitalist economies but also from natural disasters, pandemics, wars, erosion of empires, collapse of political and economic experiments. Technological stagnation is most certainly found under such circumstances, but what about technological retrogression? Documenting technological retrogression can be done by historians, digging into past recessions, and social scientists could analyse contemporary adaptations to recessions.

I want to make crystal clear what this book is for the reader to adjust expectations accordingly:

> This book is meant to be a manual of instructions: This is how technological retrogression can be found, documented, explained and how it may inspire new research of economic recessions.

> The methodology is most important: Without the work history method and the production system approach the theory of technological retrogression would not have been written.

> The book contains a rough sketch of how Schumpeterian evolutionary theory can be developed by taking technological retrogression into consideration.

I hope to invoke an interest in technological retrogression and encourage new empirical investigation. The best way to further my analysis of technological retrogression is through new empirical research. Over the years I have collected examples of technological retrogression in various parts of the world and different economic sectors. I have fragments of information from mining; transport and construction in Africa; textile industries in Asia; shifts to labour-intensive agriculture in Europe. Lack of research funds stopped me from exploring this further and for instance develop type examples. Readers who find the phenomenon of interest should note that producers may turn to technological retrogression *by necessity*, which characterizes all cases found in this volume. Another justification, found among capital owners, is that it may be profitable to reduce labour productivity – if labour is very cheap compared to capital. I term this technological retrogression *by profit opportunity*. And producers may themselves, voluntarily, for some reason, for instance, choice of lifestyle, select low-productive technologies of the past. I have termed this technological retrogression *by choice*. But there is no nostalgia in my book. Whatever justification put forward by producers, when one factor of production is limited by nature, diminishing returns lurk in the shades. Technological retrogression is an engine of increased social inequality.

In his 1890 *Principles of Economics* Alfred Marshall – the founder of neoclassical economics – indeed had good reasons when he suggested that nations tax diminishing returns industries and pay subsidies to activities subject to increasing returns. Such a tax would prevent technological retrogression.

INTRODUCTION

THE CONCEPT OF TECHNOLOGICAL RETROGRESSION

Point of departure

On any working day in many coastal Third World countries, big, busy trawlers may be observed on their way to deep-sea fishing grounds, as they pass a fleet of small wooden crafts, being ignored by the patiently rowing fishermen aboard. Faced with this striking contrast between high- and low-productive methods of fishing, most observers infer that modern times are coming; the days of picturesque fishing methods are counted. The basis of the inference that traditional fisheries are dying is – of course – the historical experience of fisheries' industries of developed nations over the past century. What can be learned from history is, however, limited, and what can be learned by studying patterns formed by production equipment dispersed on the surface of the sea is even less. The above snapshot provides us with information on the situation today. The investigation of diffusion of technologies in a few Asian fishing villages has taught me that the *past* may be as hidden as the future.

Sitting in a Colombo café in 1980, reading a Sri Lankan newspaper article treating the 'Catamaran's dramatic come-back', my curiosity on retrogression processes was roused and my investigation started. The catamaran, which according to Norwegian standards is (wrongly) considered a primitive craft, was said to experience a renaissance on the north-western coast of the island:

> The weatherbeaten old hoboes of the sea – the traditional catamaran – which had more or less been elbowed out by mechanized fishing craft, have made a dramatic come-back to Negombo's beaches. With the advent of the three-and-a-half ton fishing boats and plastic craft with outboard motors, it looked as if it would be the end of road for the old outriggers. But now the fishermen with mechanized crafts are faced with the high price of fuel and do not venture out as much as they used to […] A number of the fishermen who operated mechanized crafts have

now turned to the old dug-outs again in an endeavour to beat the fuel crisis. (Karunaratne 1979)

Why did this occur? What would be the consequences in the fishing villages? My point of departure when searching for explanations is the following questions: Faced with the superior production capacity of Western modern technologies, and in view of the powerful forces of economic and sociocultural change associated with their spread, why are relations of the production systems prevailing before technological modernization started, being reproduced? Is it just a matter of time before all becomes modern? Alternatively, do I observe a frozen transition with a future unknown? Theories of *technological change or diffusion of technologies* which are inspired by modernization theories still dominant in economic thought cannot explain the processes. To my knowledge, technological retrogression is not described or analysed in the most central works on how technology relates to socio-economic change: losers seldom have prominent roles in the optimistic plays depicting technological progress.

Understanding which *direction* technological change took and takes, the interplay between technologies and their cultural, social, economic and natural environments must be examined: one must dive beneath the surface. An attempt to do so is my master's thesis on technological changes within Sri Lankan fisheries over 30 years (Endresen 1983). Changes were studied by reconstructing employment figures in two villages on the southern coast. In both, *stagnation of technological advance* was observed, and there was ample evidence of a *reversal* of the process. After a period of relatively rapid diffusion of industrial technology, the process slows down. Artisanal fisheries (signifying low-productive, labour-intensive and capital-extensive techniques) do not disappear; on the contrary, a *combination* of artisanal and industrial fisheries gains in importance. In the early 1980s, the shares of industrial, artisanal and combination forms of technology were approximately equal. During the 1970s came a more dramatic course of events: fishermen using industrial technology started to return to artisanal fisheries, events which indicate that a process of *technological retrogression* was at work. *Within* artisanal fisheries, a similar backward movement could be observed; the use of sails on the crafts had almost stopped; the artisanal fleet more and more consisted of rowing crafts which have a much shorter range.

The statistics which normally are used to reconstruct technological change are boat statistics. The technological mobility of labour described above cannot be captured in this manner: There is a *hidden intra-industry mobility of labour*, which is part of a process of social and economic differentiation in the village society. The latter is documented by analysing living standards in the fishing communities. If one searches for an explanation of these phenomena within a diffusionist modernization perspective, the explanation of non-adoption of new technology may be that capital for further modernization is lacking, or that traditional attitudes prevent fishermen from accepting modern technology. However, when modern technology is adopted and used for years by the fishermen, who *then* return to artisanal fisheries, with the reason stated that *they may earn more by producing less*, other explanations are called for. It is especially intriguing when these fishermen are young and seem healthy.

How general is the process described? Is the Sri Lankan experience unique, or can technological stagnation and retrogression be found in societies in similar circumstances – or may it occur in other places for other reasons? Fortunately, the modernization hypothesis can be empirically tested in other contexts. I selected Malaysian fisheries for my PhD study. Malaysian fisheries are in many ways similar but in most ways different from Sri Lankan fisheries. The similarity is the external influence of the increased price of oil which probably triggered technological retrogression in Sri Lanka. Also similar is the modernization ideology of the government planners of fisheries development. The major difference is the scale of technological modernization. In Sri Lankan fisheries, small modern crafts were introduced, and there are comparatively fewer types of technology in use. Malaysia has experienced large-scale modernization of fishing technology for a long period of time. Whereas the separation of Sri Lankan fisheries into an artisanal and an industrial form of technology could easily be defended, the many technologies in use in Malaysia make the categories low, intermediate and high form of technology more appropriate. The higher degree of complexity of Malaysian fisheries caused by the wide variety of technologies in use puts to test my work history method of reconstruction of technological change.

Theories to guide my empirical investigation were lacking. I therefore had to formulate my own theory of technological retrogression, which is the justification for publishing the book you are now reading. My investigation of technological retrogression in Sri Lanka started in the early 1980s; my PhD thesis was defended in the mid-1990s (Endresen 1994). Since then I have kept eyes and ears open to processes of modernization reversed in many contexts; the small study of Russian agriculture referred to in Chapter 1 is a case in point. It is furthermore my contention that technological retrogression will be one of many long-term effects of the financial crisis of 2008 that has hit the real economy of Western Europe, especially since the supply of cheap, mobile labour continues to increase. When effects of economic recessions are studied, whatever triggered them, one should be aware of survival strategies leading to technological retrogression, deepening poverty. But then one needs to go beyond aggregate statistics and modernization ideology.

Conceptual clarifications

The concept of technology has a tool component, techno, and a knowledge component, logy. There are two levels of knowledge involved. The first is knowledge linked to the immediate operation of a tool (e.g. found in instruction manuals). Knowledge on how production should be organized for tools to function is the second level. Figure 1 presents the concepts of technological *change*. *Retrogression of tools* refers to, for example, 'from tractor to horse', whereas *retrogressive mobility of labour* may refer to retrogression at sector level as well as counter-historical current flows of labour from secondary and tertiary industries to agriculture. Choice of technology is analysed at the level of the production unit and economic sector and may also involve geographical mobility of labour. In theory, technological retrogression may cause entire subsectors to retrograde. Technological retrogression may, furthermore, lead to the withdrawal of producers from the market and to production for subsistence.

Why do producers choose production equipment that lowers labour productivity? Clearly the relative cost of capital versus the cost of labour is a key issue. However, the motivating factors behind the choices should be empirically established; the empirical examples that are discussed in this book bring evidence that producers do this *by necessity* rather than by choice. However, other producers may go for this among other options, in which case they retrograde *by choice*. A motivation which may be of importance during economic crises, when labour is abundant, is retrogression *by profit opportunity*. Then the dynamics of factor substitution are at work: hiring cheap labour is more profitable than technological improvements.

Diffusion of technology

Diffusion of technology, within a locality or from one locality to another, presupposes that individuals *adopt* the technology in question and make use of it. In the present studies, this means that investors (for instance, active fishermen, local fish merchants or absentee owners) firstly adopt. They must be convinced of its advantages and must among other factors have access to capital and labour. But labour is a production factor with special characteristics: the new technology must be economically, socially and culturally acceptable to potential *crewmen*. In this thesis, diffusion of technology is approached by investigating transfers of labour from one production unit to another, the intra-industry mobility of labour. The relative importance of the technologies over time is estimated by studying (reconstructed) employment figures.

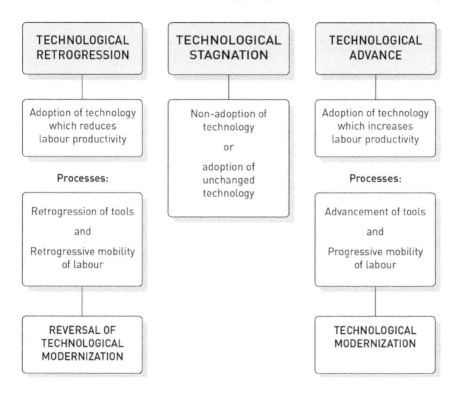

Figure 1 Technological change, the concepts.

Technologies may diffuse smoothly in a population, or the process may be impeded for some reason. When I claim that the communities studied have stagnated in their technological advance, it means that the process of diffusion of modern technology has slowed down or even stopped. This description of the process of technological change reveals that I expect diffusion of modern technology to follow some sort of normal course; in fact, it indicates a belief in *predestination*: one expects artisanal fisheries to disappear and high-productive modern boats to take over. The basis of such a modernization hypothesis is an empirical generalization of the process of technological change within *industrial* countries. The *underlying model* of diffusion of technology is made explicit in Figure 2. The figure is based on the logistic curve depicting the pattern of diffusion of innovations over time. This is an

> S-shaped […] curve (which) depicts the diffusion process as being slow at first because only a small number of people possess the item of information. It then picks up momentum as a larger number of people

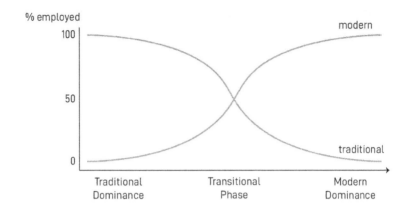

Figure 2 Ideal spread of modern technology.

act as transmitters and then ultimately levels off as the population becomes 'saturated'. (Lloyd and Dicken 1977, 63)[1]

Three phases are identified. During the first phase, when modern technologies are introduced, traditional technologies still dominate the scene. During the next, the transitional, modernization gains momentum and lastly, modern technology has replaced the traditional. Traditional technology is now a dying remnant. In the illustration of the general sequence, neither the length of each phase nor the timing of the transition between one phase and the next are predicted.

According to the Swedish geographer Torsten Hägerstrand, a population can, with respect to an item of information, be divided into three categories: non-knowers, knowers but non-adopters and adopters of the information (Lloyd and Dicken 1977). These will be found in the two last phases of the above model. But in the present context, the categories need a reformulation: it may be useful to split up the concept of knowers but non-adopters into future-adopters, former-adopters and never-adopters. Producers of the last two categories have rejected the innovation.In the early phase of

---

[1] Lloyd and Dicken (1977, 62, figure 2.38) show the logistic curve based on Hägerstrand's simulation model of diffusion of information in an agricultural landscape. It is important to note that Hägerstrand's model is not deterministic, since it is stressed that there is a *probability* but not a *certainty* of diffusion, which increases with diminishing distance from the person who possesses the information. Lloyd and Dicken (1972, 142) claim that 'Empirical studies of the rate of diffusion of a number of innovations – for example, the spread of hybrid corn in North America [...] and the spread of messages [...] have been found to correspond closely to the logistic curve.'

technological modernization, one would expect technical difficulties and adjustment problems which may hamper diffusion:

> Innovators and early adopters face technical and managerial problems that have been ironed out by the time the late adopters install the new equipment. (Nabseth and Ray 1974, 16)

This may lead to the formation of combination forms of technology: some fishermen who need time to adjust may for a period work aboard both old and new crafts. People are, however, more than the labour they trade, which sometimes makes the choice of words a difficult matter. When fishermen combine technologies at different productivity levels over time, *flows of labour*, forming economic linkages between technologies at different productivity levels, result. The terminology may indicate that human beings are objectified, treated as equal to commodities. This is not my intention. In capitalist societies, *human labour power* is a commodity but *human beings* are not – not even a 'thinking commodity'. I consider people decision-makers, that is, not *solely* victims of blind, cultural, social or economic forces.[2] If I did not, I would be unable to discover that some of them choose technologies which are inferior in terms of productivity. I would have assumed that their freedom of choice was zero and (joyfully) limited my research on fishing societies to abstract theoretical circles.

At the societal level, aggregate outcomes of individuals' actions (their concrete choices and adoption of technologies) can be studied in terms of technological advance, retardation, stagnation and retrogression. This characterizes the direction of change: societies may modernize technologically – progress; if modernization slows down, they move very slowly forward – retard; they may stagnate or move 'backwards' – retrograde. New recruits to an industry should be expected to go for the most advanced technologies. If *many* young recruits do the opposite (where they for generations have been exposed to modern technology), this could be analysed in terms of *relative reversal* of modernization.

Technological advance and retrogression may be considered converse processes. In cases where the technological gap (a vast difference in technology levels in terms of labour productivity) is closing, the process is termed technological *convergence*. But productivity levels may also move further apart, in the process of technological *divergence*. Transfers of technology from industrial countries to developing countries may result in coexistence of low- and high-productive technology, and unless indigenous technologies disappear

---

[2] This is more precisely expressed by Giddens (1984, 3): 'To be a human being is to be a purposive agent, who both has reasons for his or her activities and is able, if asked, to elaborate discursively upon those reasons (including lying about them).'

or are radically modernized, this leads to extreme divergence, to technological *polarization*: from a situation where productivity levels were relatively equal, a widening of the gap occurs. As stated earlier, societies with these characteristics are here termed technologically heterogeneous, in contrast to the (relative) homogeneity in industrial societies on the one hand and tribal societies on the other. If high forms of technology take over and low forms of technology vanish, a closing of the gap, a technological convergence, will result in technological homogeneity. And what should be particularly stressed in the present context is that technological convergence may also result from a process where *productivity levels converge at the lower level*, which may be the outcome of dramatic reductions of productivity combined with high forms of technology.

The chapters

In ancient Rome, Janus was the god of doorways, beginnings and transitions; he therefore gazes at the future and the past at the same time. Reading this book, the relevance of the cover image of a god of transitions will become evident. According to Plutarch in *The Life of Numa*,

> [Janus] [...] is said to have lifted human life out of its bestial and savage state. For this reason he is represented with two faces, implying that he brought men's lives out of one sort and condition into another. (quoted in Gill 2020)

This book contains a foreword by Erik S. Reinert, my preface, this introduction and six chapters. The introduction presents the way in which the concepts of technological change are applied and provides a brief account of diffusionist theory of technological change. As stated above, the phenomenon of technological retrogression was not recognized or well understood, and there was no social theory explaining technological retrogression when my quest started. This, I believe, is mainly due to the persistence of the idea of progress in social theory, forming scientific blind spots treated in Chapter 1. Furthermore, circumstances under which technological retrogression may occur are sketched here. How technological retrogression relates to Schumpeterian thought is briefly discussed and will be revisited in the final chapter of the book.

In Chapter 2, I seek to derive explanations of technological retrogression from general theory, discussing how technological heterogeneity is understood in these bodies of thought. Three approaches to heterogeneity are thereby derived, inspiring my empirical analysis.

Persistent belief in progress is one possible explanation of the ignorance regarding technological retrogression, another is its *statistically hidden* character. In statistics, technological modernization by some producers may outweigh retrogression and produce an aggregate illusion of *stagnation* and even *modernization*. To uncover and analyse technological retrogression, I have designed the work history method where producers' choices of technology over time are followed and understood in terms of shifting production systems. The production system approach and the work history method are presented in Chapter 3.

In Chapters 4 and 5, empirical evidence of technological retrogression in Sri Lankan and Malaysian fishing villages is presented, providing the main foundation of 'A Theory of Technological Retrogression', formulated in Chapter 6. This final chapter concludes with a discussion of technological retrogression understood as 'Schumpeterian dynamics in reverse'.

Chapter 1

CHALLENGING LINEARITY AND IRREVERSIBILITY

Grand narratives of progress

The reversal of modernization has been given little attention in social science.[1] In this chapter this is discussed in terms of preoccupation with progress, dominant in Western thought. This idea may overshadow any doubts we may have and make it difficult to observe modernization in reverse: Do we only observe what we are 'programmed' to believe in? Do we have 'progressive lenses'? If so, it is difficult to challenge linearity of history, or evolutionism, that societies move – eventually – in the same direction. A discussion on how technological retrogression may be studied as well as a brief introduction to the empirical evidence presented in later chapters follows. The chapter then introduces how technological retrogression can be cast in Schumpeterian terms, the 'Schumpeter in reverse' question treated in the preface.

The grandest perspectives within history and social sciences concern the evolution of human society and the rise and fall of civilizations. Might the phenomenon of technological retrogression be discussed in terms of such grand narratives? For instance, could it be an indicator of decline or decay during the fall, or a process running counter to general conceptions of the direction of evolution? We would then look for evidence of this phenomenon during periods when empires disintegrate and vanish, and during prolonged crises of societies. Grand narratives are more concerned with *progress* than with decline. In *The History of Progress*, Nisbet claims that between 1750 and 1900, the idea of progress 'reached its zenith in the Western mind in popular as well as scholarly circles. From being one of the important ideas of the West it became the dominant idea' (Nisbet 2009, 171). Progress provided the developmental context for ideas such as equality, social justice and popular sovereignty. Philosophers of that time, Turgot, Condorcet, Saint-Simon, Comte, Hegel, Marx and Spencer, saw history as a slow, gradual but

---

[1] The main arguments of Chapter 1 were published in Reinert et al. (2016).

continuous and necessary ascent to some given end. Linearity in historical analyses was born.

Grand narratives proclaiming progress as 'an inexorable march of mankind' (Nisbet 2009, 171) do not generally obtain the status of *theory* in social science, where researchers concentrate on contemporary issues and testable hypotheses. But social science abounds with grand narratives, concepts of which are ingrained in our language, scientific and vernacular. In a historical perspective, postmodernists' proclamation of the death of grand narratives is very recent and has yet to obtain hegemonic status. What should be credited to postmodernists, however, is that their questioning of grand narratives has inspired a renewed critique of the idea of progress, hegemonic in Western thought for nearly three hundred years. *Progress* is not something we think *of* when discussing societal change; it is *what* we think (Eriksen 1991). It thus has become the category structuring our thoughts. When this is understood by scholars, we become aware of a pattern of thought which may delimit what we observe and therefore distort the conceptualization of change.

The written history of industrial development in the West is the optimistic demonstration of technological progress par excellence. When the general traits of the process of development are discussed to identify the variables which promote economic growth, technological change is considered a crucial factor. Comprehensive analyses demonstrate how smart nations have used technological progress to catch up in the race (Abramovitz 1986). In studies by Gerschenkron, Schumpeter and Rosenberg, the concept of technological *change* even comes across as being the same as technological *progress*. In this manner the history of technology is firmly linked to *the belief in progress* characteristic of Western thought. Where traditional technologies survive in industrial nations outside the sphere of art and in museums, they are considered anachronist residuals, kept alive by idealist craftsmen to bear witness of our past. Some theorists even go further; in Dillard et al.'s economic history, technological optimism becomes technological determinism: 'Technological changes are interdependent, cumulative and irreversible' (Dillard et al. 1977, 209, my translation). He argues that a reversal from large- to small-scale production 'from a technological point of view is impossible' (Dillard et al. 1977, 209, my translation). Technological imperatives limit our choices and even make *economic* development irreversible.

Before the stage of modern relative technological homogeneity is reached, society has escaped the stage of traditional technological homogeneity by going through a stage of transition. According to theories of modernization, this process is inescapable: 'All of the present relatively nonmodernized societies will change in the direction of greater modernity' (Levy 1966, 31). Eisenstadt (1973) terms this a theory of convergence: *Development* is progress towards greater modernity, Western social structures and mass consumption being the (usually tacitly understood) *aims*, as in Rostow (1971). Undeveloped nations represent earlier stages of developed nations. Technologically heterogeneous societies are, in Eisenstadt's terms, transitional. This perspective is termed *developmentalism* by Taylor (1992), 'developing countries will become developed'. It is, however, evident that development here equals *evolution*, that developmentalism is but a form of evolutionism. Anthony Giddens defines evolutionism as

> the explication of social change in terms or schemas which involve the following features: an irreversible series of stages through which societies move, even if not held that all individual societies must pass through each of them to reach the higher ones; some conceptual linkage with biological theories of evolution; and the specification of directionality through the stages indicated, in respect of a given criterion or criteria, such as increasing complexity or expansion of the forces of production. (Giddens 1984, xxvii)

According to Giddens, in one variety or another, social evolutionism has been most influential within social science. In the works of Sahlins and Service (1960) the biological analogy is evident:

> In both its biological and cultural spheres evolution moves simultaneously in two directions. On the one side, it creates diversity through adaptive modification: new forms differentiate from old. On the other side, evolution generates progress: higher forms arise from, and surpass, lower. (Quoted in Giddens 1984, 231)

The process of modernization is considered both inevitable and irreversible:

> The evolutionist process is like the historical, or diffusionist, process in that both are temporal, and therefore irreversible and non-repetitive. (White 1959, quoted in Giddens 1984, 230)

Scholars still celebrate progress, searching for definitions that capture its essence. Sztompka (1990, 258, emphasis in the original) denotes progress as greater freedom, progress-conducive agency and self-transcendence which means society and individuals '*going beyond itself, overcoming limitations, breaking through constraints, crossing "frontiers"*'. Two fundamental traits of the human world explain this tendency: *creativity* and sociocultural *transmission* of experience in historical span. He underlines two important features of progress, the first is *unevenness*:

> The rhythm of human history is certainly uneven. There are prolonged periods of stagnation, inertia, slow movement, minor changes. And from time to time those eruptions of sudden transformation, thresholds between epochs. Just think of those exceptional periods marked by acceleration of changes which are later called the miracles of progress: Athens of the fifth century BC, imperial Rome, Aztek, and Maya Empires, European Renaissance, China of Deng Siao Ping, Soviet perestroika – to mention just a few. (Sztompka 1990, 259)

The periods of abrupt change are considered evidence of gradual emancipation of human agency, allowing history to jump forward. However, for our specific purpose, his stressing of what we may term *contingency of progress* is important:

> There is no necessity of progress, it is not pre-ordained that people will be willing and able to exercise their creative capacity. The constraining natural, structural, or historical conditions, or the suppressed motivations for activism [...] may prevent creativity from flourishing. And similarly, the process of cumulation, passing on of tradition may get disrupted, both at the biographical and at the historical level [...] In such cases, stagnation or regress rather than progress will be a likely result. (Sztompka 1990, 258)

Sztompka claims that a scientific theory of progress is possible within his paradigm; he builds on morphogenesis-structuration theory. The conception of progress within this theory puts human agency into the equation when construction and reconstruction of societies are analysed. This goes beyond historical thought that stresses the agency of dominant personalities, or the workings of blind forces in class struggles. The theory is part of postdevelopmentalist thought, where we find among theorists of Third World development an explicit questioning of progress: What concrete progress has modernization, following integration into the world economy, brought to Third World societies? The idea of progress is at the heart of modernization theory, where *developmentalism* dominates: every society progresses towards greater modernity. But do they? Within neo-Marxist development thought, developmentalism has been questioned since the days of Baran (1957). Amin (1976) thus introduces the concept of retrogression in agricultural technique, inspiring the analysis of causes of decline. He describes a situation where modernization is reversed; average labour productivity of the production unit is reduced; it is characterized by *more men and less capital*:

> [The] extraverted orientation of the economy dooms agriculture to stagnation, sometimes even to retrogression. [...] The increase in the density of population in the countryside leads to retrogression in agricultural technique, for progress in agriculture is usually expressed in the use of more capital and fewer men per hectare. (Amin 1976, 206)

This is the closest I got to a theoretical treatment of technological retrogression by a scholar.

According to Sztompka (1990), what may prevent progress should be studied at the biographical as well as the historical levels. Firstly, individuals may be socialized into passivity, or harsh lessons from past failures can result in limited capacity for innovation. These are conditions which limit creativity. Secondly, the process of 'cumulation', passing on of tradition, may be disrupted, and therefore, the transfer of human experience over time may be prevented. The role of institutions such as schools, church, media is crucial here. This may be understood in terms of knowledge loss over generations.

Constructing a testable theory of reversal of modernization

Paradoxically, to construct a theory of decline we must search for knowledge in literature on progress. Decline seems not to be considered an object of interest but is rather seen as unfortunate and sporadic occurrences; decline becomes an appendix to progress. However, when modernization is divided into cultural, social, political, economic and technological change and investigated empirically, constructing sweeping generalizations of human progress becomes more difficult. To take but one example, during the last few decades there is ample evidence in Europe of racial hatred and violence, and regrowth of right-wing parties inspired by fascist ideologies that results in crises of parliamentary democracy. Economic setbacks following the financial crisis of 2008 fuel politico-ideological regress. However, there is no need to proclaim the irrelevance of the concept of progress. Equal political rights may easily be defined as human progress, trafficking of vulnerable people a step in the wrong direction. At the societal level, with the spread of racial violence and exploitation of workers, we need to reflect upon the possible ephemeral nature of progress: Allowing these phenomena to persist is a sign of societal regress. The necessity of including *values* in our deliberations, based on discussions of moral and ethics, is evident. Furthermore, progress in one domain may cause regress in another. Thus, what is needed is always to cater for the possibility of counteracting forces and contingencies when a trajectory of change is sought to understood and study the outcomes of changes in terms of dilemmas.

If wearing 'progressive lenses' when changes are studied, decline may be overlooked. The dominant idea of progress hampers our ability to observe and conceptualize regress, reversal and retrogression. We therefore need to operationalize the concept of *decline* rigorously and confront social reality. The theory of technological retrogression is an attempt at constructing a testable theory of reversal of technological modernization. This theory has gained new relevance due to economic setbacks in Eastern Europe during the transformation to capitalism. In rural Western Europe, the relevance of the theory is linked to de-industrialization after the financial crisis (Tregenna 2016).

Revisiting the concepts of linearity of historical change and the importance of technology for progress may be fruitful. As understood by Nisbet (2009), with the triumph of Christianity, a linear conception of change surpassed ancient cyclical conceptions. With the Enlightenment, the Christian linearity conception which includes a prophecy of the *end of time* waned, and the modern secular conception of linearity now dominates. The belief in eternal progress of society came with the triumph of Science; hegemonic history since the Industrial Revolution can be read as a narrative of continuous scientific progress, carrying progress in every other sphere of society. And nowhere has the idea of progress been more pronounced than in the narrative of technological change. Nowak (1990) uses technology as the example of progress:

> It is relatively easy to find examples in the history of mankind of simple, uni-dimensional directional changes, and quite a few of them are quite longitudinal. Development of science or technology [...] when regarded in isolation from other analogous processes seem to correspond to the old beliefs in the permanence of human progress. (Nowak 1990, 237)

Here, a distinction should be made between *invention* and *diffusion* of technology. Only through the latter process, the progressive potential of new technology can materialize, and it presupposes that producers adopt and adapt the new technology to solve their production problems. If they stick to the old by preference or because they lack the means to modernize, progress of science and technology will remain but potentials at the drawing table. This is consistent with Sztompka's (1990) underlining of the *contingency of progress* discussed above.

In the above quotation, Nowak brings into our discussion yet another dimension, namely, 'other analogous processes', social change in other spheres of society occurring simultaneously. Technological progress may depend upon other forces of change, and, also put in motion change in other domains of society. The latter, how technological progress spurs human progress through improvement of productive capacities, has been a major theme in grand social theory for centuries. Abramovitz (1982, 254), however, underlines that the classical economists 'did not accept the notion that technical advance and capital accumulation would continue at a rapid pace indefinitely' or result in 'indefinite advance in material standards for ordinary people'.

Another entry point into our discourse of decline is changes in the composition of GDP or the workforce according to economic sector. Here, we confront our conceptions of societal evolution: a society that is predominantly agricultural is considered lower on the development ladder than industrial countries. This fits well with the overwhelming evidence of the importance of industrialization for economic growth. Sejersted (1979) analyses economic growth during industrial transformation in terms of 'surplus of transfer', which stems from the shift of labour from traditional to modern, from primary to secondary occupations. Consequently, a shift in the opposite direction, where labour flows into agriculture, would result in 'transfer loss'. Sejersted is here close to Marshall's (1890) distinction between activities characterized by increasing returns and activities prone to diminishing returns.

Necessity, choice and profit opportunity

What motivates producers to adopt technologies which lower labour productivity? The concept of *motivation* is here applied to underlying causes at the structural level (structural coercion; ideological trends; profitability considerations). What actors themselves express as being the reason why certain choices were made could be termed *purpose* or *justification*. If producers are forced to abandon modern technology and go for technologies that are inferior in terms of labour productivity, it should be considered *technological retrogression by necessity*. But technological retrogression may be the result of a lifestyle *choice*, like when the Amish adopt and preserve production equipment of the past aiming to replicate the society of a bygone century. Apart from motivations of *necessity* and *choice*, there is the motivation of technological retrogression by *profit opportunity*. When availability of capital reduces, the substitution of capital for labour becomes more viable; instead of investing in machinery, cheap labour can be hired, and production becomes *more* labour intensive. If workers are employed instead of buying machines, it is done because *it makes economic sense*: It is more profitable. The direction of technological change is thus a question of the relative cost of labour and capital. If labour becomes extremely cheap, this may also lead to a change of *produce*. This motivation may become important during periods of economic recessions and political turmoil. Where there is an oversupply of labour, wage levels may drop to what the most desperate of workers are willing to accept (Ricardo 1817). However, when technological retrogression is understood, reproduction of labour *below subsistence level* is of significance. In Chapter 2, in the section discussing the transition to capitalism in the colonial context, this phenomenon is treated. The contrast to industrial societies is great. Here working class' struggles resulted in increased price of labour, spurring technological progress. Understanding technological retrogression by necessity, which is the main purpose of this book, the concept of *lock-in* of producers in production systems/places as applied in Erik S. Reinert (1980) is of utmost importance.

Empirical evidence of technological retrogression

The most thorough verification of the existence of technological retrogression is presented in Chapters 4 and 5. Retrogression was widespread in Asian fishing villages. In one case, this was due to price increase of imported inputs, in another it was due to disastrous ecological effects of technological modernization. Diminishing returns coincided with the major precondition in both cases; a severe lock-in of primary producers caused by lacking diversification of the economy. The modern crewmen were the first to turn to traditional boats as a survival strategy, but this did not lead to labour shortage on modern boats. In the societies in question, labour supply was almost unlimited; workers were willing to work for very low pay. The owners of modern boats exhausted their capital funds before they finally gave up and went for traditional technologies. However, the traditional sector they (re)turned to was not as productive as before: Local knowledge such as sailing skills and old fishing techniques was lost during the modernization period. Harsh economic realities led to retrogression in these cases, it was thus retrogression by necessity.

There is historical evidence of retrogression in Europe. During financial crises of the eighteenth century as well as during the Great Depression in the 1930s, Norwegian fishermen had to move from modern boats to traditional ones, becoming less productive and poorer (Bull 1988, 163). In both cases, de-industrialization, capital shortage and lock-in were factors of explanation. Capital shortage during the latter period led to incidents of *primitivization* in Norwegian manufacturing as well. Small apparel producers survived during the hard times by squeezing labour and reducing technology levels (Bull 1988).

The results from a pilot study on technological retrogression and poverty in contemporary rural Russia are included in Papalexiou (2015).[2] She concludes

---

[2] Two unpublished papers from my pilot project in 2014. From the 1990s, Elena Bogdanova, Retrogression in the Russian countryside. Review of newspaper "Selskaia

that the *shock therapy* (opening of the economy, liberalization, land reform) led to a sharp rise in the price of agricultural input factors, such as harvesters and cars. Food imports increased and prices fell. At the same time, subsidies were removed, creating a capital squeeze preventing investments in machinery to secure efficient production. Monoculture in large production units now exists side by side with many smaller farms with a multitude of produce, and rural poverty persists. But this small-scale agriculture does not constitute the modern, competitive farming that the reformers had in mind. It relies mainly on manual labour and serves as a survival strategy in the absence of employment or income from the indebted agricultural collectives (Kalugina 2014 in Papalexiou 2015, 15). The parallels to the Asian cases are clear; lacking diversification, lock-in, capital shortage, poverty traps. The technological choices made are good for the immediate survival of the producers, but less so for sustained growth and development. It is a crux of thought that some perceptions regarding rural poverty in Russia (such as reluctance on the part of villagers to change their way of life) echo the flawed explanation of lacking modernization found in literature on the cases of Asian fisheries studied, that of stubborn traditionalism.

Challenging Schumpeterian thought

The theory of technological retrogression is new; it is at odds with conceptual frameworks that seek to capture technological change in classical (including Marxist), neoclassical as well as evolutionary economic thought. Technological change and economic progress are often associated with economist Joseph Schumpeter (1883–1950). According to Schumpeter, economies turn from decline to development when entrepreneurs start adopting new technology, sweeping away old technologies in gales of *creative destruction*, setting in motion the upswing. The result is increasing returns and economic progress. The phenomenon of technological retrogression challenges this theory, but at the same time, it can be formulated in Schumpeterian terms: Schumpeterian mechanisms do not *only* operate by creating economic progress; they may also function in reverse as technological retrogression. A choice of technology of production may lead to reduced productivity and economic decline. With technological retrogression, processes of increasing wealth have been put in reverse, with increasing poverty as a result; the concept of destructive destruction (Reinert 2007) is applicable here. The theory of technological

Zhizn" 1996 and 1999. St. Petersburg: Centre for Independent Social Research. From the 2000s, Olga Tkach, 'Rural life'. Newspaper overview based on random sampling of 2009, 2011, 2013 and 2014. St. Petersburg: Centre for Independent Social Research.

retrogression thus contrasts retrogressive economic dynamics of technological change to progressive dynamics as developed by Schumpeter.

Cast in Schumpeterian terms, technological retrogression may be considered the resurrection of 'dead' technologies. The concept of resurrection may have positive connotations, but in the theory of technological retrogression there is no nostalgia. Although considered good for short-run survival, I consider technological retrogression detrimental to economic growth, social and regional development. Thus, progressive Schumpeterian dynamics have an 'evil twin'; retrogressive dynamics are set in motion where (un-)favourable contextual preconditions prevail. Producers, incapable of escaping crises through innovation, do not cease to exist (except, it seems, in economic theory). They try many survival strategies, including technological retrogression, resulting in diminishing returns and economic decline. Both dynamics can be cast in Gunnar Myrdal's (1957) term *cumulative causation*, positive and negative, depicting spiralling effects of economic upturns and downturns. Whereas cyclicality of capitalist economies is of major importance in Schumpeter's mainly optimistic theory of technological progress, many different triggers in addition to cyclicality of capitalism are relevant in its retrogressive twin process; collapse of political systems, exploitation of labour, trends in lifestyle produced by ruling ideologies.

Technological retrogression results from producers' adoption of technology which reduces labour productivity. The theory of technological retrogression presented here seeks to understand the technology component of *decline*, trapping societies in cumulative spirals of low income, low capital accumulation, low investment. Producers experience physical hardship associated with low-technology levels and daily struggle to keep ends meet and provide education for their children; in short, they experience immiseration. Migration may provide an escape; technological retrogression results where this option is lacking or perceived fruitless. The discovery of this phenomenon raises questions of its causes: what motivates such technology choices, what triggers such processes and what are the contextual preconditions?

As explained above, a major precondition of technological retrogression is lock-in of the producers in production systems/places. In this regard, a distinction should be made between 'voluntary' technological retrogression and retrogression induced by structural coercion. The latter may be desperate measures when other options are (or are perceived to be) non-existent. Labour mobility may be restricted, or producers believe that they have nothing to gain by moving out. In the case of voluntary retrogression there *are* other options, the producers may be said to have *locked themselves in* – to production systems of the past. Their choice is laden with dilemmas if widespread; for instance, in agriculture, those pertaining to food for growing urban populations. A future scenario of polarization emerges, 'idyllic' low-productive old-fashioned producers at the one extreme, and super-industrial, high-productive production units at the other. This spurs reflections on the causal relationship between technological retrogression and socio-economic marginalization, and, thereby, socio-economic polarization and increased inequality. Furthermore, where technological retrogression involves return to organizational models of the past, this may affect the political leverage of labour and curb social progress.

Chapter 2

PERSPECTIVES ON TECHNOLOGICAL HETEROGENEITY

Understanding time–space edges

The Asian societies I have studied were characterized by coexistence of technologies at very different productivity levels. Then how is such technological heterogeneity understood in theory? The most general conception concerns processes in the field of tension formed when phenomena which originate in different societies meet. In Giddens's (1984) terms, such encounters form time–space edges, which may be defined as 'critical interfaces of historical and geographical transition' (Spengen 1992, 7). Connections between societies of different structural types 'may be conflictual as well as symbiotic' (Giddens 1984, 377). The fishing societies I have studied have all experienced dramatic encounters when technologies originating in the West were introduced in the low-technology settings. While searching for an understanding of the outcomes in terms of structural change, I try to find out which – if any – explanations are offered to the unexpected technological changes I came across. What explanations to the processes where modernization seems to reverse can be detected in the general development debate?

When outlining how central theorists understand structural properties of technologically heterogeneous societies, the discussion by necessity attains a very general character. Should technologically heterogeneous societies be considered *dual societies*, as suggested by *modernization theorists*; are they composed of two different sectors, a traditional and a modern? Then technological heterogeneity indicates an incomplete modernization process, caused by lack of capital for further technological modernization or by traditional attitudes towards modernization in the population. Alternatively, are the producers that are pushed out of modern production less productive? In general, when explained in the spirit of modernization theory, technological changes which do not confirm to the ideal (Western) model are transitional problems, bound to disappear when market forces have fully penetrated the economy.

By appearance, technological retrogression is the rejection of modern technology; by substance, however, it is a strategy of the exploited and marginalized poor to uphold their standard of living. When faced with the inadequacy of modernization theory to explain my empirical findings, I approached radical schools of economic thought.

The transition of various pre-capitalist modes of production into the capitalist one has been central in the Marxist development debate for more than a century. But the main concern has been the transition process within Western societies: the emergence of the capitalist mode of production, internal changes caused by it and its dominance in the Western world. In this classical transition debate the spread of capitalism to (and especially within) the colonies received little attention. Basing a judgement solely on what can be found in Marx's writings on this issue, he may be considered both a dual and a modernization theorist: Technological heterogeneity should then be understood as a structural trait of societies where an expanding and progressive capitalist mode of production has met with the backward pre-capitalist modes; and in the process, the latter are destroyed.

In the Marxist discourse on the nature of developing societies, there are several positions. To try to identify *a single* perspective on technological heterogeneous societies held by Marxists would be impossible. Their views diverge, and in addition, Marxist theorists are difficult to categorize due to a formidable conceptual confusion. In the obscure theoretical landscape, interesting observations and understandings can however be found by studying Marxist development theory. One position (which I most certainly do not need to explain the findings) is the orthodoxy of Marxist modernization theory sketched above, where pre-capitalist modes of production are being destroyed by progressive capitalism. In societies where pre-capitalist modes stubbornly refuse to die, *perverted capitalism* prevails; but soon they will be on the right trail. 'They are *en route*' (Foster-Carter 1978, 48).

Inspired by Marx and positioning themselves in relation to his works as well as to modernization theories, some theorists are studying the effects of capitalist penetration in the Third World. The capitalist mode of production is by then considered structurally linked to non-capitalist modes, which explains the technological heterogeneity of these societies. Capitalism is thought to dominate economic, political and social life; a general understanding held both by non-orthodox Marxists who advocate and those who contest a *peripheral capitalist* thesis. Their views on whether capitalism in Third World social formations is unique in history may differ, as do their views on other structural properties, but there may be consensus regarding a central point: Reproduced non-capitalist relations (including artisanal technologies) may play a central role in the reproduction of capitalism in Third World social formations. In this matter their view sharply contrasts that of the modernization theorists, who consider such remnants part of waning traditional sectors.

As will become clear, I find no power of explanation in modernization theory when applied to the empirical material. Traditional mindset or rationality cannot explain technological retrogression. But I found that fisheries planners and technologists harbour such views; and technological retrogression found in Russia as well was explained in terms of traditionalism, reluctance to embrace changes. For more than a century, a plethora of economic theories which explain economic growth and development of Western countries have been formulated, and they have inspired the transfer of development models to developing countries. Governments in developing countries still emulate successful industrial countries in search for economic growth and prosperity, seemingly oblivious to the failures of the past and the resulting social polarization.

A probable hypothesis is that modernization *thinking* is still alive, no matter how many times the *theory* is pronounced dead by academics. Recall the discussion in Chapter 1 on whether the belief in progress, linearity of history, has become ingrained in our thinking. The distinction between modernization theory and modernization ideology should be invoked, the latter depicting a belief system which motivates actions. We should therefore not bury modernization thought too deeply if we want to analyse its transformation into ideology.

When European experiences were sought generalized by modernization theorists and applied to the contexts of developing countries more than 50 years ago, radical academics started to prepare its burial. Especially, scholars that originated or had strong ties with developing countries pointed at flaws and shortcomings of modernization theory. Since I conclude that Marxist theories of peripheral capitalism have the greater explanatory power, I am in the burial committee as well. Then why do I start this volume with the diffusionist model of technological change (Figure 2), a model close to the core of modernization theory? The answer to this question is *methodology*: A useful model should not be discarded because you judge it infested with a flawed theory. It is a theory, a tool, not a creed. It can be falsified. The diffusionist ideal model is serving as a contrast to village reality and enables me to visualize discrepancies between expectations and reality. The changes seemed to follow the well-known track, but then something curbed the transition. So, the model is useful.

But modernization theory is treated here for yet another purpose; it serves to unveil similarities between classical Marxism and modernization theory: they are both linear. This is not surprising; the roots of Marxism are deeply embedded in European soil. But the main reason that modernization theory needs to be treated here is that radical theorists took the theories as their point of departure in their critiques. The resulting debate on the structure of societies in transition is well suited to inform my empirical research. It would, however, be interesting to analyse my empirical findings in the light of contemporary development theory. But this is judged not to bring my Schumpeterian interpretation of technological retrogression any further. I leave the updating task to contemporary development scholars.

One backward and one progressive sector

The modernization theory which prevailed during the post–Second World War era contributed to a technology optimism frequently found within fisheries planning. This optimism is inherent in theories on how technological changes relate to economic development. Typical examples can be found within the Schumpeterian tradition of economic thought. By transferring ultra-modern technology, Third World nations are thought to be able to radically improve their position within the international division of labour (Perez 1985), or in a more moderate version, *some* of the countries may leapfrog (Soete 1985) into modernity. Emile Vercruijsse (1984) underlines that modernization theorists attribute the same developmental potential to all societies, since they assume that every society, when time has come, will change towards modernity. This is an expression of linearity of development, which is challenged in this book. They elegantly conceal the capitalist nature of the transformation, but the ideological character of modernization theory is exposed

> since, in complete contradiction, it matches a theory of universal indigenous development with a diffusionist practice. (Vercruijsse 1984, 14)

The very purpose of applying the label 'traditional society' or sector is 'to bring out a society's resistance to modernization' (Vercruijsse 1984, 13). Here, reference should be made to the analyses of the Luddite riots in nineteenth-century England, where workers violently opposed the introduction of modern technology, allegedly because of their reactionary attitudes, but most probably because of the labour-displacing nature of the technologies introduced.

The notion of fundamental differences between traditional and modern societies can be traced to early sociological theories of backwardness (Eisenstadt 1973). Characteristics of the modern societies are a high degree of differentiation; they are dynamic, expansive, specialized and urban. Traditional societies represent their negation: They are static, restrictive, un-differentiated and agrarian. The typical modern person is an action-oriented entrepreneur; the typical traditionalist is a passive, non-innovative, un-adaptable and conservative person, with an irrational view of economy and a preference for immaterial value (McClelland 1961; Lerner 1958). In development theory after the Second World War, these ideas are clearly visible in Parsons' (1951) theory of action. Cultural changes associated with development from traditional to modern society imply the breakdown of traditional social values, to be replaced with modern: Collective orientation, which is one of the *pattern variables*, is gradually replaced by self-orientation. This means that individuals' prospects of profits become more important than what is best for the community. Likewise, particularism turns into universalism, which in fishing societies may imply that a better qualified and clever non-relative may be preferred as crewman to family members. For the fisherman preferred, it is no longer what he was born, but what he has achieved, which matters, which indicates that at the societal level, ascription changes into achievement orientation.

These theories provide us with the ingredients of a modernization recipe: the opening up of the economy, transfer of capital from the modern world to secure the provision of efficient technology and the eradication of traditional attitudes towards modernization among the inhabitants of the backward countries. Among attitudes to be changed is the persistent preference for large families. The pie to be baked is the transition to modernity. The increased surplus generated by the higher productivity of modern technology will automatically generate the betterment of the inhabitants' standard of living: It is supposed to trickle down to all layers. Within this frame of analysis, the *power* dimension of redistribution of economic surpluses is hardly discussed, nor are the conditions of those left behind in the traditional sector interesting: It is considered just a matter of time before the backward traditional sector gradually vanishes as labour is absorbed by the modern sector.

William Arthur Lewis may stand as a representative of this school of thought, although his observant analysis of *Economic Development with Unlimited Supplies of Labour* (1954) makes him an atypical one.[1] In Lewis's model productivity and wages in the traditional sector (which also is termed agrarian or subsistence sector) are low compared to the modern sector (which also is termed the capitalist sector). When labour is transferred from the traditional to the modern, a surplus of transfer (Sejersted 1979) and therefore economic growth is created. An initial barrier to development is a *lack of capital and a capitalist class*; both can, however, be imported. Capital accumulation in the modern sector is secured by the low wage level, kept low by the *almost unlimited supply of labour from the traditional sector*. The traditional sector is in Lewis's model characterized by *underemployment*: Labour can be withdrawn from, for instance,

---

[1] Being a critique of neoclassic economic theory, Lewis's analysis is a continuation of the works of Smith, Ricardo, Marx and Malthus. My interpretation of his work is inspired by Brenner (1966), Arrighi (1970), Hodne (1979) and Leeson (1982).

traditional agriculture without affecting its productivity. Population increase and the liberation of women secure growth of the modern labour force. Labour surplus keeps the wage level low in the modern sector and because of the initial poverty in the traditional sector, only minimal wage differentials are required to start the flow of labour into the modern sector.

According to Lewis, modernization of society will spread from bright cities expanding their modern industries to their dark, backward hinterlands. Simultaneously, modernization may occur *within* the traditional sector, because of contacts between, for instance, agriculture and industry. The modern sector will expand until the traditional sector is absorbed. The only hindrances predicted by Lewis are decreasing capital accumulation in the modern sector, due to an increase in the wage rate or to technological progress within the traditional sector. Also, union action within the modern sector and increasing prices of agricultural products may curb capital accumulation. But these hindrances will delay the process for a limited time only. When the labour reserve is absorbed, market forces will take over: The society has become modern.

Lewis understood that the capitalist sector has objective interests in *keeping the wage rate down* in the traditional, for instance, by curbing technological progress:

> The owners of the plantations have no interest in seeing knowledge of new techniques or new seeds conveyed to peasants. [...] The imperialists invest capital and hire workers; it is to their advantage to keep wages low, and even in those cases where they do not actually go out of their way to impoverish the subsistence economy, they will at least very seldom be found doing anything to make it more productive. (Lewis 1954, 149)

In this way, poverty in one sector can be linked to wealth in the other. Lewis, however, considers this to be transitory problems.

The theorists who take Lewis's dual model as their point of departure in the 1950s and 1960s do not realize the analytic potential of the *relation* between the sectors described by Lewis. The model becomes simplified rather than developed: In some analyses of transitional (transitory or dual) societies, technological heterogeneity is considered an indication of people living in *separate economic spheres* and even *different worlds*, a progressive modern and a backward traditional. Development in these societies first and foremost becomes a question of removing traditional attitudes and values.

An example of the increased importance of sociocultural variables at the expense of economic is Albert O. Hirschman's analysis in *The Strategy for Economic Development* (1958). Rejecting Lewis's major explanatory factor, lack of capital, he claims that the cause of underdevelopment is 'the persistent preference for the traditional' (Hirschman 1958, 127). Inhabitants of the backward countries lack the will to improve their lot, which must, together with a *growth perspective*, be transferred from the developed nations. Hirschman obviously thought the sectors unrelated, and his analysis does not represent a break with the idea of automatic spread of the modern sector. The thought strikes him, however, that it may take some time:

> There is reason to believe that certain preindustrial economic activities have today a far better chance to survive than was the case during the rise of industry in Western Europe. The forces of industrialization tend at present, far more than formerly, to *leave the preindustrial sectors alone* for a prolonged period rather than attacking them frontally. (Hirschman 1958, 126, emphasis added)

Technological development opens new opportunities for investment; modernization of the activities of the traditional sector no longer is the only option. Schumacher (1973) even pointed, without a treatment of its causes, at what he termed the *disintegration* and the *poisoning* of the traditional sector, causing mass unemployment and migration to urban slums. He argues that development planners should concentrate on the development of intermediate technologies, appropriate for the use within the traditional sector:

> The 'dual economy' in the developing countries will remain for the foreseeable future. The modern sector will not be able to absorb the whole. (Schumacher 1973, 176)

When the theorists treated here indicate that the transition to modernity may take longer time than expected, they are less in conformity with mainstream modernization thought than when they analyse the causes of slow progress. The major causes outlined are *internal* to the society in question: lack of capital, unrestricted population growth and traditional attitudes producing resistance towards modernization. If the fishermen's choice of technologies which are inferior in terms of productivity is sought to be explained in the spirit of modernization theory, it could be linked to discourses on the importance of cultural values in the making of peasant rationality. What is decisive for their choice is not necessarily as high an income as possible, but for instance the way of life aboard traditional crafts. This may be termed a non-income-optimizing or non-maximum-yield rationality. Essentially, the culturally defined rationality hypothesis implies that certain *values* are attributed to artisan production, values that are not attributed to industrial production. In fishing societies, such values may be related to social organization of the production process. There are technical constraints to social organization; properties of tools may determine how the production process is organized. When type of boat is chosen, size of crew is predetermined as are work practices and inter-crew relations determining when to start work, who decides where to cast the nets and so on. For crewmen, technological modernization may thus imply a change from a more to a less independent position. Their influence aboard the craft may be reduced, and they may even experience deskilling as regards knowledge or physical skill required. Life aboard mechanized and non-mechanized crafts is not the same. Nor are the working hours: Modern boats may have shorter or longer fishing trips than traditional. The ultimate argument when explaining the process would therefore be that being unwilling to pay the cultural cost of higher productivity, the fishermen return to traditional fisheries, thereby sacrificing material progress.

The destruction of antiquated modes of production

The belief that all societies follow similar development trajectories, evolutionism, is central within Marxist development thought:

> The country that is more developed industrially only shows to the less developed, the image of its own future. (Marx 1867a, 7, my translation)

But the popular contention that Marx shares with modernization theorists a totally developmentalist view of social change is perhaps overplayed (Harrison 1988). It should also be stressed that the observed similarities are superficial: Modernization theorists and Marx neither share the assessment of the causes nor the effects of the diffusion process.

Marx's view is founded on the analysis of what he considered the inevitable spread of the capitalist mode of production. The motivating force is the capitalists' urge for profits and the means are labour exploitation and technological progress. Since technological change affects all social relations, it will lead to the extinction of cultures:

> The bourgeoisie cannot exist without constantly revolutionising the instruments of production and thereby the relations of production, and with them the whole relation of society. […] It compels all nations, on pain of extinction, to adopt the bourgeois mode of production; it compels them to introduce what it calls civilization into their midst, i.e. to become bourgeois themselves. In one word, it creates a world after its own image. (Marx and Engels 1848, 37–38)

Capitalism is here seen both as a destructive force, eliminating all non-capitalist modes of production, and at the same time a progressive force, having a *civilizing* effect. The spread of capitalism implies that all non-capitalist modes of production will be eradicated. This is many Marxists' interpretation of Marx. The appearance of capitalism

> signalled the more or less immediate and inevitable disintegration of pre-capitalist modes of production, and the subsumption of the agents of these modes under capitalist relations of production. (Wolpe 1980, 2)

One could claim that the spread of the capitalist mode of production corresponds to the modernization theorists' spread of the modern sector, that only the choice of words differs: What is termed by the modernization theorists integration of traditional societies into the modern world, in Marxist terminology, is destruction of pre-capitalist modes of production by capitalism. However, whereas a fully developed market integration and mass consumption society characterizes the final stage, explicitly or implicitly stated by modernization theorists, capitalism in Marx's view represents the stage in which the productive forces have reached a level which makes socialism possible. It is important to note that the concept of *pre-capitalist* mode of production has several denotations. It may signify a mode historically preceding capitalism, a logically preceding mode and a technologically inferior mode of production (Foster-Carter 1978). According to Jensen (1988), Marx recognized all three criteria.

Marx's definition of mode of production is sufficiently vague to allow for a vast amount of interpretations, forming several schools of followers. There seems to be agreement that the concept at least comprises *the combination of relations and forces of production*. If the concept is used in the *restricted* sense (Wolpe 1980), these are the only components:

> A mode of production is an articulated combination of relations and forces of production [...] The relations of production define a specific mode of appropriation of surplus-labour and the specific forms of social distribution of the means of production [...]. 'Forces of Production' refers to the mode of appropriation of nature, that is to the labour process. (Hindess and Hirst 1975, 10)

To establish the level of the productive forces, the labour process must be identified. This implies studying the instruments of labour, the direct producers, the objects of labour and the division of labour (Vercruijsse 1984). Laclau as well includes relations and forces of production only in his definition:

We [...] designate as a mode of production the logical and mutually co-ordinated articulation of:

1. a determinate type of ownership of the means of production;
2. a determinate form of the appropriation of the economic surplus;
3. a determinate degree of development of the division of labour;
4. a determinate level of development of the productive forces. (Laclau 1971, 34)

Contemplating the huge operationalization problems involved, that these rather wide definitions are considered restricted is somewhat unanticipated. However, theorists applying the concept in an *extended* sense (Wolpe 1980) add *dynamic forces of change* to the static description above. Balibar (1970) and Bettelheim (1972) consider

> the mode of production [...] to be constituted by the combination of the relations and forces of production together with the mechanisms of reproduction or laws of motion derived from those relations and forces of production. (Wolpe 1980, 7)

Modes of production are thus abstract entities which become manifest in concrete societies; the latter are normally termed *social formations* in Marxist literature. (The concepts of social formation, economic formation (Meillassoux 1980), economic system (Laclau 1971) are here considered synonyms.) If the concept of social formation is understood as an abstraction of the concrete society with a history, a specific mode of production identified becomes a label on *structural principles* of society. Structural principles are defined by Giddens as

> principles of organization of societal totalities; factors involved in the overall institutional alignment of a society or type of society. (Giddens 1984, 376)

A capitalist society is a social formation where the capitalist mode of production is manifest. Basic characteristics of the capitalist mode of production are a high level of the productive forces and the division of labour, in combination with specific production relations such as private ownership of the means of production, private appropriation of the surplus of production (profit), labour free of any form of serfdom as well as deprived of the ownership of the means of production. A general law of motion of the capitalist mode of production recognized by most Marxists would be the necessity of capital accumulation for the reproduction of the mode. The heightening of the level of the productive forces implies technological progress; to improve implements of labour and knowledge to increase the amount of surplus value is the major competitive strategy of capital owners in capitalist societies.[2] This strategy is termed *relative* surplus value production as opposed to *absolute* surplus value production; the latter strategy does not imply technological progress, but increased exploitation of labour by for instance a prolongation of the working day (Asheim 1985). Relative surplus value production is considered the more advanced form; it is a characteristic of the capitalist mode of production. The change from absolute to relative surplus value production is a major explanation of the heightening of the level of the productive forces under capitalism.[3] Not only can increased labour productivity be obtained by means of this strategy, it has a positive political side-effect as well, since machines are more easily controlled than workers. The latter argument is by some Marxists considered a major cause of the labour-saving bias of technological advance under capitalism.

The view that the capitalist mode of production continuously expands, and in the process disintegrates and destroys non-capitalist modes, is referred to as orthodox Marxist.[4] It is particularly vivacious among Marxists who consider the industrialization of Asian countries the final proof that capitalism is progressive. They reject, as did Warren and Sender (1980), the notion of underdeveloped countries.

The cause identified by Marx of the spread of the capitalist mode of production beyond its area of origin is

---

[2] Amin (1976, 62) terms this '[The] "endogenous" nature of the progress of the productive forces' a distinctive feature of the capitalist mode of production; 'when an entrepreneur introduces a more advanced technique, the other entrepreneurs are obliged to follow his example'.

[3] Marx distinguishes between situations of *formal subsumption* of labour by capital and situations of *real subsumption* of labour. In cases of formal subsumption, 'given the pre-existing, unchanged mode of labour' (Vercruijsse 1984, 90), surplus value can only be increased as absolute surplus value. In the capitalist mode of production, labour is *really subsumed*, and surplus value can be increased by the continuous increase of relative surplus value.

[4] According to Wolpe,

The analysis of imperialism, particularly as formulated by revolutionary parties in the metropolitan capitalist countries, tended to assume that capitalist expansion implied, in a straightforward way, the destruction of pre-capitalist modes. [...] [Over] a long period of time this view was the unproblematic basis of, particularly Western European Marxism. This interpretation reappears in Brenner (1977) and Avinieri (1969). (Wolpe 1980, 5, and Note 1, 42) the tendency for capacity to produce to increase much faster than capacity to consume, a tendency which is constantly being overcome, by means that reduce the rate of profit. (Amin 1976, 188)

In the competition for markets, crises of overproduction occur, lowering the rate of profit. The solution may be a prolongation of the working day and/ or productivity increases achieved by technological advance. A crisis may also lead to the expansion of markets, either by creating new wants to increase mass consumption or by engaging in trade with non-capitalist societies. Relations between the capitalist mode of production and non-capitalist modes may thus be of different types: Both the market linkage referred to above and the plundering of the riches typical of early colonialism (primitive accumulation) imply the spread of capitalism by means of *exchange relations*, not necessarily leading to the transformation of the non-capitalist mode(s) of production affected into a capitalist mode.[5] A transformation, however, occurs when capital is imported and for instance invested in plantations; then *capitalist relations of production* are introduced. When capitalism spreads beyond the sphere of exchange into the sphere of production, this leads to the *penetration of capitalism*, and ultimately to the destruction of the pre-capitalist mode of production.

Marx's major concern was to explain the formation and dynamics of the emerging capitalist mode of production, an internal European historical process. History is analysed as a succession of modes of production; the modes thoroughly described were the feudal and the capitalist. According to Taylor (1979), Marx treated what he termed the *Asiatic mode of production* very briefly. The relationship between capitalist and non-capitalist modes when the former is externally imposed by means of colonialism was never central in his works (Meillassoux 1980; Wolpe 1980; Foster-Carter 1978). The impression one gets from the above citations is that the process of destruction of pre-capitalist modes of production takes such short time that the period of transition becomes of no significance. But in some of his writings he advanced a more differentiated view; Marx thus was less orthodox in this matter than many of his followers. As regards the development of colonial agriculture, he stated that

---

[5] In the political sphere, exchange relations of this type could lead to the *reinforcement* of existing power structures rather than to a transformation. A case in point is the in the first instance *strengthening* of the position of traditional African leaders caused by the slave trade (Dupré and Rey 1980).

the appearance of capital as an independent and leading force [...] does not take place all at once and generally, but gradually. (Marx 1894, 781)

According to Wolpe (1980), in addition to trade relations, Marx mentioned that the pre-capitalist modes of production may have a *conditioning effect* on the capitalist, and he also found that capital formation within non-capitalist modes of production could provide a basis for capitalist development. Power struggles in the colonies would sometimes lead to the destruction of the pre-capitalist mode by force. In addition to violent resistance, the capitalists met with indirect resistance when striving to recruit free labour to their enterprises:

It is otherwise in the colonies. There the capitalist regime constantly comes up against the obstacle presented by the producer, who, as owner of his own conditions of labour, employs that labour to enrich himself instead of the capitalist. The contradiction between these two diametrically opposed economic systems has its practical manifestation here in the struggle between them. (Marx 1867b, 765)

He claimed that capitalist penetration could be temporarily hindered because of the

obstacles presented by the internal solidarity and organization of pre-capitalist, national modes of production to the corrosive influence of commerce. (Marx 1894, 328)

Albeit the above analysis, there is no reason to claim that Marx considered the development potentials of the colonies to be fundamentally different from those of the developed world. Marx 'appeared convinced of the pervasiveness of capitalism' (Harrison 1988, 64). There is thus reason to believe that the above penetration problems met by capitalism in the colonies were considered transitional. The capitalist mode of production will take over, but the speed would differ: both due to a varying strength of internal resistance and because the 'dominance of capital is not established all at once' (Wolpe 1980, 4).

Marx's analysis of the relationship between the modes of production in Western Europe raises questions which are of particular relevance in the debate on the articulation of modes of production in the Third World. In Western Europe,

the capitalist regime has either directly conquered the whole domain of national production, or, where economic conditions are less developed, it, at least, indirectly controlled those strata of society which, through

belonging to the antiquated mode of production, continue to exist side
by side with it in gradual decay. (Marx 1885, 765)

There are considerable conceptual difficulties here. How can something
belong to an antiquated mode of production in gradual decay, when the
mode, evidently, has been *transformed* by the expansion of the capitalist mode?
When directly or indirectly controlled by capitalism, is it still pre-capitalist?
How transformed can it be and *remain* (the same) mode of production, capable
of being reproduced as a (coherent) totality? This brings us to the problem of
the side by side existing modes of production.

A reasonable interpretation of the orthodox view would be that a nation in
transition to capitalism consists of an area where an expanding capitalist mode
of production has taken root, another area which is under attack (becoming
capitalist) and an area which has not (yet) been affected by capitalist expansion.[6]
Here, pre-capitalist mode(s) of production still prevail. Alternatively, the latter
area is affected, that is, the prevailing mode(s) of production are in decay. In
this case, the country consists of an expanding capitalist mode of production
and mode(s) of production in transition.

When reading some Marxist literature, it seems that pre-capitalist modes
of production continue to manifest themselves as coherent systems long after
the introduction of the capitalist mode of production. This indicates that
there is no question of a *penetration* of capitalism into the (total) economy;
rather that (in liberal terminology) *enclaves* have been introduced, occupying
a limited space, alongside the non-capitalist modes. They do not escape the
dualist contention of coexisting modes of production.[7] To me it is, however,
unthinkable that a transformation did not commence when relations were
established between an enclave and the hinterland. The actual size of the
territory where capitalist enterprises were established is of little significance;
small enclaves such as Malacca and Singapore exercised profound influence
on enormous hinterlands by virtue of their relations with their rulers' mother
countries. Even in the early days of imperialism, economic relations between
enclaves and hinterland were many-fold: The imperialists bought or conquered
the land; they traded with the interior; used native labour, slaves or free men;
and so on. This must have affected the hinterland societies – to a smaller
or greater extent. There were changes in cultural, production and ecological

---

[6] 'Area' could here signify both the spatial (the territory) and the economic sphere.

[7] According to Ruccio and Simon (1986, 213), 'the various modes of production are
seen to exist alongside but essentially independent of one another. This position has
traditionally been called "dualism" and Frank's original rejection of it is shared by the
articulation of MOP theorists.'

systems. Although hardly (historically) identifiable, an important qualitative change came when external relations started to *dominate* economic activities in their sphere of influence, when societal change was conditioned by these relations. Then non-capitalist relations are no longer reinforced due to their relations with emerging capitalism but are dissolved and destroyed.

The interpretation of the orthodox position in spatial terms demonstrates that viewed superficially, the connotations of two modes of production coexisting seem to be an equally dualist contention as the notion of coexisting sectors of the modernization theorists. What is the difference between the *absorption* of the traditional by the modern and the *destruction* of the pre-capitalist mode of production by capitalism? Whether *sector* equates mode of production clearly depends on *which components the entities include* and on the perceived *nature of the relations* between them. Recalling the modernization view, the economic linkage between the entities identified was the transfer of labour from the traditional to the modern sector. If sector is substituted by mode of production, the orthodox Marxist position appears *only if* 'the subsumption of the agents of these modes under capitalist relations of production' (Wolpe 1980, 2) denotes the absorption of labour into capitalist enterprises, or the (sudden) transformation of indigenous economic enterprises and institutions into capitalist ones; that is, the formation of capitalist productive forces and relations of production. In the analysis of hindrances to the occurrence of the latter event (the transition to capitalism), the path of orthodox Marxists and articulationists divides: The former can be found close to the modernization theorists' positions, the latter forcefully contest their views.[8]

The transition to capitalism in the colonial context

Escaping dualism

Non-orthodox Marxist development theorists who study the effects of capitalist expansion from an articulation of modes of production angle sustain Marx's view on the driving forces of the capitalist mode of production, but strive to escape the dualism inherent in his position. In general, they may escape dualism, but seem not to escape evolutionism; see for instance Rey's stages in

---

[8] In development theory, dependency theorists are sometimes separated from later articulationists based primarily on a controversy over the thesis of peripheral capitalism. I have, however, classified those who have a mutual starting point in Marx's concept of modes of production and who consider Third World societies as composed of articulating modes or components of modes, as articulationists. This is close to Ruccio and Simon's (1986) concept of 'The Mode of Production School'.

capitalist expansion in developing countries (Dupré and Rey 1980). A critique of the position is found in Ruccio and Simon (1986, 214).

The purpose of including Marxist development theories here is not to seek the validation of Marx's (or any other theorists') developmentalism. A search for characteristics of developing countries which would fit into such categories would result in severe oversimplifications and mistakes. For instance, the notion is of a *natural economy* being destroyed by capitalism (Bradby 1980) or of capitalism and primitive societies (Terray 1972). Thus, this part of the articulationists' discourse is of no significance here. The purpose of my empirical investigation is *not* to determine whether the societies in question can be characterized as previously *lineage* or *petty commodity* in articulation with capitalism or whatever mode can be deduced from Marx.[9] There is no point in substituting one stage theory for another; evolutionism and linearity *as such* should be distrusted. What is relevant here is the articulationists' analyses of *mechanisms which may lead to a prolonged presence of non-capitalist relations*, and thus to delayed transitions. In other words, the search is for an understanding of Bettelheim's mysterious statement:

> Inside social formations in which the capitalist mode of production is not directly predominant, [...] the main tendency is not to dissolution of the non-capitalist modes of production, but to their *conservation-dissolution*. (Bettelheim 1972, 298, emphasis in the original)

The articulationists hold a wide variety of views.[10] It is difficult to discern whether, to what extent and on which issues their disagreements (or even agreements) are significant since the discourse is characterized by conceptual confusion: With Marx's vague statement that some strata of society, although belonging to an antiquated mode of production, continue to exist side by side with a capitalist while being in gradual decay, he would have felt very much at home in the discussion of the articulationists. However, they all underline the

---

[9] An example of the latter is Amin's (1976, 22) four pre-capitalist modes, the 'primitive-communal', the 'tribute-paying' (of which the feudal is a developed form), the 'slave-owning' and the 'simple petty-commodity' mode of production. He does not, however, advocate their historical sequence and characterizes attempts of drawing 'any sort of analogy between identical modes of production integrated in formations belonging to different epochs' as absurd. Marx's historical materialism, where he portrays the succession of modes of production, should not be considered a testable theory.

[10] In the category of articulationist I here include Terray (1972), Alavi (1975), Cardoso (1975), Coquery-Vidrovitch (1975), Amin (1976), Scott (1976), Banaji (1977), Bartra (1979), Deere and de Janvry (1979), Taylor (1979), Bradby (1980), Dupré and Rey (1980) and Meillassoux (1980).

uneven character of the transition to capitalism in the Third World, and seem to share a dual purpose: The analysis of the mechanisms by which the *capitalist* mode of production is reproduced includes an analysis of the mechanisms of reproduction of *non-capitalist* modes, or of components of such modes:

> The 'articulation of MOP's' approach, as it has been termed, tends to explain the phenomenon of underdevelopment in terms of the relationships among and between capitalist and noncapitalist modes of production. (Ruccio and Simon 1986, 213)

In the encounters, non-capitalist relations may play a crucial role in the reproduction and expansion of capitalism. An extreme position is found when examining articulationists' roots in Marxist theory. Luxemburg (1913) claims that the capitalist mode of production cannot persist unless it continues to expand and exploit non-capitalist societies. As a mode of production capitalism is incomplete and *parasitic*:

> Capitalist production cannot exist without the labour of other social formations. [...] Accumulation is more swift and violent than under pure capitalist social relations. (Luxemburg 1913, 113, my translation)

Articulationists focus attention on the modes under attack. Examining their ability to hold the position necessitates an inquiry into the strengths and weaknesses of non-capitalist relations, which the penetrating power of capitalist relations of production is conditioned upon. Most articulationists would argue that the *subordination* of non-capitalist modes to capitalism should be underlined, but their disagreements, however, mount on other important issues.

Firstly, at what level of abstraction should the concept of mode of production be conceptualized, and which indicators of the presence of a mode should be recommended? The concept is by some theorists applied at the level of the social formation, and in the narrowest application, it seems that each valley of a landscape could be said to contain its own mode of production. The latter suggests that the production process is confused with the labour process: a sin often committed by Marxists, according to Godelier (1977). There is thus disagreement on what indicators of the presence of a mode of production should be used. If the indicator of a mode of production is 'different forms of co-operation as determined partly by the instruments of labour', which was advocated by Terray (1972), it would imply 'the identification of as many modes of production as there are labour processes' (Vercruijsse 1984, 10). A translation into a liberal language (which here solely means understandable) is probably requested by the non-inaugurated: This would probably parallel the reductionism appearing where tools are used only as an indicator of technology, after which technology is only used to identify economic sectors, giving the absurd result of as many economic sectors as there are types of tools. In the same manner, based on single indicators, Marxists may construct an endless multitude of modes of production. The labour process only (or technology only) is an insufficient indicator of a mode of production. However, given the emphasis on the level of development of the productive forces in Marxist theory, it is unlikely that the technologies in use would be *excluded* when reconstructing a mode based on combined indicators. To the contrary, technological heterogeneity is a prominent indicator of the presence of more than one mode of production.

A related problem is the distinction between *mode* and *form* of production. The content of the concept of form varies. Some theorists would apply form at the same level of abstraction as mode but would add that a form of production cannot dominate in a social formation. (They would say petty commodity *form* and capitalist *mode* of production.) Other theorists, however, use the concept of form of production when operationalizing the concept of mode of production. A mode is then an ideal type with a low empirical content; a form of production is closer to empirical reality.

Secondly, there is disagreement on whether reproduced relations of non-capitalist modes of production form *coherent systems*, or if they are singular relations of dissolved systems, bearing witness of non-capitalist modes of the past. The criterion of coherence is essential since it focuses attention on whether the relations are capable at reproduction as coherent systems or should be considered incomplete. Jensen (1988) distinguishes between three positions in the debate; the first are theorists who consider Third World societies as composed of *articulating coherent* modes of production; the capitalist mode, however, dominates (Rey's position). Other theorists find that when capitalism enters the scene, the pre-capitalist modes of production are completely *transformed*; the resulting society is an amalgamation, neither capitalist nor non-capitalist (Alavi's position). A third position is that of theorists who find that a (dominant) capitalist mode of production articulates reproduced (singular) components of dissolved non-capitalist modes (the position of Amin and de Janvry). I will refer to their position as the mixed mode of production position.

Peripheral capitalism

A third issue of the discourse on the nature of transition to capitalism concerns the validity of the thesis of peripheral capitalism. Is capitalism in the Third World *peripheral* and thus unique in history? One position is that laws of motion of the capitalist mode of production in the First World are different from those of capitalism in the Third World (capitalism itself is peripheral). Another position is that laws of motion of capitalism are the same (everywhere and at all times), but outcomes of the penetration of capitalism in the First World are different from outcomes of the penetration process in the Third World (the social formation is peripheral capitalist): Contextual differences shape different outcomes. In the first position one finds several theorists of the dependency school, a prominent spokesman among them is Samir Amin.

According to Samir Amin in *Unequal Development* (1976), capitalist expansion in the Third World does not lead to the formation of capitalist societies like those of centre countries, but to *peripheral capitalist* societies. Peripheral capitalism results from the way in which developing countries were integrated into the world economy, in the process of capitalist penetration in a *colonial context*. The processes of underdevelopment continue after Independence. Dependency theory thus represents a break with linearity and developmentalism ingrained in modernization theories. Where the latter describe the backwardness of developing countries, Amin seeks to explain the deviations of processes of change in these societies from a normal (centre) capitalist course: Where modernization theorists observe overpopulation, he observes structural unemployment; that is, the formation of a huge reserve army of labour and lacking outlets of labour made superfluous by technological advance. Whether experiencing increased economic differentiation or not, the economies of Third World countries are characterized by disarticulation, lacking linkages between economic sectors. Strong external linkages explain weak internal; this *extraversion* of the economy conditions the transition.

The differences between centre and peripheral societies indicate more than a delay in the development towards capitalism; they are structural. Dependency theory challenges orthodox Marxism in particular, by contesting the simplistic view that capitalist expansion by necessity leads to the eradication of non-capitalist modes of production. Transformation is incomplete and obstructed due to the role assigned to Third World countries in the international division of labour, that of suppliers of cheap labour and raw materials. Therefore, structural features of Third World technologically heterogeneous societies still originate within the capitalist as well as within pre-capitalist modes of production.

Pre-capitalist social formations were stable structures where different hierarchically arranged modes coexisted. But where capitalism enters the scene 'the capitalist mode tends to become exclusive, destroying all the other' (Amin 1976, 22). This argument is however only valid in *centre* social formations, which become fully capitalist since capital accumulation is secured by the formation of a viable internal market. A major indication of a complete transition is according to Amin that a *commodity economy* has developed. His definition of the capitalist mode of production underlines this stance; social production, labour power and the means of production become commodities to be exchanged. In the process, producers become proletarians, they are separated from the means of production which are appropriated by a capitalist class. In peripheral capitalist social formations, pre-capitalist modes of production are not eradicated but transformed:

> the capitalist mode, which is dominant, subjects the others and transforms them, depriving them of their distinctive functioning in order to subordinate them to its own, without, however, radically destroying them. (Amin 1976, 22)

Capitalist relations dominate; from domination results the eradication, transformation or reproduction of components of pre-capitalist modes of production according to accumulation needs of capital. Thus, in the process of capitalist expansion,

> the agricultural communities, maintained as reserves of cheap labour, are being both undermined and perpetuated at the same time, [the society is] undergoing a prolonged crisis and not a smooth transition to capitalism. (Meillassoux 1980, 199)

Reproduction of labour in the pre-capitalist sector

There are major structural differences between an *autocentric* model, which characterizes centre capitalist social formations, and an *extraverted* model, which characterizes peripheral capitalist social formations. In centre capitalist societies, increased labour productivity results in wage improvements and (ultimately) in the formation of a middle class. In peripheral capitalist societies, this link disappears since the peripheral society

> will by every means – economic and non-economic – be made subject to this new function of providing relatively cheap labour to the export sector. [...] The wage rate in the peripheral export sector will [...] be as low as the economic, social, and *political* conditions allow it to be. (Amin 1984, 208, emphasis in the original)

Here, Amin is close to Baran's (1957) analysis of wages. Baran's understanding is Ricardian; building on *the iron law of wages* which signifies that the wage level may diminish to what the most desperate of men can accept.[11] That this level may be *below the subsistence level* was recognized by Ricardo, but his conclusion was Malthusian, since he anticipated that the resulting misery would reduce the number of workers and thus lead to an increase in the wage rate. In contrast to Malthus, Ricardo thought that industrialization would modify this pessimistic picture: In an industrialized society, production volumes would increase faster than population, 'and hence wages may remain above the subsistence wage for an indefinite period' (Brue 1994, 46).

In Amin's (1984) analysis of Third World societies, a complete industrialization is considered hindered, and the wage rate in manufacturing industries is lower than the labour productivity justifies. The *extraverted* nature of the economy explains that technological advance not necessarily leads to a general increase in the wage rate. Capitalists in the export sector consider it unprofitable to raise the wage level to strengthen internal demand; on the contrary, it is lucrative to secure the reproduction of a large pool of under- and unemployed poor:

> The high level of unemployment ensures a minimum wage rate which is relatively rigid and frozen both in the export sector and in the luxury goods sector; wages do not emerge both as a cost and an income which creates a demand, vital to the central model, but on the contrary figure only as a cost – demand itself originating elsewhere, from abroad or from the income of the privileged social classes. (Amin 1984, 211)

Hence, if politically possible, the wage rate in the export sector may decrease to a level below what is needed for labour reproduction. The cause of this artificially set wage level is that labour is being reproduced in the pre-capitalist sector. The existence of reproduced relations of non-capitalist modes of

---

[11] In 1766, Turgot formulated a theory where he held that 'competition among workers lowers the wage to the minimum subsistence level' (Brue 1994, 46). Ricardo's version a hundred years later was termed the 'iron law of wages'. He differentiates between the *natural* and the *market* price of labour. The natural price 'is that price which is necessary to enable the labourers, one with another, to subsist and to perpetuate their race, without either increase or diminution' (Ricardo 1817, in Baran 1957, 46). The market price of labour, determined by supply and demand, will fluctuate around the natural price. The long-run tendency is that workers receive the subsistence minimum:

in the long run the worker only gets a minimum wage. [...] When the market price of labor rises above the natural price, a worker can rear a large and healthy family. As population increases, wages fall to their natural price or *even below*. When the market price of labor is below the natural price, misery reduces the working population and wages rise. (Brue 1994, 46, emphasis added) production may secure a *wage subsidy* to producers of the export sector. To capture this mechanism, de Janvry and Garramón introduced the concept of *functional dualism*:

> Labor costs can be further reduced by maintaining the subsistence economy that assumes the cost of reproduction of the labor force. *Functional dualism* between modern and traditional sectors thus makes it possible to sustain a level of wage below the cost of maintenance and reproduction of the labour force – a cost which would determine the minimum wage for a fully proletarianized labor force. [...] The reinforcement of functional dualism is what Baran and Frank have labeled 'the development of underdevelopment'. (de Janvry and Garramón 1977, 34, emphasis in the original)

Non-capitalist modes of production do not die; they are functional for capitalist accumulation and expansion by lowering the cost of labour reproduction. The reproduction of labour in the pre-capitalist sector hampers the formation of a prosperous middle class and the eradication of poverty. To the extent that First World capitalists and consumers benefit from these relations of production, Third World producers are *super-exploited* through the mechanism of unequal exchange of values. By dependency theorists of a 'deterministic stance' (Hesselberg 1986), transition towards a fully capitalist society is considered 'blocked'.

Technological backwardness and marginalization

Technological advance in peripheral capitalist societies faces considerable hindrances. In the past, some colonies experienced an active de-industrialization, and others were prohibited from starting industrial production by law. Limited transfers of advanced-modern technology due to patenting and extremely high prices are by dependency theorists seen as the continuation of colonial dominance, manifestations of 'neo-colonialism'. According to Amin (1984), the world capitalist system is inherently polarizing. Applied in the sphere of technology, the integration of Third World countries into the world system implies that the level of technology in the traditional production of these countries stagnates, while simultaneously, advanced modern production progresses:

> As regards the level of development of the productive forces, it will be heterogeneous (whereas in the self-reliant model, it was homogeneous), advanced (and sometimes very advanced) in the export sector, and

backward in 'the rest of the economy'. This backwardness (maintained by the system) is the condition which allows the export sector to benefit from cheap labour. (Amin 1984, 208)

A systemic irrationality is thus demonstrated, since factor endowments do not determine technology choice, in which case labour-abundant settings should favour labour-absorbing and not labour-displacing technologies. This explains the extreme heterogeneity of such social formations.

A major aspect of the *extraversion* of the economies of the Third World is their vulnerability to increased prices of imported input factors. As expressed by Singer and Ansari,

As far as the poor countries are concerned, world inflation has been a mixed blessing. The prices of some of their most important export commodities have risen, but so have the prices of manufactures, food, fertiliser, and oil. [...T]he overall effect has been negative. (Singer and Ansari 1978, 23)

This argument concerns several processes which are not necessarily related. Firstly, they point at price trends of the world market price of export commodities and at the greater difficulties which poor countries have (as compared to the rich) to adjust. According to Reinert,

In the case of the world system during the last century, wages and prices in the industrialized center countries have been inflexible downward, while the prices of wages in the periphery have been reversible in real terms. As a result, any international crisis will hit the periphery much harder than it hits the rich inflexible center countries. The use of selective protectionism by the center in times of crisis only reinforces this effect. (Reinert 1980, 220)

The oil price shock, which 'considerably aggravate(s) the problems of unemployment and mass poverty' (Singer and Ansari 1978, 21), is a case in point. The increase in oil prices was accompanied by an increase in the price of wheat, fertilizer and manufactured goods, which came in addition to the problems arising when much more of their export earnings had to be spent on oil imports. Secondly, developing countries may also 'import' economic problems due to the economic policies of industrial countries; periodically they may import inflation, for instance. If the price of essential input factors is affected, a likely effect would be the stagnation or retardation of technological modernization.

A corollary to technological is social polarization: The penetration of capitalism leads, on the one hand, to the formation of a wealthy elite which is continuously getting richer and, on the other, to the formation of large poor segment of society. Poor rural producers are unable to benefit from the positive effects of technological modernization, while at the same time, the prospect of improving their living conditions has deteriorated during modernization. This *marginalization* process, 'a series of mechanisms of various kinds which impoverish the masses' (Amin 1984, 211), is considered a precondition for the continued exploitation of the Third World by the First.[12] It also guarantees increased incomes to the local privileged classes which, through the adoption of Western consumption patterns, strengthen relations between the elites of the First and the Third World in all spheres of society.

In dependency theory, technological backwardness is thus *not* considered a remnant, an indication of the presence of a residual traditional sector. Quite the contrary, Amin (1976, 1984) maintains that technologies are *kept* backward; traditional technologies are continuously being reproduced since they are functional for capitalist accumulation. In primary production, low profitability (and thus a low rate of investment) may secure the formation of a labour reserve as well as cheap foodstuff, serving the interests of urban economic and political elites. The external orientation and the distortion of demand towards luxury consumption by the elites explain why subsistence production is being neglected by development planners. Investments in such production are not considered well paying, and therefore its modernization is impossible. This is how technological *stagnation* in primary production may be analysed within this paradigm, but more dramatic courses of events are also sought explained. Amin claims that extraversion may force agriculture into stagnation and '*sometimes even to retrogression*' (Amin 1976, 206, emphasis added). As I stated in Chapter 1, this is the only reference made in the literature studied where a process is denoted 'retrogression' and linked to structural features of Third World societies. The explanation factor pointed at is population pressure on land:

> The increase in the density of population in the countryside leads to a *retrogression in agricultural technique*, for progress in agriculture is usually expressed in the use of more capital and fewer men per hectare. (Amin 1976, 206, emphasis added)

---

[12] Mechanisms mentioned are 'proletarianization, semi-proletarianization, and impoverishment without proletarianization of the peasants; urbanization and massive increase of urban unemployment and underemployment' (Amin 1984, 211).

Here he describes a situation where modernization is reversed; average labour productivity of the production unit is lowered; it is now characterized by more men and less capital. But it is not *necessarily* a situation where *technological* retrogression can be identified. Where more labour is added to a fixed plot of land, labour productivity decreases after a certain point, unless, simultaneously, new technology is introduced. Area productivity may increase, however, if intensification does not lead to a reduction of the quality of the soil.

According to my definition, the situations of reduced labour productivity referred to by Amin are cases of technological retrogression if a retrogression of tools (in the production unit) or a retrogressive mobility of labour (from one production unit to another) can be identified. Hypothetically, a peasant farmer may experience that his technologies become less sophisticated for a variety of reasons. Increased prices of input factors, for instance pesticides, may reverse part of the green revolution as he returns to manual weeding, or lower the rate of fossil energy consumption on the farm. Insufficient demand or reduced prices of the produce may also lead to retrogression of tools – if it results in lacking capital to maintain machines, for instance. A retrogressive mobility of labour occurs for instance if the peasant's sons move to other production units where labour productivity is lower. This probably sounds more unlikely than it is; they may start new farms on less fertile soils. A similar solution open to *some* peasants facing labour surplus problems or reduced incomes is to increase the size of the land holding. Normally, the land firstly cultivated would be the best suited for a certain crop. If the land added to the production unit is of a lower quality, the farmer meets with a *resource quality depletion* problem which may reduce average labour productivity without involving the technological level of the farm.

Since in Amin's analysis population pressure is underlined, *overpopulation* is given explanatory power. But in what sense are the localities in question overpopulated? Population growth representing constraints to capital formation is considered *a major cause* of stagnation of technological advance within the modernization paradigm: Developing countries are considered overpopulated in the *absolute* sense. Amin, however, finds that localities may be overpopulated in the *relative* sense and considers the phenomenon a symptom of marginalization rather than a cause. Marginalization of the producers thus becomes

the manifestation of a specific law of overpopulation of the periphery, which itself results from the extraversion of the peripheral economy and the mechanisms that exclude from production an increasing section of these countries labour power. (Amin 1976, 246)

Adding more labour to a production unit with a fixed capital level, and technological retrogression to reduce costs, may be peasant farmers' strategies to avoid population pressure in situations where there are *no outlets of labour* to other industries, a 'lack of a way forward through autocentric industrialization' (Amin 1976, 211). All may result in modernization reversed, reduced average labour productivity, but not necessarily to a reversal of capitalism to a pre-capitalist stage. On the contrary, it may be the manifestation of the peasants' deeper integration into a *peripheral* capitalist economy where market forces work against their interests. In the normal case (during the transition to capitalism in centre social formations), technological advance in agriculture was a prerequisite of industrial growth. It served the two-fold aim of providing labour to manufacturing industries and food to a growing urban population. Labour made superfluous by technological advance in primary production was absorbed when other industries expanded. In contrast, when capitalism penetrates Third World social formations,

> The distortion of the traditional mode evicts part of the population from the land, proletarianizing it, but without creating a demand such as to provide employment for this surplus of population caused by the subjecting of the precapitalist structures to the requirements of foreign capital. (Amin 1976, 211)

Where alternative employment opportunities are lacking, peasants' children may also choose to stay on the land, just as fishermen's sons may choose not to leave the village. Avoiding urban slums, they try their luck at home although returns to labour approach zero and they continuously are getting poorer. However, the solution of reduced average labour productivity by *adding surplus labour to the production unit* is more feasible on a farm than on a boat; in the first case, soil erosion may sadly result – but a boat might sink. Fleet expansion or a bigger boat would be needed, not necessarily leading to reduced labour productivity. But this might be the outcome of increased scale of production if expansion occurs where resources are seriously threatened.

Explaining technological retrogression

Diminishing returns

Theoretical discussions on situations where producers face diminishing returns were central in the classical economic thought of Ricardo and Malthus.[13]

---

[13] Turgot was the first to formulate a theory of diminishing returns and the Intensive Margin (see below), which was later developed by Ricardo in his theory of rent (Brue 1994). Reinert phrases a modern version of this theory:

Maintaining that some of their arguments still are valid, Erik S. Reinert claims in *International Trade and the Economic Mechanisms of Underdevelopment* (1980) that the phenomenon of diminishing returns has been neglected economic theory:

> After the great colonial expansion [...] the concept of diminishing returns withered away from the science. Faced with the almost unending prairies of the New World of North America, how could anybody attach any importance to decreasing returns resulting from people having to resort to inferior and marginal land? (Reinert 1980, 101)

In the following centuries, the societies in which economic thought was formed were characterized by the growth of manufacturing industries:

> The carrying capacity – in terms of both number of human beings and ecological sustainability – is infinitely higher in an industrialised nation than in an agricultural nation. Even a relatively inefficient manufacturing sector provides much greater welfare to a nation than having no manufacturing sector at all. (Reinert 2004, 159)

Increasing returns to scale reached immense proportions – and the theory of diminishing returns was neglected.

In view of the above discussion on population pressure on land, Ricardo's distinction between *rent at the extensive and at the intensive margin of cultivation* may be of relevance. These are two qualitatively different situations in which the law of diminishing returns may operate. As interpreted by Reinert,

> *The Extensive Margin* diminishing returns take place when poorer and poorer quality of one factor of production [...] are brought into production, and equal amount of productive effort [...] produce progressively less in final output. (Reinert 1980, 99, emphasis added)

This type of diminishing returns faced the farmer in the above example, where land of a lower quality was added to the production unit (the resource quality

---

As equal units of one of two factors of production (e.g. labor and capital) is added to another *fixed* factor of production (e.g. land), a point will be reached beyond which equal quantities of the variable factors of production added, although increasing the total return, will yield a less than proportionate return to the variable factors. In other words, the marginal productivity of all factors involved will decrease, also labor productivity. (Reinert 1980, 98, emphasis in the original)

depletion situation). Here, average labour productivity of the production unit was reduced without involving the technological level or the number of producers. But situations where these factors *are* changed may also be analysed in terms of diminishing returns:

> In the case of *the Intensive Margin* diminishing returns, amounts of labor and capital are successively applied to the same physical quantity of a fixed factor of production. [...] Beyond a certain point, further application of labor and/or capital will be attended by progressively smaller increases in product. Finally, the decreasing increases will converge toward zero. (Reinert 1980, 99, emphasis added)

This may be termed *the labour/capital pressure situation*. Situations are described in which negative scale effects operate. According to Reinert (1980, 52) this will invariably result when expanding the utilization of *God-given resources* such as 'fishing, mining, agriculture, [...] the only activities which operate with one fixed factor of production – fish, ore, and land, which is given by nature'. There is however a difference between non-renewable and renewable resources. Any resource regulation measure in the case of ore would eventually fail with continued exploitation, but this is not the case with biological resources.

According to Alfred Marshall in *Principles of Economics* (1890, 246), diminishing returns may affect any production, and not only production:

> The notion of the marginal employment of any agent of production implies a possible tendency to diminishing return from its increased employment. Excessive applications of any means to the attainment of any end are indeed sure to yield diminishing returns in every branch of business; and one may say, in all the affairs of life.

This is 'The law of or statement of tendency to Diminishing Return' (Marshall 1890, 98). Marshall however recognized the major difference between agriculture and mining, where one factor of production is fixed, and manufacturing, where 'the supply of machines may be increased without limit' (Marshall 1890, 249). The concept of *tendency* in the above formulation is of importance: Exploitation of a natural resource will be driven into diminishing returns, but measures can be taken to avoid this. Marshall's example is farmers who move on to new land or exit the industry:

> As his sons grow up they will have more capital and labour to apply to land; and in order to avoid obtaining a diminishing return, they will want to cultivate more land. But perhaps by this time all the neighbouring

land is already taken up, and in order to get more they must buy it or pay a rent for the use of it, or migrate where they can get it for nothing. (Marshall 1890, 98)

But what if you are *stuck* in a place or economic activity, and exit is no option? Reinert analyses such situations in terms of lock-in. Building on the classic and neoclassical theory, Reinert's key argument is that productivity improvement must be maximized to achieve economic development, and that 'different economic activities contribute to economic development in widely divergent degrees' (Reinert 1980, 27). He argues that primary production and mining are often subsidized in industrial countries to keep up real wages. The aim may be to protect workplaces, for national food security reasons or to uphold a preferred settlement pattern. If agricultural or forest produce, fish and minerals are to be produced while simultaneously curbing the effects of diminishing returns, the solution is the *diversification* of the economy: economic growth based on manufacturing industries and *redistribution* of surplus to primary production and mining. He demonstrates how undifferentiated developing countries may 'specialize in becoming poor' because their economic activities are driven into areas of diminishing returns. Technological and thus economic backwardness is caused by and continues due to the role which developing countries obtained during colonialism as producers and suppliers of raw materials: These economic activities are bad for economic growth due to *inherent properties of the produce*. In addition, to a varying extent, production is mechanizable, and 'unmechanizable economic activities will over time come to appear as labor intensive' (Reinert 1980, 30); therefore they are less fitted to promote economic development. Since they are subject to diminishing returns, basing economic growth on their exploitation cannot result in lasting progress.

Reinert explicitly attempts to produce a non-Marxist explanation of underdevelopment; but the situations of reduced labour productivity he describes may well be considered cases of backwardness maintained by the system, the position held by Amin.[14] Reinert argues that in diversified economies, economic activities will not expand into diminishing returns; where this irregularity may occur, the adjustment is to 'force up the price of

---

[14] It is difficult to avoid dependency theory when tracing Reinert's roots in development theory. He agrees with 'the unequal exchange school' that 'the key to the process of polarization of world income in the two groups – center and periphery – is to be found in the institution of international trade' (1980, 18) and aims at bridging the communication gap between Marxists and non-Marxists where theories parallel, that is, 'the realities referred to are the same' (1980, 235).

the product maintaining the average national return to both labor […] and capital' (Reinert 1980, 106). Marginal resources are utilized much longer in developing countries because real wages are *reversible*. They are *not* in industrial countries 'where strong labor unions (can refuse) to take the cut in real wages' (Reinert 1980, 219). Here, economic activities subject to diminishing returns 'die a natural death in the competition for labor with other economic activities' (Reinert 1980, 178).

Situations where the producers face diminishing returns and have few alternative employment opportunities are by Reinert analysed in terms of a lock-in effect. Describing the diseconomies of scale in the banana industry of Ecuador in the late 1960s (an example of the Extensive Margin), he concludes that

> In a situation with a large oversupply of cheap labor such an immiserizing development may continue for decades. Real wages in a country like Ecuador are reversible until the level of physical subsistence is reached, since there is no employment in alternative activities giving a better pay. (Reinert 1980, 177)

However, technological change may counteract a tendency of diminishing returns. In the tin mining industry of Bolivia, the introduction of more advanced technology made previously unprofitable mines profitable, but since these new mines are of a lower quality than the old, the average labour productivity of the industry is reduced. (Reduced labour productivity was here the outcome of technology choice; this should therefore be termed technological retrogression at industry level.) This is an example of the Intensive Margin: As more marginal mines are being exploited, labour productivity came under attack. Technological change could result in increased labour productivity, but this

> will depend on the outcome of the race between the diminishing returns pulling worker productivity down and technological development which works to bring productivity up. (Reinert 1980, 190)

In such situations, average labour productivity may increase when annual production contracts.

The above race could be observed in the third case of diminishing returns described, namely in the Peruvian cotton growing industry. Here, technological development

> *was completely dwarfed* by the negative effects of the increase of scale of operation. Specialization in sugar as well as in cotton in the international

division of labor has proved to run the economy into negative scale effects, which, in spite of important technical improvement, kept labor productivity steady or decreasing, with resulting negative consequences for the real wages of the common man. (Reinert 1980, 227, emphasis in the original)

Reinert's analyses are at industry and nation levels, which implies that variations in the strategies of different production units must not necessarily be discussed. Neither are different strategies of the actors within production units a focus; owners and various groups of workers will experience the effects of diminishing returns differently and react differently. However, he points at what happened in the mining industry of Bolivia after the collapse of the state mining company: Many mines were taken over by small firms with more primitive tools.[15]

The discourses on diminishing returns, found in classical and neoclassical economic theory, and discussed by Reinert (1980), place the processes of technological retrogression in a more open theoretical landscape. Modernization may thus reverse due to labour productivity reductions as producers start to exploit more marginal resources (the resource quality depletion situation) or when productive assets are added to a, in terms of resources, fixed production unit (the labour/capital pressure situation). There may be interesting similarities as regards the ultimate *causes* of reduced labour productivity in the different settings Reinert describes and mine; ultimately, the mechanisms to be analysed are what keeps the level of technology low and reproduces poverty in Third World societies.

Gaining more by producing less

A major question in my analysis of fishing societies concerns *stagnation* of technological modernization; why are all fishermen not found aboard modern boats where modernization started ages ago? The principal question, however, concerns *reversal* of modernization. Both forms of technological retrogression – retrogression of tools and retrogressive mobility of labour – lead to an absolute reduction of labour productivity as seen from the level of the producer, the production unit, the industry and/or the nation. The first form demands primarily an analysis of craft owners' choices. To explain the latter, I must figure out why some fishermen aboard modern boats believe they gain more by producing less. And I must find out why they turn to artisanal fisheries instead of exiting the industry when leaving industrial fisheries.

---

[15] Erik S. Reinert, personal communication, October 1993.

Explaining stagnation as well as retrogression involves finding out why some old relations of production systems refuse to die. By sketching briefly how structural features of technological heterogeneous societies are understood in selected development theories, I have tried to capture possible explanations. It may be inferred that *my selection of theories* explains why I have not found an explicit treatment of such phenomena. However, the selection is not narrow, I have searched high and low. My stubborn conviction that one of these days I would stumble over a dusty copy of *Retrogression Processes Explained* next to *The Rise and Fall of the Roman Empire*, I had to renounce as time went by. All development theories treated discuss stagnation phenomena; but as regards the problem of retrogression, I have tried to find out what explanations they *would have offered* if they had recognized the process. My discussion therefore by necessity has attained a general and at times speculative character, since I deduced from the logic of the theories explanations of a process which is not explicitly treated. The brief mentioning of a retrogression in agricultural technique due to a special kind of overpopulation in peripheral capitalist societies (Amin 1976) is an exception. How the theorists' arguments are extended is within reason and justified because they treat related phenomena.

The theorists hold widely divergent views on structural features of technologically heterogeneous societies. Whether the object of analysis was termed modernization or the expansion of the capitalist mode of production, in a neutral language (if existing), it is a process of diffusion of relations from an area of origin to a new area. In the new area, old may give way to new, or may continue to exist, unchanged or transformed. The motivation of the diffusion, the resistance to it and the structural outcomes were focused. The resulting societies were considered *dual* societies (where a backward and a progressive sector prevail); or *perverted capitalist* societies (in which the capitalist mode of production coexists with dying pre-capitalist modes), or they were considered *peripheral capitalist societies* (where the capitalist mode of production articulates coherent or singular components of dissolved, non-capitalist modes).

Explanations of technological stagnation offered by *modernization theorists* are capital shortages, population growth (aggravating the constraint of capital shortage) and unwillingness among the inhabitants to accept modern technology. This is probably where explanations of retrogression would be searched for within this paradigm. As regards negative attitudes towards new technology, the Luddite riots, where workers violently opposed the introduction of labour-displacing technologies, should be kept in mind. A related but less dramatic explanation is that producers of the traditional sector possess a traditional rationality. The argument would be that the change to modern technology presupposes shift of rationality which fishermen who firstly accepted modern technology, but later returned to traditional, could not endure. An implication is that the fishermen could have acted otherwise, that they freely chose to retrograde. The culturally defined rationality hypothesis implies that a preferred traditional way of life rather than improved standard of living was decisive for the fishermen's choice of an inferior technology. Moreover, the hypothesis that technological retrogression may be the outcome of a process where less productive workers are being pushed out of the modern sector could also be deduced from a modernization perspective.

Due to the variety of approaches, Marxists would offer several explanations of the phenomenon of technological retrogression. If presented to *orthodox Marxists* as the conscious rejection of modern technology, they would probably suggest that this may indicate *an active resistance* to capitalist penetration. There is historical evidence that political struggles against capitalist relations of production have resulted in the rejection and even destruction of capitalist implements of labour. An alternative within this paradigm would be to explain technological retrogression in terms of capital owners' change from the strategy of relative to absolute surplus value production: In extreme situations capitalists who cannot compete with the improved technology weapon turn to increased labour exploitation. One of the forms this can take may imply technological retrogression.

Some advocates of the *peripheral capitalist thesis* would probably go along with these arguments, but extending this theory to encompass technological retrogression also implies to further Amin's (1976) argument of prolonged technological heterogeneity: Backwardness in terms of technology may be maintained by the system and is not necessarily the aggregate result of free choice of a low-technology level. The major factor of explanation offered is that transition to a fully capitalist society is hindered (or even blocked), since the reproduction of non-capitalist components of society (for instance, artisanal technology) is functional for capital accumulation. An explanation of technological retrogression offered within this paradigm is thus lacking outlets of labour made superfluous during capitalist expansion. The explanatory potential of Reinert's (1980) concept of lock-in, the labour/capital pressure hypothesis, is thus most relevant.

Applying the three approaches to heterogeneity

I have outlined above three perspectives on societies characterized by technological heterogeneity: modernization, orthodox Marxism and dependency theory. The theorists advocating these views disagree when establishing the precise nature of such societies, the causes and consequences of technological heterogeneity and, above all, when analysing the direction of change: Are productivity differences levelling off, are there processes of technological convergence? And if so, how *long* will the period of transition be? Alternatively, are there processes of technological divergence, of technological polarization preventing a transition? These questions about social processes and their future outcomes follow logically from the attempts of the theorists to interpret structural properties of such societies. There is, however, a long step from these grand theories to what may be termed real phenomena or empirical reality. But I believe that the only justification of the existence of academic discussions on grand theories of social change is that it is possible to *trace* at the empirical level structural properties which theories recognize: Undertaking empirical analyses, the confrontation of theories with real phenomena is the only way to move forward in our attempts to substantiate or falsify theories. Grand theories are, however, too general to be more than very general guidelines in the field; more testable theories of the middle range must be formed. The intermediate theoretical level, where I tentatively explain technological retrogression, is the very outcome of my research and is thus found in the final chapter.

So far, I have explained how I came across the phenomenon of technological retrogression and discussed the rather inadequate explanations found in grand theory. The next step is to find out how theorists studying *fishing societies* have understood their structural features; I may thereby find a model with which to approach empirical reality. The approach must facilitate the identification of the mixed character of the societies, as well as enable the understanding of the technology mix at the level of the producer. Subsequently, I arrived at the conclusion that a new approach should be designed, the production system approach presented in the next chapter. But first I substantiate why I consider already existing approaches inadequate.

The three theorists are carefully selected to illustrate theoretical points made. Are the fishing societies of developing countries *dual* societies? The sector approach is very common: Tempted by superficial observations such as the contrast between industrial and artisanal production equipment, and influenced (consciously or not) by modernization theories, scholars continue to claim that within Third World fisheries, there are *two sectors*, an expanding modern and a traditional in trouble. The conceptual difficulties involved in this contention are here demonstrated mainly by reference to the concept of linkage in Jean-Philippe Platteau's article 'The Dynamics of Fisheries Development in Developing Countries: A General Overview' (1989).

The thesis of peripheral capitalism may provide a fruitful starting point in studies of fishing societies, which is demonstrated by Johan Galtung in 'Development from Above and the Blue Revolution. A Study of the Indo-Norwegian Project in Kerala' (1980). He analyses effects of the introduction of modern technology in terms of centre–periphery relations and stresses effects of extended market relations for village development. The empirical content of his study is limited; the aim is to sketch an analytic framework in which structural features are sought captured by means of economic cycle models. The fishing societies, he claims, experience *expansion of traditional economic cycles.*

In contrast, Vercruijsse's comprehensive empirical study in 'The Penetration of Capitalism. A West African Case Study' (1984) is primarily a historical reconstruction. His aim is to understand changes in two Ghanaian fishing societies in terms of *articulating modes of production.* Vercruijsse takes an explicitly Marxist point of departure, and his work provides a basis for the discussion in the final chapter on whether the fishing societies I have studied can be fruitfully analysed in Marxist terms.

A preoccupation with dualism

The belief that Third World fishing societies contain a traditional and a modern sector is widely held. The inference that such observed technological heterogeneity indicates the existence of *separate economic spheres*, for instance *sectors*, is an a priori assumption which *may* or *may not* be true. However, analysing the way in which the social scientists use the concept of sector, it seems that, in concrete analyses, sector is *reduced* to contain technology only, or even just technique. And then, in the general discussion, sector (which still only contains the technology or technique in question) is *expanded* to cover a more comprehensive entity, such as what I term production system – and even to cover mode of production.

The reduction of the concept of sector to include only *technology* is also apparent in Kurien (1978). After describing the traditional sector of Kerala fishing villages, which forms the base of the economy, he contrasts it with another sector:

> The modern sector has a relatively shorter history. [...] *The producers of this sector are also by and large traditional fishermen* numbering about 65 to 70 thousand and operating around 11 to 12 thousand small mechanized boats. (Kurien 1978, 1559, emphasis added)

What is traditional about *these* fishermen? Their minds? Their way of life (when they are not fishing)? Here, the *scale of operation* is confused with productivity level of technology, which becomes evident when he later contends that 'A third sector, which we term as the ultra-modern sector, is now in the making' (Kurien 1978, 1559). This sector consists of large boats. Does each new technology bring with it a separate economic sphere, which justifies the use of the concept of sector? That separate economic spheres exist within the fisheries industries of developing countries can, according to Platteau, be defended only

> when the modern mechanized sector forms a self-contained whole with practically no connection with the small-scale fishing communities. (Platteau 1989, 585)

But Platteau questions dualism within fisheries development. On the contrary, he contends that

> Fisheries development provides one more proof that the distinction between 'modern' and 'traditional' is both misleading and ideologically biased. (Platteau 1989, 592)

His argumentation against dualism is, however, less convincing than his conclusion, since he advances the view that there exist 'linkages between the modern and artisanal sectors' (Platteau 1989, 585). In his article, no distinction between artisanal (or small-scale) and traditional fisheries is made. An inconsistency thus appears. Are not sectors separate economic spheres, as I have put forward? Although he does not explicitly say so, Platteau tries to solve the puzzle of the 'mixture' by distinguishing between 'sectors which are separate' and 'sectors which are linked'. The latter he advocates, the former he identifies with modernization theory which he contests.

Neither Platteau nor I claim that separate economic spheres do *not* exist in Third World countries, forming situations of absolute duality. But they are perhaps harder to detect than what Platteau thinks:

> A sizeable sector of this kind – that is one which is completely, or almost completely, cut off from the artisanal fishing sector – exists in numerous developing countries, including those of Africa. (Platteau 1989, 585)

What does 'almost completely, cut off' mean? That the only economic relation is the transfer of labour from artisanal fisheries to industrial? Has, for instance, the possibility of a reverse movement of labour been studied? The size of the industrial versus the artisanal fleet may remain the same during such labour transfers. Platteau describes what may be termed absolute duality as a situation where there are *no linkages* between the modern and the traditional sectors. In such situations, the modern sector is characterized by very sophisticated technology, trained personnel, long-lasting fishing trips, an urban elite market and foreign consumers, strict quality control, tied to modern processing plants, distribution owned by foreign multinational corporations. He claims that where there are such ultra-modern sectors, there may simultaneously be another modern sector: a 'semi-industrial' one, which may be *interconnected* in various ways with the traditional sector.

Although extensively used, neither the concept of 'linkage' nor 'interlinkage' nor 'interconnection' is defined by Platteau. These concepts, which all signify relations, I consider synonymous. *Economic linkage* I define as follows: When values are transferred from one economic unit to another (for instance, between sectors), an *economic relation* is created. For the relation to become a linkage, it must be repeated: An economic linkage, then, is a *continuously reproduced relation involving a transfer of value*. When a relation involves a transfer of value, but is not being repeated, the term '*one-time transfer*' may be used, denoting a *non-reproduced economic relation involving a transfer of value*. The concepts of 'linkage' and 'one-time transfer' are reserved to denote intra-fisheries industry relations only, such as relations between fishing technologies at different levels (for instance transfer of labour from artisanal crafts to industrial boats). Economic linkages between the fisheries industry and other industries are termed *backward or forward linkages*. An example of the former is the relation between the shipbuilding yards and the fishing gear industry, an example of the latter is the relation between fish production and fish processing.

Then a closer look at what Platteau terms linkages between sectors. According to him, the most obvious linkages are the following:

> Artisanal fishermen – especially from among the younger generations – may work as crew labour on board the mechanized boats, either on a part-time, or, more generally, on a full-time basis. (Platteau 1989, 586)

I would assume that the moment an artisanal fisherman *permanently* works aboard a modern boat, he ceases to be artisanal, he *leaves* what Platteau terms the artisanal sector. It is a one-time transfer of value in the form of labour, not an economic linkage. If the fisherman has two jobs, the one on an industrial and the other on an artisanal craft, either simultaneously or for instance by seasons, he is not solely an artisanal or solely an industrial fisherman – he is both. If these are 'linkages', what are the entities which are linked together? Can individuals belong in several sectors simultaneously? In my terms, such flows of labour indicate only a linkage between *technologies* – unless there are other characteristics present which make it advisable to include technologies in greater entities such as sectors or production systems. Platteau is aware of these conceptual difficulties. When artisanal fishermen start to work on modern boats, he claims that an interpenetration of the modern sector with the small-scale fishermen communities leads to an *absorption* of the latter in the former (except when artisanal fishermen work as part-time boat crew members to supplement their incomes from artisanal fishing and to stabilize their employment opportunities throughout the year). (Platteau 1989, 587)

A second relation found by Platteau occurs because artisanal fishermen

may acquire mechanized boats [...] and, in the process, a transfer of savings may possibly take place from the artisanal to the modern sector. (Platteau 1989, 586)

This is again a one-time transfer, not a linkage. That it is unlikely that this transfer of value in the form of capital will be repeated is supported by what Platteau himself has written on the low rate of capital accumulation in artisanal fisheries. A third example can be found:

[Artisanal crafts] may also, in some cases, work in concert with small vessels; for example, acting as ferries to transport boat crews and catches to and from mechanized vessels anchored some distance from the beach due to lack of berthing facilities [...], or when they use their crafts as 'mixture canoes' to bring to shore by-catches (mixtures) they have purchased at high sea from trawler captains [...], or when bait fishing and specializing in supplying bait to mechanized boats, or transporting their traditional craft by mechanized vessels to help them reach distant fishing zones. (Platteau 1989, 586)

The only example of a linkage between industrial and artisanal – not sectors, but technologies are found in the cases referred to above – is when artisanal fishermen supply industrial boats with bait: That is an example of a division of labour according to technology, but also an example of a transfer of value in the form of goods. Producers using different technologies are linked through the market. None of the others are examples of linkages *within* the fisheries industry, but of *relations* between the fisheries industry and the transport industry. The time a fishing boat is used (fulltime or part-time) for transport of goods, the vessel should not be considered part of the fisheries industry, but the transport industry. This is the case whether the goods transported is fish, cereals or tourists, such as can be seen in fishing villages close to beach resorts. Also, when fish is *bought* at sea (not captured), the artisanal craft is a transportation vessel while bringing the fish to shore, whether it is used in fishing operations at other times, or not. The men aboard are not artisanal fishermen during these operations. If they buy the fish themselves, they are fish traders and transportation workers. If they buy for somebody else, they are merely in the transport business. When big fishing boats transport artisanal crafts to the fishing banks, this is, from the point of view of the artisanal fishermen, a minor modernization, comparable to when outboard engines are attached to the crafts. Whether the industrial fishing boats are paid for their services or not, they are, during the towing, in the transport business *as well as* in the fisheries' industry, since they are on their way to the banks where they will be doing fishing. However, some linkages observed by Platteau are linkages indeed:

> They (artisanal and modern fishermen) may use the same distribution networks, the same processing and service facilities and even manufactured inputs (e.g. ice to take on board of artisanal canoes) provided for the modern sector; conversely, fish from the industrial fleet may be purchased, and even possibly smoked, by small-scale traditional middlemen. (Platteau 1989, 586)

Which entities are linked in these examples? What he first observes is artisanal fishermen's integration into an extended market, forming a forward linkage between artisanal fishermen and modern markets and marketing systems. He also describes how artisan production has backward linkages to modern industry (the ice supply). Then again, he describes forward linkages between industrial production and artisan processing plants.

I am not saying that the economic relations observed by Platteau cannot be considered economic relations between traditional and modern. All of them may be. *But they are not economic relations between two (coherent) economic spheres.* Most of Platteau's examples of linkages are excellent examples of new economic opportunities being created: They are examples of *economic differentiation*, forming forward and backward linkages because of technological modernization and an extended market.

I do believe that there are fishing societies in which artisanal fisheries are reduced to an anachronism, for instance, kept alive solely because of their exotic appeal to tourists. Nor will I exclude the possibility that situations of absolute duality may exist. Maybe somewhere in an Asian coastal village, idyllic conditions persist: The artisanal fisherman patiently catches his fish by using his old traditional craft and gear in inshore waters, delivers the catch to a female fish vendor who sells it at a reasonable price to consumers within or close to the village. If he works together with his father or his son, the value of the catch is shared according to expenses involved in production, as well as to the crewmen's various needs. When his income is insufficient, he goes to the pawnbroker for a loan until his next big catch. He is by no means affected by the doings of his next-door neighbour, the industrial fisherman, who catches his fish by trawling offshore, sells his catches to the fish merchant from the capital city and who at hard times survives on the goodwill of his bank.

In such situations, there are few conflicts of interest between industrial and artisanal fishermen. But violent clashes between producers using technologies at different productivity levels occur, indicating that the idyll, if it ever existed, is broken for one or several reasons. Frictions are manifested as *visible* struggles, or more subtle *invisible* mechanisms: For instance, when the volume of fish increases as a result of the introduction of modern technology, the *price* of fish may be negatively affected, unless a protected market is kept alive by the state. Also, conflicts regarding *resource exploitation* may occur, for instance if greed or decreasing resources push trawlers into inshore waters, where they destroy the breeding grounds of the species usually caught by artisanal fishermen. Both market integration and resource competition, as well as state neglect of low-productive technologies, may lead to a situation where artisanal fishermen no longer can produce sufficiently to keep up their standard of living.

The existence of a sector presupposes a greater entity of which it is a part; there must be at least one more sector present. In studies of the development of Third World fisheries, what is the greater entity which is divided into a traditional and a modern sector? The fishing society? The technology of the fishing society? For the concept of sector to make sense, it must be possible to classify individuals (firms, technology types, systems of redistribution) accordingly. In concrete empirical analyses, this is difficult. Fishermen cannot be said to belong to the one or the other sector in question – *unless sector is reduced to technology only*. Appearances are, however, deceptive: The fisherman you classify as traditional today may have been modern yesterday. Even where such a mobility of labour between the various technologies is not found, there is reason to question the concepts of modern and traditional fisherman. You may decide that the *precise denotation* of 'modern fisherman' (the core of the concept) should be 'fisherman who uses modern technology'. Nevertheless, the concept has *connotations* which are not easily eliminated: The modern fisherman is expected to be linked to the modern world, and the traditional fisherman is expected to be purely traditional in all his ways. It is a manifestation of our preoccupation with dualism; the connotations of modern and traditional are products of theoretical positions within the modernization paradigm. However, the two-way mobility of labour between technologies at different productivity levels erodes the concept of sector at its core – the technology.

The difficulty involved in categorizing fishermen reminds me of Frank's attack on the myth of feudalism in Latin America. He describes a 'fluidity in owner/worker relations', as exemplified by a single worker who is simultaneously (i) owner of his land and house, (ii) sharecropper on another's land [...], (iii) tenant on a third's land, (iv) wage worker during harvest time on one of these lands, and (v) independent trader of his own home produced commodities. (Frank 1969, quoted in Foster-Carter 1978, 76)

As said before, it would probably be wrong to claim that *no* society contains separate economic spheres, such as sectors. What I do think is, however, that in the technologically heterogeneous Third World fishing societies, absolute duality, where the only relation is (in the terminology of modernization theorists) the absorption of traditional sector labour by the modern sector, may be hard to find. There is dualism inherent in the concepts of traditional and modern sector. Even if one distinguishes between situations when sectors are separate and when they are linked, the connotation of *sector* continues to be a (coherent) economic sphere. When the concept is used without capturing reality, it becomes just a hard-dying misconception, inherited from modernization theory. My contention is that the phenomena which Platteau understands as linkages between economic sectors are adjustments of artisanal fisheries to the penetration of capitalism. It might be better understood when studied in terms of economic differentiation in fishing societies.

The categorization of theorists into paradigms cannot solely be based on the way in which they apply their concepts. It would be very unfair, on the basis of their use of the concept of sector, to place Platteau (1989), Kurien (1978) or, for instance, Meynen (1989) within the modernization paradigm; they should, however, be criticized for not clarifying their concepts. They ask the right questions, for instance, when Platteau (1989) explicitly attacks the dominant modernization ideology in fisheries' planning and outlines what kind of research should be undertaken in Third World fishing societies:

What are the precise mechanisms and contractual arrangements through which small-scale fishing communities have been incorporated into national, regional and international markets? How do they secure access to crucial production factors, and to what extent are they able to insure against new risks and uncertainties? In the process, what degree of independence are they obliged to forsake? (Platteau 1989, 591)

In Galtung's (1980) analysis, these are fundamental questions; in particular, the effects of market integration are central.

Expanded relations

Galtung's (1980) view on the consequences of technological modernization in fishing societies is based on research undertaken in India. Admitting that he goes beyond his empirical basis, which is the experiences of the Indo-Norwegian fisheries development project in Kerala, he presents a general theory of modernization of Third World fishing societies. The introduction of modern technology, leading to a Blue Revolution, he considers the major motive of the development effort:

> The basic *idea* is the introduction of *new* technology. This is the *sine qua non* of the entire project: the new technologies justify the experts. (Galtung 1980, 351)

In Galtung's terms, fishing societies to where Western modern technologies are transferred undergo a transition from a traditional to a modern economic cycle. The concept of economic cycle is meant to capture major aspects of fishing, namely relationships between nature and producer, fishing; between producer and consumer, marketing; and between consumer and nature, waste. In Figure 3, the traditional economic cycle is sketched. A major feature of the traditional economic cycle is low production volume and very little catch per producer. Its limited extension led to a low degree of *alienation* in society:

> The fisherman standing on the beach in the early morning, about to launch the canoe, has all points in the cycle within his horizon. He himself was the producer, nature was in front of him, the consumers right behind in the village, and in some of the neighbouring areas. [...] The cycle was not only an abstraction in their minds, but could be observed in their immediate and concrete surroundings. (Galtung 1980, 345)

The traditional economic cycle is also characterized by (a relative) ecological balance with little resource depletion and pollution. Furthermore, uneven accumulation, where fish merchants acquire a major proportion of the accumulated wealth, is also pronounced.

As I understand Galtung's model, the basic feature of modernization is the *geographical expansion* of relations and a simultaneous transformation of nature, producers and consumers. This he examines by studying the process of fish production, marketing and the formation of waste products. The cycle expands

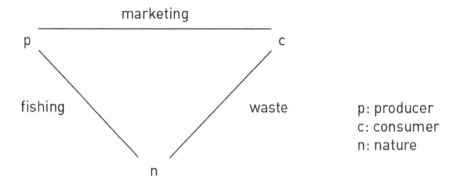

Figure 3 The traditional economic cycle for fisheries.

Source: Galtung 1980, 244.

far beyond the level of the village, to the world level, both where nature, producers and consumers are concerned. (Galtung 1980, 346)

Geographical expansion in the exploitation of nature is evident when harvesting of fish is undertaken further out and deeper down. As regards consumption, markets are no longer local or regional but remote; elegant seafood captured is enjoyed by modern consumers of wealthy nations. In Figure 4, the process of expansion is sketched. The nature of *knowledge* changes as well, since it is no longer locally generated: The modern fisherman has become an industrial worker, the skill required is learnt in technical courses. In contrast, knowledge of traditional fishermen is internalized:

> Expertise based on dozens, hundreds of generations of accumulated experience, filtered through complex communication processes. (Galtung 1980, 353)

In development projects there is a bias against utilizing such local expertise – as well as local leadership and local capital. The very idea is alien to planners since the purpose is to pave the way for non-local innovations.

In Galtung's model, change is both demand-driven, induced by consumers of rich countries, and supply-driven, induced by producers of modern technology and development 'experts' who transplant Western models in Third World contexts. The modern and the traditional economic cycles are similar, since they contain the same basic components, but the similarity is superficial:

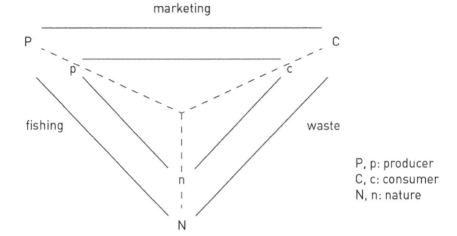

Figure 4 'Development', expansion of economic cycles.

Source: Galtung 1980, 347.

The cycle has been modernized; not only in the sense that it has indeed been expanded, and integrated into the world economy in general, but also in the sense that all elements in the cycle are 'modern'. What is caught is caught with the most modern technology, by modern fishermen, marketed with modern techniques to modern consumers. The cycle is of almost unlimited extension, reaching so far and so widely around the world that hardly anyone understands more than a tiny segment of it. (Galtung 1980, 350)

In his discussion of the effects of the expansion process, Galtung firstly points at a steep increase in 'GVP (gross village product) per capita' (1980, 350), a consequence of increased production. But he argues that the value expansion does not necessarily benefit all villagers: With modernization, social inequality rises tremendously. In the case studied, he even argues that paradoxically,

the consumption of fish among those who needed this source of protein most did not go up, there are even indications that it went down. (Galtung 1980, 350)

Increase in demand may lead to an increase of prices, so that the fisherfolk's produce becomes too expensive for their own consumption. There is *need* for protein, but no *demand* in 'the language of money' (1980, 348). When it comes to what modern consumers define as luxuries, the fisherfolk were alienated from their own produce:

> Shrimps and lobster [...] became abstract entities, nicely wrapped up with foreign texts, rather than concrete things available for the local population. (Galtung 1980, 349)

What he describes is part of a marginalization process as defined above: while at the same time unable to benefit from modernization, some villagers are negatively affected.

Galtung evaluates the consequences in what he terms a 'Centre–Periphery' perspective. The Centre of the model (the national elite, the donor agency or the producers of modern technology) gains the most from technological modernization. This is where administrative functions, financing and research are located. Very often these functions 'are found at the same place, in a private or public corporation' (1980, 353). The value transfers make the Centre grow; profits and experiences are accumulated. The periphery gains as well, by receiving '*solutions, decisions and investment*' (1980, 354, emphasis in the original), but there are negative effects: Since *production* is located there, the periphery is left with the adverse effects of modernization: depletion of resources and pollution: 'a high proportion of the total costs of running the process have been dislocated towards the periphery' (1980, 355). There is also the important problem of increased technological dependency. When technology is imported, the village (and the nation) becomes dependent on non-local supplies of spare parts and maintenance. But this is a price which they may be willing to pay:

> The Center may put at its disposal more capital, for expansion of the technology introduced, or for introduction of even more modern technology. This dependency pattern is relatively clear: only Periphery countries with very clear goals and strategies *of their own* will be able to resist this. The strength of the Center is in part based on the weakness of the Periphery. (Galtung 1980, 354, emphasis in the original)

Technological dependency may be counteracted by nationalizing economic enterprises. But to a poor Kerala fisherman, what may a change of power from London to New Delhi signify? As Galtung phrases it, there is a centre and a periphery within the Periphery. He does not share planners' belief in a *trickle down*, neither to the poor of the villages nor to the village itself:

The ideology of 'industrial growth today, benefits for everybody tomorrow' will sound as obvious to the center as it is meaningless to the periphery. (Galtung 1980, 356)

When the produce is exported to industrial countries, the value exit from the village is especially high. He finds it improbable that hard currency earnings will flow back to the villages, since centrally articulated demands, such as industrialization and defence, will be given priority:

Those who articulate the need for capital goods near the power centers speak with a considerably louder and more articulate voice than those who suffer from malnutrition in the backwaters of Kerala. (Galtung 1980, 356)

In conclusion, Galtung finds the new economic cycle both alienating and exploitative, and the contribution to a more equal distribution of wealth insignificant. On the contrary, the producers' share of profit (as well as that of local entrepreneurs) is less than what accrues to other actors in the expanded economic cycle: exporters, authorities, developers and manufacturers of modern technology. This, in addition to increased income inequality within the villages, Galtung maintains, 'may contribute to a revolution which is not blue' (1980, 356).

There are unsolved logical problems in Galtung's model. While arguing that a change from a traditional to a modern economic cycle occurs, he finds that 'some of the villagers continue as before' (1980, 350). Does he perceive that during the transition period, the village contains two separate sectors, one characterized by a limited and the other characterized by an expanded economic cycle? This is unclear; there is, however, evidence that he regards these societies as *dual*; he in fact concludes that they are 'typical examples of dual societies and dual economies' (1980, 357). But his concept of dualism is not a corollary to the modernization theorists' concept. For instance, Galtung considers traditional producers 'a *labour reserve* to be drawn upon for shrimp peeling purposes when the catch is particularly good' (1980, 357, emphasis added), which means that labour may enter, leave and re-enter the modern economy. This is closer to the notion of reproduction of labour in the traditional sector. Galtung does not extend his analysis of what this duality signifies to the producers apart from a comment on what it feels like to be exposed to the wonders of the modern world while being unable to share the benefits: After the introduction of modern technology, traditional fishermen go on fishing

with the old methods, or with the old methods slightly improved [...]
with the demoralizing shadow of the glittering affluence of modern
ocean-going vessels, ice factories, insulated vans, etc., before their eyes.
(Galtung 1980, 357)

This brief sketch of Galtung's theory clearly shows his roots in dependency
theory. Studying villagers as well as the village, he demonstrates the effects
of capitalism when imposed from outside. His focus on external relations is
somewhat at the expense of internal; he only briefly treats what later became
central in the development debate, namely the contents of the notion of
reproduction of labour in the traditional sector. A strength of his approach
is the focus on imbalances of power; the villagers' reduced influence on the
direction of development with productivity increase due to technological
modernization is seldom treated in literature on fisheries. In the following
chapters it will become clear that I owe much to Galtung's approach. I find
it, however, difficult to capture structural features of societies experiencing
a transition in his model. For instance, to what extent and how do *traditional
fishermen* enter the modern cycle? I believe the difficulty arises when he seeks to
capture structural properties by including *individuals* (the producers) as well as
relations in the models. The *mixed* character cannot be captured since individuals
are in this respect quite indivisible phenomena, a difficulty which becomes
apparent if fishermen who are somewhat modern and a little bit traditional
are placed in the producer's position of Galtung's schema. When structural
properties are sought revealed, *relations* should be the object of analysis; but
when *effects* of changes of structural properties are studied, the object should
be experiences of individuals and groups.

An articulationist's approach

The relevance of Vercruijsse's (1984) study to my research problem is
immediately understood when reading his questions of departure:

> Is it possible to assess, with any degree of precision, the extent to which
> capitalist production has made inroads in the canoe fishing sector, or to
> distinguish between aspects that have retained a pre-capitalist character
> and those which have taken on a capitalist character? And if it is correct
> to say that canoe fishing has not been completely cast in a capitalist
> mould, why is it that capitalism has come to a halt at an intermediate
> point? (Vercruijsse 1984, 6)

Vercruijsse (1984) considers Ghana a peripheral capitalist society; the changes in the fishing societies are considered part of the development of capitalism in Ghana during the past century.[16] Class relations, which are the outcomes of colonialism, explain the extraversion of the economy (peasant production of cocoa for the world market; the formation of a wage labour force in mining and capitalist cocoa farming). This extraversion conditions both private and state modernization efforts in fisheries; the single most important factor of explanation of the penetration of capitalism in fisheries is the increased demand for fish caused by the growth in other economic activities.

Vercruijsse's project is to analyse how capitalism is linked to pre-capitalist mode(s) of production. The outcome of the articulation process is the transformation of pre-capitalist modes of production into *transitional forms*, in which pre-capitalist relations continue to be reproduced.[17] Since a form combines capitalist and pre-capitalist features, it attains a hybrid character, but it is an integral (coherent) unit as regards production and reproduction. The domination of capitalism (through the alliance between state and capital) over pre-capitalist modes of production 'enables the appropriation of pre-capitalist surplus as capitalist profit' (1980, 22). In his analysis, Vercruijsse distinguishes between the canoe fishing sector and the modern sector; the latter is controlled

---

[16] A contention in the second chapter of Vercruijsse's study may lead the readers to believe that he *contests* the peripheral capitalism thesis:

Particular focus will be placed on those social formations in the periphery which have as a special characteristic that they articulate capitalism with pre-capitalist modes of production. *Their peculiarity does not spring from the special features of "peripheral" capitalism* [...] but arises from the nature of the articulation as well as from the domination of indigenous capitalism by metropolitan and international finance capital. (1984, 16, emphasis added)

The domination referred to is precisely what defines peripheral capitalist social formations, according to Amin. Since Vercruijsse in his analysis contrasts effects of capitalist penetration during 'autocentric' and 'peripheral' capitalist development, the above contention should probably be interpreted as, capitalism as such (the laws of motion) is not 'peripheral', but *contextual differences* during the spread of capitalism under (old- and neo-)colonialism produce the special characteristics of peripheral capitalist societies.

[17] As regards the debate on the definition of *mode* versus *form* of production, Vercruijsse's position is that they in essence are the same (when empirically reconstructed, the same indicators must be applied), but that a form of production is always articulated, never dominant in a social formation (by Marx, such forms are referred to as 'notional'). Whereas the reproduction of a mode of production is based on the relations of exploitation which characterizes it, the forms do not follow this logic: They are subordinate to the reproductive needs of the dominant mode of production. He therefore considers the forms he identifies as transitional.

by local capitalists and multinational companies. He does not consider this sector completely cut off from canoe fisheries, there are 'interconnections [...] creating a division of labour [...] in the interests of capital-intensive fishing' (1980:12). In particular, he stresses that government policies have favoured the modern sector. In the present context, however, the discussion on linkages between these economic spheres is less important than his understanding of the mixture of capitalist and non-capitalist relations within the *canoe fishing societies*. Far from being a backward traditional sector, canoe fisheries have through technological modernization acquired considerable labour productivity increases; larger canoes, multipurpose nets and outboard engines have been introduced. But still many socio-economic relations are non-capitalist. The canoe fishing societies thus have been

> transformed towards a more capitalist form of production, but this does not mean that they were converted into anything resembling a modern capital-intensive fishing industry. On the contrary, as a form of production canoe fishing has retained many *singular, precapitalist features*. (Vercruijsse 1984, 6, emphasis added)

Vercruijsse searches for an explanation of the stagnation of capitalist penetration in the special way in which capitalism articulates pre-capitalist modes of production. Articulation becomes manifest in the

> peculiar system of exchanges which have come to join capitalism and pre-capitalism in canoe fishing. (Vercruijsse 1984, 10)

He arrives at this conclusion through the empirical reconstruction of three transitional forms of production: *tenga, adii* and *ahwea*. In each form, the labour process is analysed, the basic indicators are technique of fishing and the corresponding relations of production.[18] None of the forms of production are completely transformed; to a varying extent, capitalist relations are found. The crucial process of free labour formation is not completed; labour retains an intermediate position. He finds such peculiarities (which are peculiar only if a complete transformation is expected) when analysing distribution and exchange systems, capital supply and the role of state interventions as well.

---

[18] Following Balibar (1970), Vercruijsse maintains that the relations of production are more than *ownership* of the means of production; it must be made clear who set the means of production to work, who controls the distribution of the product (i.e. who appropriate the surplus) and in which form is the surplus being appropriated. The latter may reveal exploitative relations, and thereby the struggle between classes.

The *tenga* form of production has many pre-capitalist features. The crewmen have their own nets which are linked together while fishing, and they are therefore heavily dependent on each other. The crews normally form stable fishing teams, and there is little basis for private control over the production process. The owner of the boat has little influence; for instance, democratic decisions are made on when and where to go fishing. The fishwives play a crucial role as financiers and middlemen, therefore, much of the surplus created in *tenga* fisheries remains within the local community. The commercial role of the women may also secure the fishermen's control of exchange relations through kinship ties. However, both the existence of many petty financiers and the egalitarian sharing of the catches inhibit the accumulation and concentration of capital necessary for further investments.

While reconstructing the *tenga* fisheries as a form of production, Vercruijsse finds that some fishermen work part of the year in *adii* fisheries, but there as hired crewmen. This indicates that the *tenga* form of production articulates the more capitalist *adii* form of production. The mobility of labour between the forms Vercruijsse considers a major indicator of their articulation, and this reveals the mixed nature of the relations:

> Under one form of production fishermen are petty-commodity producers who pay the boat owner for having rendered a service to them; under the other form, the same fishermen enter into some kind of employment relationship with the boat owner. (Vercruijsse 1984, 145)

Adii fisheries represent a break in the development of canoe fishing, since big investments in boats and gear were necessary. Capital is more concentrated; the boat owner also owns the gear and is therefore in full control of the fishing operation. The crewmen are hired, but the form is not fully capitalist since a share system (as opposed to wage remuneration) is predominant, and the process of free labour formation is incomplete. There are other pre-capitalist features as well; like in the *tenga* form of production, distribution of the catch value is partly controlled by the fishwives. Together with share systems, these are *remnants* of a pre-capitalist mode of production.

Technologically, *ahwea* fishing is a furthering of the *adii* fisheries, but it is even more capital intensive. Big multipurpose nets and big mechanized boats are used. It is carried out throughout the year at a large scale. Absentee ownership is common, and the crewmen have specialized functions aboard. As compared to the two other forms, the position of the crewmen in *ahwea* fisheries indicates a high degree of exploitation; Vercruijsse finds that the crewmen's share of the catch is very low. In *adii* as well as in *ahwea* fisheries, productivity is much higher than in *tenga* fishing, and the ownership structure facilitates capital accumulation. This indicates the development of capitalist forces as well as relations of production. But here too, some pre-capitalist features are reproduced, since the owners encourage the crewmen to invest in motors (due to frequent breakdowns), thereby spreading the risk. Vercruijsse concludes that Ghanaian fisheries represent an

> odd, theoretically unexpected, case of capitalist penetration. In canoe fishing the transformation of the productive forces is outrightly capitalist, while the social relations of production [...] are not yet completely capitalist. (Vercruijsse 1984, 12)

After having identified pre-capitalist features and their reproduction, and described how the forms of production articulate, Vercruijsse searches for features of *two ideal type of modes of production* as described by Marx, *the pure petty commodity mode* and *the pure capitalist mode*. At the level of the social formation, capitalism is said to articulate the *petty commodity* mode of production. The subsumption of labour by capital is incomplete; capitalism has not fully penetrated and transformed the pre-capitalist mode of production. This is a characteristic of peripheral capitalist social formations.

It will be recalled that the articulationists have widely divergent views on the question of *coherence*: Some theorists claim that the reproduced non-capitalist relations do *not* form coherent systems but are reproduced as singular relations which articulate a mode of production. Others maintain that non-capitalist relations form coherent systems (like the *tenga* form of production described). Vercruijsse admits, however, that in contact with capitalism, the form has been deformed. So far, I can follow his argumentation, but when he concludes at the higher level of abstraction, he seems to construct *separate economic spheres* by forcing a diverse and complicated empirical reality into the dichotomy of a pure capitalist versus a petty commodity mode of production. I find this an unnecessary, dogmatic, exercise. Vercruijsse arranges relations analytically to form systems (forms of production). The forms are mutually exclusive as regards technology, but do not exclude the producers from moving between them. There is reason to assume that the relations identified may be analytically arranged to form *one system* only: Firstly, the same producers may be classified into both (the tenga fisherman may be an adii fisherman as well). Secondly, what is observed as regards the producer's relations to technology is valid for his market relation as well (the fish-wives' strong position in both forms). To follow this line of questioning further, the empirical material presented is, however, insufficient.

Vercruijsse's approach explicitly involves the historical reconstruction of modes of production, using a set of indicators of their presence. Here, the danger of reductionism lures; whereas he *claims* to have captured a societal totality, his *indicators* are (when all is said and done) merely technology, market relations and ownership of the means of production. I am thus not entirely convinced that Vercruijsse's indicators have captured more than *a few essential features* of the totality. This does not reduce the value of his work; ultimately, I am convinced that this is all that *can* be done – by one social scientist. Whether applied in an extended or restricted sense, the reconstruction of a mode of production is a formidable exercise. To reconstruct empirically *all* relations between social, ecological and cultural value systems is, by its very nature, multidisciplinary (and impossible).

An appraisal of the approaches

I have searched for an approach which would enable identifying at the empirical level the structural features of technologically heterogeneous fishing societies. A side effect of my questioning the notion of separate economic spheres is that most of what is written on technological modernization in fishing societies is not useful for this purpose. This does not mean that studies taking an explicit or implicit *sector* point of departure do not convey essential understanding of the effects of technological change; the only implication is that the mixed character of the relations in the societies I have studied cannot be captured.

Several interesting points of view were found when studying Galtung's (1980) approach, especially as regards effects of extended markets. But his approach cannot be used to capture the mixture either: The transitional phase, whether short or long, was hardly touched upon. When the transition appears immediate (or is kept in a black box), there is no room for the observation of a mixture neither at the producer nor the production unit nor at industry level.

The approach of Vercruijsse (1984) comes closer to an understanding of transitions. The empirical analysis of the fishing societies clearly shows the diversity of relations; relations and artifacts of different origins are found, captured by the concept of the hybrid character of the forms of production. Also, by pointing at mechanisms by which non-capitalist relations are reproduced, he explains the prolongation of the transition period. It should therefore be concluded that by using his approach, the mixed character of the societies in question can be understood. But Vercruijsse's approach is not designed to capture individual action in detail. His is an *extensive* reconstruction in which he traces the history of social relations. To document individual action implying technological retrogression my approach must be more intensive. And what is gained in depth must often be sacrificed in breadth – though not always entirely. The production system approach developed in the next chapter is designed to place the producers' choices of technology into a broad societal context. What I have sacrificed is not the broad picture of the producer's relations, but a thorough historical perspective needed to describe how these relations evolved.

Chapter 3

PRODUCTION SYSTEMS AND
WORK HISTORIES

The production system approach

We have moved from the grandest of theory, the philosophical discussion of linearity of history, to theories of development: modernization theory and theories inspired by Marxism. How students of fishing societies were inspired by these bodies of thought was treated next. This chapter presents the next step in the operationalization ladder: How do we, in the challenging context of fieldwork, identify relations so that we can conclude on societal properties and processes? I have designed for this purpose 'the production system approach', which enables identification of relations. The traditional production system is contrasted to the industrial system, which entered the village with the modernization of technologies and integration into remote markets. I conclude that fishermen, whether traditional or modern in terms of technology, cannot easily be put into the one or the other category in terms of production system, thus supporting the 'interconnected relations' stance. This chapter also describes in detail the 'work history method', crucial in discovering technological retrogression. The fishermen's technological pasts were documented, providing a rich empirical material which is explored in the next chapters.

The concept of production system

A production system may be defined as interrelations of relations essential to the reproduction of a localized group of people's material existence, such as natural resources, labour, technology, capital and mechanisms of surplus distribution. A community's social and economic relations with the larger society are also part of their production system; the economic relations with the world outside include flows of capital; labour and commodities, as well as the social relations necessitated by these flows. For instance, social relations of a political nature, such as state regulation of resource exploitation, may condition the economic activities of rural villages. The extent to which production systems are integrated into the larger society varies in time and space. If only new technology is accepted (and other relations of the production system within which the new technology originates are avoided), the system is kept partially closed (*selective modernization*). Such societies exist; whereas some Amish communities are closed to new technology, American and Canadian Mennonites may protect their culture by keeping constant everything *but* their technology, which they import from the outside world. It follows that the concept of production system denotes *social* and *economic* relations within a society. Only those attributes of nature which are of economic interest to human beings (resources) constitute integral parts of the production system, at the interface of social and ecological systems. Furthermore, production systems mediate between ecological and cultural value systems of societies. This is evident when people's attitudes towards the exploitation of nature, determined for instance by norms of their religion, influence their choice of technology. Vice versa, an economically determined choice of technology may transform cultural values.

The rationale of the production system approach is the contention that relations of production systems have special characteristics determined by their *origins* or the nature of their *adoption*, which have profound impact on the livelihood of the producers. In the Malaysian case the first major problem concerned the nature of the system of the fishing village studied. It is assumed, and substantiated below, that the production system is characterized by a mixture of relations and artefacts of different origins, among which are technologies at different productivity levels. Analysing the mixture, structural properties are traced, thus judging which theoretical perspective has the greatest force of explanation. That there is a mixture is easily observed; but is it correct to assume, which I have done so far, that there exists *one* production system only? If so, can *subsystems* of the (one) production system be identified? Or maybe the fishing village contains *two coexisting production systems* – or even several systems? For instance, do artisanal fishermen live in a not-so-splendid isolation from the modern world, in a *traditional sector* of their own, characterized by low productivity and a lower living standard than their more fortunate relatives in the *modern sector*? How traditional are artisanal fishermen? Is their low productivity compensated by traditional redistribution systems such as family security nets? Perhaps their now vulnerable position is compensated by government interventions like market protection or subsidy schemes? Although they use artisanal technology, do they make use of the same marketing channels as industrial fishermen do? And vice versa, how modern are industrial fishermen? Do they from time to time make use of artisanal technology? Do they have access to traditional security nets, or do they put their trust in banks? Is labour recruited freely to the modern boats, or does kinship still play a dominant role in crew selection? Two hypotheses on the nature of the production system will structure my argumentation: the separate economic spheres and the interconnected relations hypotheses.

Separate economic spheres

The dual hypothesis claims that it is possible, within the mixture, to identify *two separate economic spheres*. Firstly, according to modernization theory, one should expect to identify *two* production systems, the traditional sector forming one and the modern sector the other. The traditional sector is the remnant of the traditional production system present before modernization started. The only economic relation between them believed to exist is the transfer of labour from the traditional to the modern sector. Secondly, orthodox Marxism expresses an equally dualist position: A capitalist production system exists side by side with a pre-capitalist production system, making manifest the structural properties of an (coherent) expanding capitalist mode of production and a (coherent) pre-capitalist one. The latter mode is losing terrain while being in decay. Thus, according to classical as well as Marxist modernization theory, the mixture is an indication of a still incomplete modernization process. If the modernization process were of a classical type, modern components (such as industrial technology) would diffuse by pushing traditional ones away; old components would be substituted by new. The process may be swift or gradual. The un-adjustable traditional components surviving are dying remnants.

From the theoretical discussion on the concept of sector can be inferred that I have serious doubts as to the validation of any dual hypothesis, implying the empirical observation of indicators of two coherent systems, able at reproduction. To take but one example, a fisherman may use artisanal technology – but all artisanal fishermen do not produce for a limited local marked, nor is it possible in the long run to avoid the intervention of non-local capitalists or national authorities. Nevertheless, a dual hypothesis should be considered, due to the importance of this view within studies of fishing societies.

Interconnected relations

In contrast to the above dualist contention, the interconnected relations hypothesis claims that within the mixed production system such separate economic spheres cannot be identified. Production system features originating in the system prevailing before technological modernization started as well as those introduced are interconnected, forming complex patterns. Some *articulationists* assume, just as the orthodox Marxists do, that the mixture is the manifestation of the co-presence of two or several modes of production, a capitalist and non-capitalist mode(s), however, adding that these are articulated in a manner which secures the *domination* of the capitalist relations. In this case the existence of *two* articulating production systems must be inferred. Alternatively, only *one* is suggested, indicating that where the capitalist mode of production meets with non-capitalist, a *new* mode comes into being, which is neither capitalist nor non-capitalist.

According to the mixed mode of production perspective sketched in Chapter 2, there is but *one* production system. This system is capitalist, but of a special brand; determined by the nature of capitalist penetration, forming a *peripheral capitalist* society. When explaining the reproduction of the production system as a mixture, evidence is sought that within these societies, a capitalist mode of production articulates with *surviving relations* of preceding modes of production. Which relations that survive are not purely accidental; only those which are functional for capital accumulation of industrial capital are reproduced. Their reproduction is linked to processes of social stratification and marginalization.

The direction of change

The second major problem concerns *the direction of change and the length of the transition period*. The analysis of the nature of the production system and its formation provides a basis for the discussion on its reproduction. Limiting the discussion to technology, the following hypotheses can be formed:

Technological progress: the society is becoming modern. What is observed is a progress towards modernity, the major trend being that industrial technology gains in importance relative to artisanal. The dominant process is one of technological convergence at the higher technology level.

Retardation or stagnation of technological progress: the society will become modern but will remain in a transitional phase for a long period of time. What is observed is a delayed transition. Artisanal technology gains in importance, causing retardation or even stagnation of the process of modernization, but still only slowing down the process of technological convergence.

Technological retrogression: the society becoming less modern. Industrial technology reduces in importance, artisanal gains, causing a movement back to former technologies. The dominant process is one of technological divergence or polarization, or even technological convergence at the lower technology level.

An *ideal type* approach

An ideal approach to the reconstruction of changes in the villages studied should be to give a detailed historical account of the development of the different relations of the production system. But there is, firstly, the problem of limited written historical sources of information as regards technological change. Then there is a question of research objective, which in my case has necessitated an ideal type approach.

The ideal type production systems sketched below are Weberian; they are not reconstructions, but constructs. Their empirical content may, however, place them in a continuum far from purely theoretical constructs, but they will never reach the opposite position, that of empirical reality. An ideal type constructed may fruitfully be used to compare our conception of important features to reality, and this

> is not methodologically questionable at all *as long as* one continuously reminds oneself that an ideal-typical *construction* of a course of events and history are two things which must be viewed as separate entities. (Weber 1971, 210, my translation, emphasis in the original)

Weber points at a specific problem in the use of ideal types in the analysis of courses of development, namely that the probability of equating the ideal type with reality is particularly high. This is of special relevance in the present context. It should also be stressed at the outset that the purpose of my constructing the two ideal type production systems is *not* to be able to classify fishermen accordingly, but to demonstrate that *this cannot be done*. Ideal types are constructed not only because there is a need to identify the origins of certain *existing* features of social reality but also to reflect upon *non-existing* features of the production system: features found elsewhere.

The first ideal type, the *artisanal*, presents essential features of the production system which prevailed in the fishing villages *before the introduction of high-productive modern technology*. To pre-empt the usual criticism: this does not signify a Year Zero. I do not believe that these villages 50 years ago were static societies, unchanged until modern technology was introduced. It is analytically possible to 'freeze' history at a point in time, then move forward to a second point and evaluate changes. Based on rudimentary empirical evidence, the artisanal production system can be constructed and compared to the present situation. In the analysis, there is however need for a second ideal type, which I term industrial and which does not exist in my study area now, nor existed earlier. This ideal type is based on my general impression of production systems within which *the introduced modern technology originates*. It sketches generalized features of common production systems within which fisheries of industrial societies exist. The hypothesis is that introduction of modern technology, originating in another production system, may be a powerful change agent, which may alter the artisanal production system profoundly, even result in the transformation of the artisanal to an industrial production system. That is, it may affect not only technology and the incomes of fishermen adopting it, but other relations of the production system as well: *Has the contemporary production system attained, as a consequence of technological modernization, feature similar to an industrial rather than an artisanal production system?*

In Figure 5 the ideal types are sketched. In the mid-section, production system relations are listed; on either side, essential features of the artisanal and the industrial production system are found. Characteristics of the artisanal production system are a low rate of resource exploitation and energy consumption, low capital/labour ratio, low labour productivity, no state regulation of resource exploitation, local markets, local but low rates of capital accumulation, private/family ownership of crafts and gear, family labour recruitment, share systems giving high returns to labour and, finally, an extensive redistribution system based on family security nets and pawnshop/moneylenders as credit for survival institutions.

Characteristics of the industrial production system are a high rate of resource exploitation and energy consumption, high labour productivity, high capital/labour ratio, state regulation of resource exploitation, remote markets, high rates of capital accumulation, both absentee and local private ownership of boats and gear, state investments (subsidies), free labour recruitment, share systems giving low returns to labour and, finally, the redistributive mechanism of state welfare measures securing survival. The artisanal and the industrial production system outlined above do have some features in common, such as private ownership of the means of production. The importance of family ownership within the artisanal system is, however, greater.

Production systems are never static but subject to internal as well as external impulses of change. The degree to which changes affect the totality of a system varies: Some changes are incremental, other changes are more sweeping, such as technological shifts, which may totally change the basic characteristics of the system. To avoid being cited in support of the myth of a stagnant traditional society, unchanged for ages, I want again to stress that impulses of change of a production system of a given society are not necessarily external in origin. *Internal* changes, for instance demographic (population decrease or growth), may not only contract or expand systems geographically, but may necessitate technological progress or change of redistributive systems to sustain the population. Climatic changes, or wars, which may cause adjustments of production systems, may originate both externally and internally.

Ideal type	Production system element	Ideal type
Artisanal production system		**Industrial production system**
Low rate of exploitation Low rate of energy consumption Low capital/labour ratio	Resources	High rate of exploitation High rate of energy consumption High capital/labour ration
Low labour productivity	Technology	High labour productivity
No or customary regulation of resource exploitation	Regulation	State regulation of resource exploitation
Local markets, supply and demand and 'tied boat system'	Markets	Remote markets, supply and demand and state price control
Low rate of accumulation Local owners Private and family ownership of crafts and gear No state investments	Capital	High rate of accumulation Local and absentee owners Private ownership of craft and gear State investments / subsidies
Family labour recruitment	Labour	Free labour recruitment
High returns to labour, 'equal share'	Share systems	Low returns to labour, 'less equal share'
Family, pawnshop, moneylenders as 'survival credit'	'Security nets'	State welfare systems

Figure 5 Ideal type production systems.

General features of the production systems

The ideal type approach is designed to capture changes brought about in the low-technology fisheries settings by the introduction of Western high technology. In this section I wish to substantiate two hypotheses: Firstly, before the introduction of high-productive Western technology, there were in the fishing villages studied production systems similar to the artisanal ideal type sketched. Secondly, some features originating in this production system are still being reproduced; the production systems thus have a mixed character.

This section is an introduction to social and economic changes, containing major characteristics of the production system found in the fishing villages studied. Although natural and cultural differences have shaped many differences, I believe that the basic features of the production systems in the two settings are similar. My understanding of fishing societies relies heavily on the empirical research I have undertaken in Sri Lanka and Malaysia, I believe, however, that the general features sketched can be recognized in many Asian fishing villages. The Malaysian fisherfolk themselves have been major informants on the old production systems in Kuala Kedah. However, any student of Asian fisheries is indebted to Raymond Firth's analyses in *Malay Fishermen: Their Peasant Economy* (1966).

The production system is sketched here to provide the context in which technological change and economic inequality in the fishing villages should be understood. Each relation deserves a book of its own. Capital formation, labour recruitment, changes in share systems, changes in and expansion of markets as well as state policies in fisheries are complicated issues which can only be briefly treated. Also, sociocultural changes, which are essential for the understanding of underdevelopment in general, are only briefly commented on. In the treatment, reference is made to the ongoing debate among social scientists studying socioeconomic changes in fishing societies, which gives a brief indication of the generality of the processes described.

Resource exploitation

The questions on resource exploitation concern linkages between the production system and ecological systems, which demand detailed studies by marine biologists and social scientists to answer. Conclusions based on fishermen's perception of the resource situation cannot be drawn. Marine ecological systems are extremely complex, especially in tropical waters, where the variety of species is enormous. Also, if one species is heavily exploited, this can have serious repercussions on other species, positively or negatively. In addition, some species migrate; the effects of overexploitation may therefore be felt far from the locality studied.

Before technological modernization, the degree of resource exploitation was limited by the supply of labour and thus dependent upon local population increase and immigration to the fishing villages. There were natural fluctuations of resources, but there is no evidence of the destruction of any species due to overfishing. According to old Malay fishermen, resources seemed to be inexhaustible. This relative harmony between resources and rate of exploitation can hardly be culturally explained, that is, viewed as the outcome of conservationist attitudes, an ideology of nature preservation. It is easier to substantiate the hypothesis that the notion of unlimited resources prevailed among the fisherfolk until they witnessed decreasing resources and the extinction of some species. Whether artisanal or industrial technology is used, fishermen seek to maximize output. This view is also held by Ling in the case of Malaysia at the time of the study:

> Optimum allocation of fishing effort is achieved only with vigilant control. Fishermen when left to their own device would seek to maximize their own returns rather than the aggregate production of the entire industry. (Ling 1978a, 2)

Hostility towards modern technology (and thus towards increased rate of exploitation) has not been found in any of the case studies to explain non-acceptance of modern technology. Thus, the *attitudes* towards resource exploitation within the two ideal type production systems seem similar. The fishermen of the past were too few, and their technologies were not efficient enough to catch all of it. My view on the fisherfolk's relations to nature is shared by Kurien in the case of Kerala:

> Though fishing is a sort of perpetual harvesting operation, the low productivity of the traditional techniques prevented any rapid depletion of the resources. (Kurien 1978, 1560)

The question of overfishing was less relevant in Sri Lanka (at the time of the survey) than in the case of Malaysia. Kedah fisherfolk viewed the rate of resource exploitation in the past to be wiser and more controllable. This recognition, however, came too late since local control of the rate of resource exploitation is long lost. It is to a large extent determined by market conditions and the capital investors' prospect of profit. Investments in modern fishing technology have been encouraged by the authorities irrespective of damages caused by increased rate of resource exploitation. The emphasis on big, mechanized boats and large-scale investments in infrastructure such as harbours is typical of the post-war modernization efforts in fisheries sector of coastal developing countries (Platteau 1989). The post-war decades have seen *uncontrolled* investments, accompanied by insufficient resource management, leading to the present overexploitation, which is often studied in terms of a *Tragedy of the commons* (Hardin 1968).

Artisanal technologies may, due to their selectivity, do less damage than industrial, but whether they are more environmentally sound also depends on the scale of operation, that is, *how many fishermen are using them*: Whether a species vanishes due to the use of primitive traps or advanced modern trawls is of no significance to the fish – but perhaps to advocates of appropriate technology? Where there are conflicts between trawlers and the artisanal fleet, regulation of trawlers only cannot solve the problem. Ling maintains:

> The use of traditional gear in place of the trawl, the provisions for the purchase of outboard engines and small boats mean that the number of boats within the seven miles zone is continually replaced and added to. To convert from trawling to these gear will merely create overexpansion in the use of another set of fishing gear. Prohibiting the fishermen from trawling within this area does not automatically mean that they will liquidate their fishing units especially when no alternative means of employment are open to them. (Ling 1976, 15)

Fishermen as well as authorities and researchers are aware of the limited success of the regulation. They agree that fishermen have not followed demarcations strictly, but have encroached upon fishing grounds of inshore fishermen, causing damage of artisanal fishermen's gears. Trawler fishermen may even try to justify their actions by claiming that 'this is where my family and I always have been fishing' – a useful feature of an artisanal production system. Artisanal fishermen, on the other hand, would often benefit from the enforcement of modern regulation.

Technology

Production and reproduction of people's material existence necessitate the provision of means and methods of production, as well as the formation of social relations into which people enter when organizing their production. The means and methods are here termed *techniques* of production, which together with social organization of the production process constitute the *technologies* applied. There is today a wide variety of technologies in use. Some are very old, such as the use of traps and handlining from rowing crafts. Other technologies, such as trawling, were introduced only a few decades ago. A distinction between artisanal and industrial technologies based on a complexity criterion cannot be made. A case in point is knowledge of production organization. Operating lift nets, the first major technological modernization in Malaysia, required *teamwork* as did the purse seining technology which came later. When the lift nets were introduced, cooperation when fishing was by no means uncommon. For example, the operation of large traps and beach seines requires close cooperation between crewmen and the divers, supervised by *master fishermen*. The question whether old technology is more simple than new should also include knowledge of nature. The detailed knowledge of the location of resources and fish behaviour may have deteriorated among common fishermen, as claimed by old master fishermen of Kuala Kedah. This process is evident in the fisheries of industrial countries: The crewmen on some of the vessels resemble factory workers who do not need such skills, and the skipper is helpless if the echo sounder does not function. The amount of knowledge and skill acquired by the Malaysian *human echo sounders*, the divers whose task was to locate the shoals of fish, and direct the crafts accordingly is enormous in contrast. Knowledge of nature, if not in demand, eventually dies out.

However, observations on the degradation of work or on the deskilling effect of modern technology (Braverman 1974) can easily be exaggerated. To operate modern fishing boats, knowledge of new fishing methods and machinery is essential. Also, most industrial production units are bigger than the artisanal ones. When many people are involved in fishing operations, new forms of labour management are necessary. In contrast to the crews of two or three men on the small *sampans*, the bigger purse seiners may have crews of 50.

A common distinction between artisanal and industrial technology is that the former is less labour productive than the latter. This is truer than the simple – complicated dichotomy; it is the very explanation for the wide diffusion of modern technology. In contrast to the artisanal fishing methods, which commonly are *stationary* gear (such as fixed nets or traps), many new methods are *active* (such as trawls), and the fishermen are therefore able to follow moving resources. Technological modernization also counteracts the seasonality of fisheries by introducing motorized and bigger boats, which increase production by reducing the number of lay days. As regards labour productivity, the contrast between the catch landed by two-men operated trawler and what is brought ashore by two handlining fishermen is immense. My categorization of the technologies into *forms of technology* is based on the labour productivity criterion.

When technologies are studied in relative detail, mixtures of relations of technologies at different levels may appear. For instance, when ice is used on board artisanal crafts, as observed by Platteau (1989), it is at the same time an example of a backward linkage to ice production and an example of a mixture of techniques at different productivity levels, that is, if fish handling aboard is considered part of the fishing *method*. It then becomes a minor modernization of artisanal technology. Also, when outboard engines are fixed to artisanal crafts, mixtures of old and new technology result. Artisanal technology is modernized by absorbing modern elements. It cannot, once and for all (places), be determined whether old crafts onto which have been attached outboard engines should be considered low or intermediate (or even high) technology. That depends on the purpose of the classification, as well as the other technologies present. In the Sri Lankan case, the line of division between artisanal and industrial technology was drawn by applying the criterion *mode of propulsion* (oars and sails or motor). Outrigger canoes with outboard engines were thus classified as industrial crafts. In the Malaysian case, this dichotomy is substituted by low, intermediate and high technology.

The choice of technology of production may rest with fishermen or non-fishermen, local or non-local investors (*absentee owners*), private or state. In addition, state or customary regulation influences the choices. Several researchers of Malaysian fisheries (Yahaya 1976, 1978; Munro and Chee 1978; Ling 1978a, 1978b; Fredericks and Wells 1981) criticize the choice of technology, their fundamental objection being that where labour is abundant, technologies should be labour intensive. The debate on the labour-displacing effect of modern technology is treated below.

Capital

Due to low productivity and cultural values which generate social equality (see Share systems below), capital formation within artisanal fisheries is slow. If no credit facilities exist, even a very clever and lucky fisherman must save money for years to buy the material he needs to build a craft. However, contrary to the popular belief among Western fishing technologists, who judge from the state in which they may find modern boats, the maintenance tradition is strong in these societies. Therefore, a wooden craft can last for more than one generation, and a fisherman may inherit his father's or grandfather's craft.

A feature of the artisanal production system is private ownership of crafts and gear, but crafts are often owned by more than one person, such as father and son, or brothers working together. When modern technology became available in the villages, some of the fishermen had a head start. Some of the craft owners had capital which could be used as security for bank loans. They also often had political influence which was useful when they applied for subsidies. Other local petty capitalists, such as fish traders and shopkeepers, used their savings to invest in modern boats. They had earlier invested in fisheries, but mostly as financiers of fishermen.

However, capital accumulated locally was of minor importance for technological modernization. The amount of capital needed by artisanal fishermen for the provision of crafts and gear is small compared to the size of investment needed to build and equip a purse seiner or a trawler. Most of the capital invested in the Kuala Kedah fishing industry came from non-local sources, of which a substantial amount was provided by Chinese investors. Increased absentee ownership of boats and capital originating in trade and manufacturing and not in fisheries were in the Malaysian fishing villages a prerequisite for large-scale technological modernization. This was, according to Platteau (1989), the case in most other societies experiencing a *Blue Revolution*. Absentee ownership is related to a process of *concentration of capital*, that is, there are fewer owners than before. The other side of the coin is the process of proletarization in fisheries resulting from technological modernization. In Malaysia,

> the proportion of paid employees among fishermen rose from 21% in 1957 to 55% in 1976. This has been more dramatic for Malay fishermen than for their Chinese counterparts. (Jomo 1991, 25)

Epple (1977) reports that in 1950, 90 per cent of the Grenadian fishermen owned boats. By 1970, the percentage was reduced to 25. However, the degree to which technological modernization leads to concentration of capital and proletarization of fishermen depends on the capital intensity of the technology introduced as well as the social context. Within Norwegian *coastal* fisheries, the ownership pattern changed slowly with technological modernization.

The massive investments expanded and changed the villages' relations with the world beyond the villages. The early years of technological modernization in the Malaysian villages can be characterized as time of free enterprise *El Dorado*. During this period, absentee ownership considerably reduced local control over production.

Market expansion

Theories of social change in rural societies define the *agrarian transition* as the change from an *ecological* to an *economic* situation. In the former, the relations determining the rural people's standard of living were those between producers and nature; in the latter, the decisive relations were those between the producers and the market. However, in fishing communities, market relations have been important for centuries. On coasts where resources were rich, specialization came early. The fisherfolk increasingly became dependent on fisheries alone. Fish were traded to meet the requirements of their diet, cereals, vegetables and meat. Establishing an ecological situation is thus difficult, but the increased importance of remote markets with technological modernization is beyond doubt.

The prime causes of technological modernization of fisheries are increased demand for fish with economic growth and increased population. Increased production resulting from technological modernization reduces prices in the long run. If production increases at a higher rate than the demand, the reaction within an industrial production system is not necessarily to limit the size of the output. The situation can be met by attempts to control or expand markets and by further technological modernization to reduce labour costs. Over time, decreasing (or even stable) prices of fish may result in economic difficulties for artisanal fishermen. When at the same time the prices of inputs increase, they are trapped in a price squeeze and they become victims of the mechanism which reproduces poverty among African peasant farmers. Vercruijsse considers this mechanism a major cause of what he terms the *dissolution of labour.*

> The *ali* and seine fishermen flooded the markets with their larger catches: if they did not exactly cause prices to fall, they prevented increased demand from raising them by any considerable degree. The livelihoods of many fishermen, which had never been much above subsistence level, were endangered. (Vercruijsse 1984, 121)

If the only way out is radical technological modernization, it implies exit from traditional occupations. The price squeeze may spur minor technological modernization as well. In Kerala, technological modernization led to the expansion of the artisanal fleet, simultaneously with the introduction of the modern prawn trawlers. The prize squeeze may thus contribute to the modernization or eradication of traditional technologies – and to technological retrogression.

An important difference between artisanal and industrial technology is the dependence of the latter on the supply of non-local goods and services, the increase in the villages' backward linkages to other areas. The energy intensity of modern technology provides the best example of increased dependence. The need for oil necessitates frequent interaction with the world beyond the village and the price of oil may determine whether the fishing trip resulted in profit or in loss.

Also, in contrast to artisanal crafts, which often are locally made, trawlers and their gear are manufactured elsewhere. Spare parts must be imported to the villages (and often also to the nation). When the boats need repair, they are moved to shipyards, or mechanics are sent for. Increased dependence on non-local supplies is now evident in artisanal fisheries as well. In the past, gear was manufactured by the fishermen themselves, and they often used materials which were available locally. Now, most of the nets, ropes and hooks are bought, as are cotton and nylon thread used for the maintenance of gear. Very few types of gear are now manufactured by the fishermen themselves. Therefore, in a 30-year perspective, the demand for *money* among artisanal fishermen has increased, and therefore their dependence upon price fluctuations of inputs:

> The market economy entraps fishermen in an exchange business where they are made conscious of the fact that capital does indeed play a significant role in almost all their dealings. (Hassan 1977, 7)

The forward linkages to the world beyond the village increased simultaneously with the production increase. Being a perishable commodity, distant trade with fresh fish could only take place after improvement in transportation technology, and cooling technology became available. Kurien gives a good description of the effects of market expansion in Asian fishing villages: Production increase, resulting from increased national and international demand, and made possible by importing Western technology, has expanded the relations in fishing communities. Whereas earlier they produced for a local market to consumers at the same standard of living as themselves, their produce can now be found in

> the luxury hotels of the US and the wedding ceremonies of wealthy Japanese. In this manner, the traditional fishermen were linked to the world market through a hierarchy of middlemen [...] [and] to an ultra-modern consumer in the developed industrial countries of the world. (Kurien 1978, 1562)

The increased information flow went both ways: The resources of the fishing villages, fish and labour, provided investment opportunities for big business. On the other hand, the fisherfolk were exposed to consumption patterns of national and international centres.

There has been an understanding among governmental agencies that increased production and market expansion might lead to a greater exploitation of the fisherfolk. The attempts to control markets have often resulted in the building of public marketplaces, where both cooperatives and private fish merchants can buy fish. Cooperatives are supposed to be alternatives to the middlemen, but to break dependency relations between middleman and fisherman demands more than the building of physical infrastructure. New systems of marketing, in attempting to break up such relationships, often fail to realize the extent of the fish merchants' role in the society. Their function as source of credit, both for investments and for subsistence, must be considered. Otherwise, the fisherfolk may bite the helping hand which wants to curb the power of the middlemen (Stirrat 1974). In Merlijn's (1989) study from Sarawak, he notes that the fishermen do not consider their relations with traders as one of exploitation and contends that institutions created by governments will never be able to match the flexibility of the middlemen. Conditions in Sarawak may differ from Peninsular Malaysia, but Merlijn probably pushes matters to extremes when he claims that

> although fishermen are more or less tied to their middleman, this tie is not necessarily permanent, has not led to any exploitation, and is not resented by the fishermen. (Merlijn 1989, 699)

Maybe he confuses whether they objectively are exploited and whether they subjectively recognize it? The view that the relation of power between Asian fishermen and middlemen is asymmetrical is widely held. For instance, Firth finds Raychaudhuri's (1980) observation of general application:

> [The fishermen] are firmly under the stranglehold of a chain of financiers not directly involved in the hauling of fish. (Firth 1981, 4)

Hassan (1977), in her study of a Kedah fishing village, concludes that features of the relationship between middlemen and fishermen typical of small-scale inshore fisheries, the *bertaukeh* system (see Security nets below), continue to be of importance after technological modernization:

> The *bertaukeh system* that governs inshore fishing continues to serve as a functional element in the entire village fishing industry. (Hassan 1977, 23, emphasis in the original)

Compared to the time before technological modernization, the boat owners' possibility to control the information they get from the buyers on market prices is reduced. The value of the catch is dependent on which market it is sold in, as well as daily price fluctuations. Market expansion has given the fish merchants a golden opportunity to manipulate prices, and thus increase their share of the value of the fish. There may also be, such as was observed in India by Kurien (1978), a concentration of capital as big business enters fish marketing: Small middlemen are either competed out or within the sphere of influence of the larger merchants (Munro and Chee 1978). Transportation cost per unit of fish may have decreased. But a general effect is that the number of links in the chain from fisherman to consumer, which each demands a share in the profit, has increased. There are in Malaysian, as in many fishing villages, complaints regarding the *exit of value* which is created locally:

> Perhaps those who benefit most from trawling are the boat owners who are not residents of Tanjung Dawai, for they are the ones who get the major portion of the proceeds from the sale of the fish landings. (Hassan 1977, 21)

Labour recruitment

Earlier, kinship ties were important when crewmen were recruited to the crafts. A son was preferred to a friend, irrespective of his skills. This is probably more economically sound than it sounds since the household normally had the disposal of its members' incomes. Löfgren (1972, quoted in Acheson 1981) argues that within an industry characterized by highly fluctuating incomes, the shock absorption capacity is greater where the family is the production unit. In addition, when there is a labour shortage, recruitment based on kinship secures the supply of labour and crew stability. Within artisanal fisheries as well as in industrial fisheries, kinship relations continue to play a significant role in the formation of crews. Bjøru (1982) comments on the paradox that kinship seems to be more important for the recruitment to the Norwegian fishing fleet than it is in the beach seine fisheries of Sri Lanka. The question whether recruitment based on kinship decreases in importance in the fisheries of developing countries is, however, still open. Acheson (1981) maintains that, in general, there is great flexibility in the recruitment pattern in fishing societies, but that inshore artisanal fisheries are often organized around a core of kinsmen.

In the Malaysian case, labour recruitment based on kinship is less functional for industrial capital. The formation of *free labour* was necessary for the owners to be able to recruit the best skilled, strongest, and most efficient fishermen. With absentee ownership, the breakdown of the family labour recruitment custom could even come overnight. When local skippers, who were hired by the non-local owners, recruited labour, family members would be preferred, but sometimes the very size of the crews counteracted this. This was evident when local Chinese owners needed crews. On these crafts, there is a mixture of Malay and Chinese crewmen. The process of free labour formation is slower in the cases where local Malays bought modern boats. To take productivity only, and not kinship, into account in selecting the crew is alien to a strong cultural tradition. However, the changes gradually came. Since the investments are much larger than before, the risk increases, and capital formation must be quick and large to enable the repayment of loans. Hence labour productivity, and therefore skill and experience, must be evaluated when crewmen are selected. The low-productive uncle – or even a lazy son – is in danger of losing the job. Even in the early 1970s, Hassan observes:

> It is quite normal that there are no strict rules in the recruitment of personnel to man a fishing unit. Although kinship ties and same locality are the main criteria in the choice of work mates, still they are not the absolute rules. (Hassan 1977, 5)

Fishermen's political organizations often follow lines of division according to technology, not the labour versus capital division. This indicates that fisherman versus state (resource management and subsidy policies) has been considered more important than fisherman versus fish merchant, or crewman versus owner. As regards the latter relation, the strong crew solidarity undermines the crewmen's identity as *wage earners*. Vercruijsse observes in the case of Ghana:

> When asked about their position, non-owner crew members will deny that they are wage-earners (in which they are quite correct) and also deny that they are employed (in which they are mistaken). (Vercruijsse 1984, 39)

Stirrat (1977) also notes the lack of a class of owners as distinct from workers in Sri Lankan fisheries. Crew solidarity, which is commonly strengthened by rituals (Palmer 1989), is the outcome of literally being in the same boat and sharing the risks with the owners. This may explain the relative persistency of share systems prevailing in fishing societies:

> After all, a crew is a group of 'co-adventurers' [...] – not wage earners. (Acheson 1981, 279)

In the case of Malaysian fisheries, Jomo links the low level of political organization to the remuneration system:

> The virtual absence of any form of independent organization of fishing crew, let alone unionization, underlines (the crew's) vulnerability, though the typical catch-sharing mode of wage payment probably has great ideological effects in terms of establishing an identity across class lines. This question obviously also has implications for the efficacy of poverty eradication measures among fishermen. (Jomo 1991, 26)

Share systems

The systems of profit distribution, the share systems, are particular to the type of craft and method used. In technologically stable situations, share systems may therefore be inherited from previous generations. The relationships between owners and crewmen were stable, based on agreement on how income from fisheries should be divided among the crewmen. Analysing the examples given by Firth (1966), Bjøru (1982) finds that in Malaysian fishing villages before technological modernization,

> returns to different inputs tended to correspond to the degree to which each contributed to the total yield. (Bjøru 1982, 15)

Although the share systems which were common before technological modernization were characterized by a high degree of stability, they were flexible. The owners thus could give additional part-shares to crewmen

> because of extra work done, or because of labour shortage, or because of his age or poverty. (Firth 1966, 257)

But Firth contends that the old Malaysian share systems were not

> merely customary structures of a haphazard kind; they follow underlying economic principles. (Firth 1966, 257)

The principle underlying when old or poor fishermen are given additional incomes is a principle of *social equity*, a notion of a fair return based on the household's *needs*. This principle was even more prominent among the Tikopian fishermen (Firth 1939):

The smaller the catch, the more equally it was shared. (Emmerson 1980, 31)

New share systems had to be designed when modern technology was introduced. The owners' increased capital costs and running expenses were sought to be estimated. Neither in the Sri Lankan nor in the in Malaysian villages studied is there consensus among the fisherfolk on the size of the owners' shares. Aboard some modern boats, there is a high turnover of labour caused by disputes on the share system between owner, skipper, and crewmen. Lifelong crew relationships, characterized by few conflicts, have become rare. A high turnover of labour may well be a general effect of technological modernization. In Norwegian trawler fisheries, a high turnover has become part of the technology (Høst 1980).

Increased economic inequality in the fishing communities has been an effect of the introduction of the high-labour-productive modern boats. The fact that owners are better off now than earlier, relative to crewmen, is the consequence of share system changes. In the Malaysian case as well as in the Sri Lankan, the owners' improved living standard indicates that their shares cover more than capital costs, running expenses and what they earn as crew members. Their increased consumption is the result of *increased profits*, disguised as return to capital. In some cases, however, it can be argued that the owners' consumption increases are at the expense of boat maintenance, that is, what should cover capital costs in the future covers increased consumption of the owner today.

If one accepts the egalitarian principle that increased production should benefit all the producers equally, the new share systems must be considered unfavourable from the point of view of the crewmen, since the owners' shares become relatively larger than the crewmen's shares, as compared to share systems in artisanal fisheries. There is evidence that such change in disfavour of crewmen may be a general outcome of technological modernization in fisheries. Based on Firth's (1966) findings from the Malaysian East coast, Bjøru (1982) calculates that the crewmen's share of the catch decreased from 62 per cent in 1940 to 40 per cent in 1963, a period during which modern technology was introduced. Similarly, she finds, based on Christensen (1977), that a Fanti fisherman in Ghana got his share reduced from 10–12 per cent in 1950 to 4 per cent of the gross value of the catch in 1972. This was a direct consequence of the introduction of outboard engines. Similarly, in the case of Korea, Sang-Bok concludes that

the gap between wealthy and poor fishermen began to widen. Most motorboat and net owners are now ranked in the upper class in the community. (Sang-Bok 1977, 123)

In the beginning, the crewmen accepted the new share systems, partly because they had no choice, but also because the owner's increased profit in a way is disguised as 'return to technology'. This is formulated very clearly by Vercruijsse in the case of Ghanian fishermen, who

> treat the ownership of boat and net as incidental, as can be seen from the terms in which the contribution of boat and net to production are expressed: 'one share *for the boat*, two shares *for the net*', terms which refer to the instruments of labour and not to the person who owns them. (Vercruijsse 1984, 39)

It is easy, if you come from a rowing craft, to be impressed by the wonders of modern techniques. In addition, in the early years of technological modernization, resources were ample, catches good and the crewmen earned a lot more than before. However, it is not the craft but the *fisherman* who is the producer of the fish and therefore the creator of value. After technological modernization, the crewmen had to accept share systems based on complicated calculations of capital depreciation, and in addition, the transactions involved in the administration of fish production became less transparent. Earlier, when prices were stable, the crewmen knew the value of the catch as well as the costs involved in producing it. They could witness the transactions between middleman and owner and would meet to share the money at the owner's home. The paper transactions between owner and middlemen, typical of the modern production system, are for crewmen less *controllable* than the cash involved earlier. Before technological modernization certain transactions earlier were more transparent, the fishing societies had a

> low level of the type of alienation so typical of modern economies of scale where each single person is just one little element in enormous, world-wide economic cycle that practically speaking nobody understands. (Galtung 1980, 345)

When the settlement is correct as well as when it is incorrect, a suspicion of being cheated prevails among many fishermen:

> There is much opportunity for genuine mistakes and also for some misappropriation of funds. (Firth 1966, 249)

Firth however argues that cheating when the catch is shared is rare, although share systems are complex. The reason for this is the owner's fear of losing the crew. Firth's argument is, however, valid in situations of labour shortage only. Where labour is abundant, the general effect is a pressure on the wage rate and, as one owner stated, 'if you accuse me of cheating, then leave'.

Concentration of capital may contribute to the lowering of the returns to labour. The position of the crewmen was better when there were many owners compared to when there are few, as reported by de Silva (1977), who studied the difference in bargaining position of Sri Lankan fishermen in mechanized versus trap net fishing.

Fixed wage remuneration (such as monthly salaries) is the most common system in capitalist societies. It is thus interesting to note that share systems still exist in the fisheries in industrial as well as in developing countries. Even in cases where a minimum wage is secured by union action or government intervention, sharing of the catch still takes place, and the share may constitute a major part of the fishermen's salary (Bjøru 1982). The continued existence of share systems can be viewed in two ways. Either, the share systems are transitional forms, which will disappear when the industry becomes fully capitalist. Or which is my view, the industry already *is* capitalist, and share systems are a reproduced old feature, kept alive because they are modified to become functional for accumulation of capital. Despite technological modernization, production of fish still contains an element of *hunting*. Annual variation of yield is much greater than for instance in agriculture. Share systems continue to exist because they *secure a spread of the risk to all those involved in production*, whereas when a fixed salary is paid, the risk is borne by the owner of capital only. This view is shared by Bjøru (1982) who emphasizes the work incentive inherent in the system. According to Vercruijsse, where the crew member is remunerated with a share of the catch, it means that

> the value of labour as a commodity is not expressed immediately through the market; (and this) has at least two consequences: first, that the amount of compensation given to crew members in kind fluctuates with the market price for fish. Moreover, if there is no catch […] the crew members have no income. The sharing system is thus not only a means of dividing the product but also of dividing the risk of production between the capital owner and the direct producers. (Vercruijsse 1984, 38)

Furthermore, there is reason to argue that with technological modernization, hired labour bears *more* of the risk of production than they did before. Increased capital intensity has led to a transfer of risk to the crewmen. Arguing that competitive labour markets, and not the type of remuneration system, are decisive for the wage rate of the crewmen, Sutinen claims that share systems are for the benefit of the owners:

Fishing entrepreneurs are unambiguously better off with the share system. It allows spreading some of the risk among the crew, thus reducing the cost of risk-bearing, and provides a work incentive that makes it less costly to extract the desired level of labour services from the crew. (Sutinen 1979, 159)

He also argues that from an employment point of view, the share system is beneficial. If it is replaced by the wage system, the total number of fishermen would reduce. But sharing the value of the catch implies sharing of the variable costs, for instance the cost of fuel, bait and foods consumed aboard during fishing trips. Normally such expenses are either deducted from the gross value of the catch before it is shared or the owner is paid a larger share which covers these expenses. In this way increased oil prices directly affect the wage of the labourers, not only those who pay the bill.

Old types of share systems, giving high returns to labour, are still common in artisanal fisheries. In the Malaysian fishing village studied, in the same manner as aboard artisanal crafts, trawler crewmen get incomes from fish caught which are not for human consumption, that is, trash fish which are sold to fertilizer factories. However, other reproduced relations of an artisanal production system are less favourable to the crewmen. An owner of a *perahu* or a *sampan* has the right to extract some free labour; his crewmen often take part in repairs of craft and gear. This is also the case on the modern boats; some trawler crews do maintenance work without any compensation.

Security nets

In fisheries, fluctuations of income are high. Therefore, the fishermen often receive advances on their payments from middlemen or boat owners. In the latter case, the advances will later be deducted from their shares. These debts tend to accumulate, since the fishermen often fail to repay at once. When prepayments from boat owners become *credit for consumption*, they cease to be just advances and become a security net. Even in fishing societies where share systems give high returns to labour, or where unequal sharing to the benefit of the less fortunate is not uncommon, there may be times when some families must survive on loans or rely on gifts from other members of the community. A security net is thus a means of survival when income from participation in income-generating activities is insufficient.

Economic security nets are a way of distributing the surplus of production according to needs, either on a regular basis, like loans for consumption, or more permanently like gifts. The most common of situations when there is a demand for security nets is when old age forces fishermen to retire. Few can rely on savings, but must be supported by their families, which may be viewed as return to previous investment in children. Long periods of illness or unemployment may also reduce incomes dramatically. In such periods, a way to tolerate being a burden to your relatives or friends is that, in the future, it may be your turn to help them. Within social anthropology, there is a long reciprocity debate on whether gifts are being returned in one way or the other. Whether they always are or not, they seem to be part of good circles of security, in which the members of the community are closely related to each other. The negation of good gifts is bad loans, creating vicious circles of debt and dependency to capital owners, such as professional moneylenders, middlemen or boat owners. It is interesting to note that owners of the industrial boats may have obligations typical of the role of capital owners within the artisanal production system. They are expected to lend money to the crewmen, not only as advances on lay days but also when larger sums are needed, for example, for marriages or funerals. However, what is a security net for fishermen may be *a means of labour control* from the point of view of capital owners. For instance, in situations where labour is scarce, the boat owners' supply of skilled fishermen can be secured through their debt. Thus, security nets must be considered part of the production system, in the same manner as share systems and labour control mechanisms.

Although there may be reciprocity between fishermen and middlemen, some relationships are clearly of an exploitative nature. For instance, fish merchants who have lent money to the fishermen sometimes buy the catch at prices below its market value; the prices are agreed upon before they go to sea. In Mankok, a fishing village on the East Coast, Bailey (1983) found that of 29 fishermen, as many as 10 delivered the catch to a buyer for non-economic reasons, that is, either kinship or friendship. In the case of Sri Lanka, Alexander (1975a) terms similar relations *the tied boat system*, but underlines that in general, the fishermen have a strong bargaining position vis-à-vis the middlemen. In the case study, I found that 26 per cent of the respondents in Kalametiya and 14 per cent in Hambantota sold the catch to a price agreed to beforehand. In Malaysia, similar relations are termed the *bertaukeh* system. The word *bertaukeh* means 'to have a *towkay*'. *Taukeh* is derived from the Chinese word *towkay*, which in Malay means

> a man, usually a Chinese, who manage and controls a business. [...] The term *towkay ikan* refers to a Chinese fish dealer who has control over the marketing aspect of the local fishing industry. (Hassan 1977, 8)

Hassan (1977) maintains that the *bertaukeh* system can be viewed as a patron – client one, in which the middleman takes care of his fellow villagers in force of his superior position, thus reproducing the traditional (feudal) *bertuan* relationship. This vigorous feature of the artisanal production system functions very well within the production system today: The *bertaukeh* system is important not only to artisanal fishermen. As regards the relationship between industrial fishermen and cooperative societies, Hassan observes that

> there is a tendency among the community members to visualise the main office holders of the (co-operative) society as being the counterpart of the *taukeh ikan* of the inshore fishing industry. (Hassan 1977, 24)

Some fishermen try to escape the obligation by selling fish illegally at sea to other dealers (Yahaya 1981) or by overestimating the amount of fish for consumption given to the crew (Munro and Chee 1978). Other ways in which fishermen may exercise countervailing power to reduce the middlemen's exploitation are described by Elliston (1967).

Some forms of social security are of an indirect type. The above example of the *share system* in which small catches were shared more equally than big ones demonstrates a way in which cultural values of social equality operate to prevent the suffering of poor households. One could claim that this is at the cost of the boat owners; they may, however, increase their share when the big catch comes. Also, labour recruitment based on kinship criteria provides a form of job security which counteracts the development of inequality based on skill or strength, which reduces the demand for security nets.

The indirect security nets may be undermined by technological modernization. Share systems with low returns to labour replace older systems, and it may no longer be taken for granted to get a job. Direct security nets may also have become weaker. For capital owners, there may now be more profitable objects of investment than economic support of fishermen, particularly where labour is abundant. Absentee ownership of boats also reduces personal relations between fisherman and boat owner, which weaken what moral obligations the owners may have to help their crewmen. Whether this implies an overall weakening of the fisherfolk's economic and social security, or if new security nets have replaced old, ought to be thoroughly investigated.

With technological modernization, not only owners' social responsibility diminishes. Nieuwenhuijs (1989) reports a weakening of the security nets of poor families in fishing villages in Kerala. Traditionally, a substantial part of the calorie intake of poor families comes from fish foraged on the beaches by children present during the landing of the catches. When catches now decrease, this customary right of children is threatened. Centralization of catch landings in harbours, which is necessary with the introduction of big modern vessels, also affects such security nets negatively.

The security nets described, both direct ones such as loans or gifts and indirect ones like share systems and labour recruitment criteria promoting social equality are features typical of an artisanal production system, still functioning. The number of needy, both in absolute and relative terms, has, however, increased, which puts severe strain on these systems. The security nets are still there, but they are inadequate. As will be discussed below, the creation of a relative surplus population, resulting in unemployment and poverty, occurs simultaneously with the weakening of socio-economic security nets.

Simultaneously with the diversification of the economy, modern security nets, such as sickness and unemployment benefit and pension plans, developed in industrial countries. Increasingly these have become crucial ingredients of the welfare state. Social security systems are, as well as state intervention in market and production, alien to capitalist ideology, which assumes that the economic growth which accompanies technological modernization will make security nets superfluous. This has nowhere been the case; but in most industrial countries, the polarization tendencies of the capitalist system have been checked by the formation of strong labour unions, to some extent limiting the exploitation of labour and spurring a more equal distribution of social surpluses, for instance by means of creating social security systems. Such systems are still way out of reach of poor Asian fishermen made superfluous by capitalist expansion. They are still non-adopted modern security nets. When such security nets are unavailable, the fishermen must rely on the old ones, or create new.

The classification problem

I have substantiated that when analysing production systems, we are faced with a mixture: some features originate in the previous production system which has similarities to the artisanal ideal type; others originate in production systems similar to the industrial. Furthermore, I now contend that two separate economic spheres cannot be constructed: No living human being or economic enterprises in the villages can be classified accordingly.

In Figure 6 I have drawn the beach seine fisherman Shamon's relations to the production system, illustrating his position in relation to the ideal types. He uses a rowing craft and a beach seine (low technology), accumulates capital slowly (if at all), works together with his uncle with whom he shares the catch equally and, when he is broke, he goes to the pawnbroker or lends money from his relatives; he seems artisanal indeed. *But* he has received a subsidy to buy

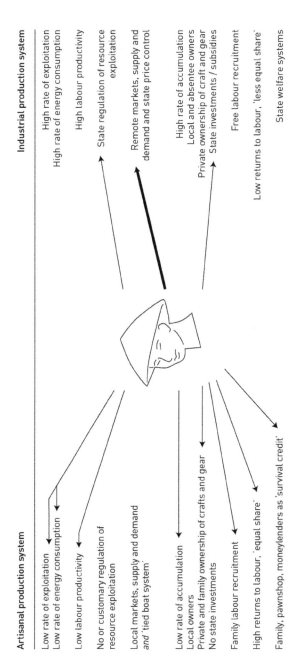

Artisanal production system

Low rate of exploitation
Low rate of energy consumption

Low labour productivity

No or customary regulation of
resource exploitation

Local markets, supply and demand
and 'tied boat system'

Low rate of accumulation
Local owners
Private and family ownership of crafts and gear
No state investments

Family labour recruitment

High returns to labour, 'equal share'

Family, pawnshop, moneylenders as 'survival credit'

Industrial production system

High rate of exploitation
High rate of energy consumption

High labour productivity

State regulation of resource
exploitation

Remote markets, supply and
demand and state price control

High rate of accumulation
Local and absentee owners
Private ownership of craft and gear
State investments / subsidies

Free labour recruitment

Low returns to labour, 'less equal share'

State welfare systems

Figure 6 Shamon and the ideal types.

fishing gear, and what is even more important is that his catch is sold at the big city markets. This is a most important economic relation, since his living standard is directly dependent not only on whether there are fish in the sea but also on its price. Shamon is very industrial in terms of market.

The case of the trawler fisherman Mahmud is illustrated in Figure 7. He uses high technology (which of course is a relative concept) and has managed to save enough money to buy his own house. His catch share is, compared to what he would have got if working with Shamon, however, less equal (lower returns to labour). But Mahmud is not exclusively industrial: He was recruited by his father and, which is more important, he must often rely upon his relatives' support or the pawn shop when his income is insufficient. In sum: Mahmud is traditional in terms of labour recruitment and security nets.

The fishermen Shamon and Mahmud cannot be classified as belonging to different production systems. This applies to the 412 other Asian fishermen interviewed. Furthermore, the artisanal production system is not present as a coherent system. Only some features are reproduced. And the industrial production system is not adopted in its totality. There are, for instance, no modern security nets in the village.

Weber points at a special advantage when using ideal types in social analyses. Where great *divergence* between an ideal type and reality is found, the result still guides the researcher towards a clearer understanding of unique features and historical significance of a certain object of analysis. In such cases,

> the purpose of (the ideal type) is fulfilled, precisely as it manifests its own *unreality*. (Weber 1971, 210, my translation, emphasis in the original)

Relations can, according to certain characteristics such as their non-capitalist or capitalist character, be analytically arranged to form an ideal type system. They may be termed ideal type system relations to distinguish them from empirically identifiable relations (real relations). If a description of ideal type system relations to a great extent captures essential real relations of the producers, there is a match. But in situations of change, unless the theoretical construct of the ideal type system relations is changed, real relations are no longer captured; there is a mismatch. The ideal type is emptied of empirical content – and becomes a description of essential relations of the past. In the present context, one cannot claim that relations of a non-capitalist character form a pre-capitalist mode of production (or that indigenous relations form a traditional sector). Similarly, one cannot claim that industrial fishermen are modern.

The difficulty of matching the producers' real relations to ideal type systems shows that the unit of analysis cannot be kept unclear in theoretical models.

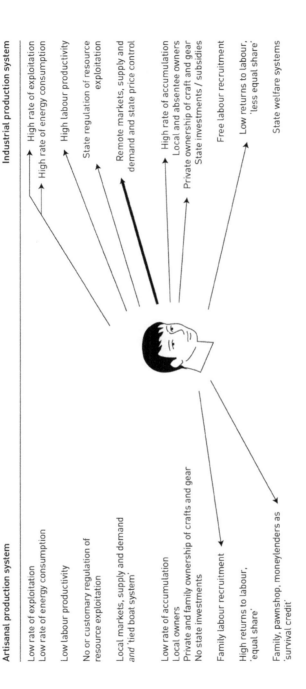

Artisanal production system

Low rate of exploitation
Low rate of energy consumption

Low labour productivity

No or customary regulation of resource exploitation

Local markets, supply and demand and 'tied boat system'

Low rate of accumulation
Local owners
Private and family ownership of crafts and gear
No state investments

Family labour recruitment

High returns to labour, 'equal share'

Family, pawnshop, moneylenders as 'survival credit'

Industrial production system

High rate of exploitation
High rate of energy consumption

High labour productivity

State regulation of resource exploitation

Remote markets, supply and demand and state price control

High rate of accumulation
Local and absentee owners
Private ownership of craft and gear
State investments / subsidies

Free labour recruitment

Low returns to labour, 'less equal share'

State welfare systems

Figure 7 Mahmud and the ideal types.

However, the problem does not affect the *logic* of such models; it arises only in empirical research where the producers' relations have a mixed character. The problem of mismatch can be solved by changing the ideal type according to the empirical findings (which is what theoretical work is all about). But to researchers, ideal types may appear more real than reality, as discussed in Chapter 1. There seem to be many a good reason to keep obsolete ideal types alive; many of them are probably ideological.

Returning to the question on the contents of the mixture, which was my point of departure, it is probably clear by now that separate economic spheres cannot be identified, and that what is observed rather supports an interconnected relations stance. The position or direction of change is still not clear. This discussion will proceed in the final chapter; the next chapter will bring empirical evidence on technological changes and standard of living in the fishing villages studied. By focusing on the mobility of labour between technologies at different productivity levels, the oneness as well as the mixed character of the production system is underlined: the fisherman who is classified as industrial today may be artisanal tomorrow.

Reconstruction of technological pasts using work histories

When knowledge of the past is a prerequisite for understanding the present, the intriguing methodological problems involved in the *reconstruction of past events and processes* arise in social science. When the time horizon of the study is the immediate past, for example, the last 20 years, social scientists rely on historians and other scientists' analyses and descriptions as well as statistical material. Severe problems arise where few historians and no reliable written sources of information exist. This is a problem which is common in Third World countries. In most studies undertaken by development researchers, knowledge of the past is gained by obtaining whatever bits and pieces of written sources can be found, often inadequately supplemented with information based on oral tradition.

However, the *systematic collection and statistical treatment* of information on past changes based on oral tradition may give valuable information of the development of social processes. The *work history method* has special relevance where an *inadequate statistical basis* limits the understanding of the recent past. Collecting information on *work histories* implies a systematic registration of the respondent's life history, his or her career from the time work started up to the present. The statistical treatment of the participants' statements, which is the core of the *work history method*, does not reduce the importance of written sources of information. The picture of the past, which is reconstructed by summing up individual experience, is controlled by confronting it with whatever written documentation available. In studies of rural development in developing countries, however, an inadequate statistical data basis is more often the rule than the exception. Participants' experiences are thus the major – and often the only – source of information.

The work history method may also have *advantages* compared with the more common reconstruction methods. Some of the individual adaptations and variations will always be lost when a general picture of a social process is set up. I contend that the work history method is superior when the aim is to reveal such variations at individual level. The two-way simultaneous movement of the same number of people between two categories, for instance, is easily revealed using this method. Usually, this will only be visible if each category is analysed in detail or if the purpose of the study is to follow people's movements.

Applying the work history method, oral tradition is no longer used as a supplement, but becomes the *major* source of information. Information on the processes is collected by using sampling techniques, which means not relying only on a few key informants like older members of the society. Testing data reliability, although limited by the quality of available statistics, becomes possible. I developed the work history method to be able to describe and analyse the course of technological change when working in the fishing villages in Sri Lanka. The method was considerably improved before I started the Malaysian study and adapted to computer processing. What inspired me to try out this idea was that reliable boat statistics for reconstructing the relative strength of the different forms of technology over time were not available. This was the case also with employment statistics; the possibility of reconstructing the changes indirectly was therefore limited. However, some use could be made of recent figures collected by the fisheries authorities, but this could only provide a rough idea of the *present* situation. The investigation was thus started by gathering knowledge on the technologies which were in use in the villages at that moment, the fishing grounds which were exploited, major species which were caught, the marketing system and the village administration, especially the fishermen's organizations.

Descriptions as well as drawings were made of past and present technologies. This background information proved sufficient to commence the interviews with the active fishermen of the villages and their households. Since the registration of fishermen was very irregular and not updated at the time of the investigations, the samples were drawn by selecting the households of every third fisherman in the Sri Lankan case and every fifth in the Malaysian. The following information was collected on each fisherman's life history:

1. Age
2. Age when he started to work

Year	Age	Time	Craft	Ownership	Method	Reasons for changes
1950			Oru with sails	Father's	Handlining	
		10 years				Better catch of modern boats
1960			Mechanised boat	Own	Longlining	
		5 years				Nylon nets more productive
1965		15 years	Same	Same	Driftnet	
1980 (present)			Same	Same		

Figure 8 The work history matrix.

3. The year when he started to work
4. The technology he used when he started: Type of craft/Methods of fishing
5. Ownership (owner/skipper, master fisherman, crewman)
6. Every change of technology he made in his career and reasons for the changes
7. Social mobility (ownership changes)
8. Geographical mobility (if he had left the village for a period) or if he periodically had other work in the village.

The information was registered on a *work history matrix* which required accuracy when filled in, in the questionnaire (Figure 8).

Simplification of the variety in the individual *work histories* registered on the matrix involves the usual problems of categorizing information. Deducing forms of technology from empirical data is not always so uncomplicated. With the increasing number of technologies in an area, the need for categories more specific than *low* and *high* arises. In addition, blending of the forms may occur, like the adoption of nylon nets on old crafts, and can blur the distinction between the categories. This is a problem which can only be solved empirically, that is, by analysing the technologies in use in an area and basing the classification on what is meaningful for the questions raised.

Establishing *extremes* is easy based on time of introduction, complexity, mode of propulsion and so on, less variation is lost if the categories *low*, *intermediate* and *high* form of technology are used. However, the concept of *high* form of technology has connotations which may be misleading. The trawlers of the Malaysian fishing villages are indeed high technology compared with their one-man rowing crafts but compared with the electronically well-equipped vessels of the industrialized countries, they would be classified as standard-modern technology. The categories used are thus time and area specific.

Career paths

The fishermen's *technological pasts*, their choices of technology over time form their *career paths*. A *modernization career path* of the Malaysian case may have this form:

$$L^c_s \rightarrow I_{sk} \rightarrow H^t_o \rightarrow H^t_c \rightarrow H^t_c$$

1941 1951 1966 1970 present

This fisherman's first job was aboard a sailing craft as a crewman in the 1940s. He later became skipper aboard an inboard boat, and in the late 1960s he got his own small trawler (which he a few years later had to sell). He now works as crewman aboard the same type of trawler. He has during his life moved from low, through intermediate, to a high form of technology. The same information is plotted in the graph in Figure 9.

Individual *career paths* may be useful when the effect of technology on the fisherfolk's standard of living is analysed. Various calculations can be made at individual level, such as number of years using *low*, *intermediate* or *high* technology, or total number of *man-years* in industrial fisheries, which can be correlated with living standard. The sample can be divided into groups like *fishermen who have always used high technology* and so on. Ownership, a dimension which is surprisingly often omitted when the economy of fisherfolk is discussed, is important in this context. A fisherman who has had his own boat in the last 20 years must be expected to be wealthier than the one who got his boat only a few months back. If official statistics were used directly for analytical purposes, both would probably be in the same category (owners today), and the important variable, *career length*, would have been ignored.

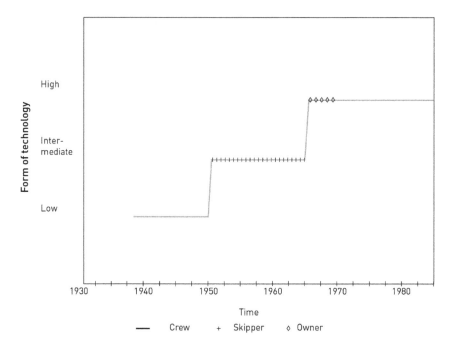

Figure 9 An example of a career path.

Forms of technology over time

Based on a representative sample of active fishermen's work histories, a reconstruction of the technological development of the village may be made. This is done by summing up the career paths, that is, by figuring out *how many fishermen were employed in the different types of technology every year*. Each fisherman's *work history* is coded according to form of technology (low, intermediate and high). Based on this, a table describing forms of technology over time can be constructed.

Since the fishermen's ages differ, the lengths of their careers also vary. The size of the samples each year varies accordingly. The contemporary sample (the number interviewed), is thus reduced as one goes back in time. When the oldest fisherman started his career in 1931 by using a sailing craft, the sample is one, that is, 100 per cent of the fishermen used low technology. As a matter of course, generalizations cannot be made on such a basis. In both the Sri Lankan and the Malaysian cases, the sample sizes increase considerably in the 1950s. The analysis of technological change based on the work history method can then start. For every year, the absolute numbers of each technology are computed and the shares of *low, intermediate* and *high* form of technology calculated.

Limitations of the work history method

In principle, the work histories make it possible to journey back to the time when the oldest fisherman in the sample got his first job. However, generalizing on this basis can hardly be justified since the sample size that year is only one. As one moves forward in time, the sample size increases as new generations of fishermen start their careers. The reduction in the sample size as one move back in history is the basic limitation of the work history method. This is discussed below, but first there is another important objection that may be made to all the variants of life cycle and work history studies, namely the limitation introduced by using people's living memory. A precondition for the use of such data is that the informants can recall the events of earlier periods in their lives. There are two serious difficulties involved; firstly that memory decays in time, secondly the problem of *telescoping*, where the time dimension is underestimated by the informant: '*events in the past are likely to be recalled as being more recent than they actually are*' (Bernard et al. 1984, 507, emphasis in the original). The faculty of memory probably varies. Most people seem to have a good recollection of *important* events like marriage, childbirth, death and some of the outstanding events in the history of the village or nation. The latter therefore must be part of the researcher's background knowledge before the field survey starts. Research of this type is impossible to undertake unless the researcher lives in the village. Knowledge of the history of the village will then increase as the work proceeds, and the respondents' memory can be aided by reference to important village events. This way to overcome (or at least mitigate) this problem is termed *aided recall* by Sudman and Bradburn (1973, in Bernard et al. 1984). Luckily, in my cases it appeared that *changes of technology* were considered such important events in the fishermen's lives that all of them could recall when they changed, and number of years they used the different technologies. The age when they made their first trip was just as easily recalled. When this was cross-checked with their wives' recollection of family events, the correspondence proved to be good. With very few exceptions, the fishermen also knew their year of birth.

The major problem of the work history method is one of representativity; that is, to make certain that the sample of fishermen each year is representative of the universe (all active fishermen in the village) that year. As explained above, the same sample of fishermen is used for statistical generalizations on events 10, 20 and in some cases even 30 years back. The population of the village has probably increased during this period, some fishermen have died and young fishermen have started their careers. What makes this an important methodological weakness is that the *leave-out of respondents may be systematic.*

Figure 10 shows the reduction of the sample from Kuala Kedah. The period from which generalizations can be justified is a matter of judgement. Here, the mid-1950s was chosen. The sample size was then about half that of the year of investigation. If the number of respondents included in the survey had been higher, it would probably have been possible to go even further back in time. The first important limitation of generalization at village level arises if the population of the village has been *unstable* during the period in question, that is, if there has been a lot of in-migration and out-migration. This is only important if the people who moved out had belonged to only one or two of the technology groups if they had stayed on in the village. Although unlikely, it is possible that all fishermen using one technique have moved or that many members of one age group left within a short period of time. Establishing an impression of the stability of the population can be done indirectly (by

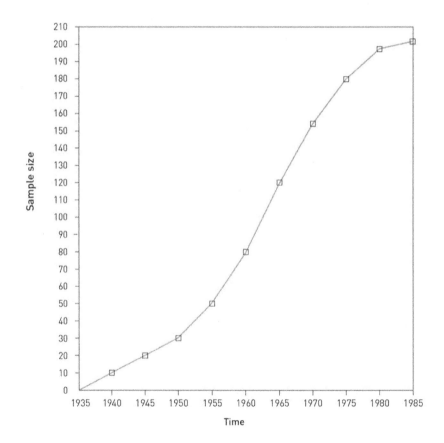

Figure 10 The decreasing size of the sample.

studying village history or by mobility studies if available) or directly by asking the sample fishermen and their wives about their place of birth. In the latter case, only in-migration would be registered.

Confidence in the conclusions may also be weakened *if mortality is higher in one group*. If, for instance, low form of technology has many of the older fishermen of the sample, it is possible that it would have had a *larger* share over time than the results of the reconstruction would show. This may be the case if the young adopt new technology quicker than the older fishermen. But adopting these methods requires capital and skill, which is more abundant in the older age groups. If this does not neutralize the above effect, increasing the number of old fishermen in the sample should be considered. Also, variations in *risk of life* in the different forms of technology may influence mortality and therefore the leave-out of respondents. This will only be of importance if the sample size is large.

In cases like these, where statistics are unreliable, the characteristics of the universe are registered before the sample is drawn. Testing of sample representativity for the year of investigation by means of the usual tests can then be done. Also, an indication of the quality of official statistics can be obtained by comparing them with the results of the researcher's own registrations. For the previous years, testing of the representativity of the sample is hardly possible. If boat statistics exist, the reliability may be low. As explained above, official statistics compared to the figures of the field survey gave *too high a percentage for industrial technology* compared with artisanal. These technologies, as opposed to artisanal, are normally *registered* since the state agencies need to monitor the various mechanization programmes. The statistics are based on lists of licensed craft, and because state subsidies are usually given to industrial boats and methods, few artisanal fishermen bother to licence their crafts. This statistical bias towards industrial technology may mislead researchers and planners who base their conclusions on official statistics only. They may conclude that the artisanal fisheries are of little importance in the economy, that artisanal technology dies as industrial is introduced.

Considerable problems are involved in the use of demographic data for representativity testing. For example, to establish the age composition of the universe in any year of the reconstruction period (for comparison with the age distribution of the samples), the demographic life cycle of the village must be known. Stability of age composition cannot be assumed, since the population in the life of a village is probably composed of younger people at one stage and older people at another. Because generalizations on past events are based on the contemporary sample, *the size of the sample when the work history method is used must be larger than is otherwise necessary*. If, for example, a 5 per cent sample would suffice to describe the contemporary situation, an increase of the sample to 40 per cent or 50 per cent of the active fishermen may be necessary for reconstruction purposes. Increasing the sample size is probably the best way of surmounting some of the difficulties described.

The methodological weaknesses to be overcome when the work history method is used are considerable. However, a high degree of uncertainty is probably acceptable if the alternative is no knowledge at all. The use of this method may uncover social processes which would have remained unknown if other reconstruction methods had been used.

Chapter 4

EMPIRICAL EVIDENCE OF TECHNOLOGICAL RETROGRESSION: THE SRI LANKAN CASE

This chapter brings you the results of my first inquiry into technological retrogression. I set out to figure out the relationship between technological modernization and level of living in Sri Lanka, but became intrigued by the news that some fishermen were returning to traditional crafts. I decided to figure out why. The empirical material has been abbreviated and thereby nuances and details are lost. A full description can be found in Endresen (1983). The work history method is labour intensive; fieldwork took about a year. I did not update the study but moved on to explore the Malaysian context brought to you in the next chapter. The snapshot provided here is thus more than 40 years of age.

Technological changes in two Sri Lankan fishing villages, Kalametiya and Hambantota in Hambantota District, were reconstructed. Technological changes from the 1950s until early 1980s are presented, and how these relate to level of living and changes in the security nets of the fisherfolk. The main finding is that diffusion of modern technology in fisheries slowed down during the 1970s, and a return to artisanal fisheries was observed. Technological retrogression within artisanal fisheries is particularly interesting: Sailing crafts become rare, and the fleet of rowing crafts expands. A comparison to the modernization of Malaysian fisheries is presented in the next chapter.[1]

The importance of fisheries for employment in Sri Lanka is small. The total population of the fishing villages was in 1981 about 270,000, comprising 68,000 active fishermen. If employment in linked economic activities such as fish processing, marketing, boat building and ice production is included, fisheries employ 2.5 per cent of the country's workforce (Ministry of Fisheries

---

[1] Major findings of my master's thesis are here included in an abbreviated form (Endresen 1983, in Norwegian, and Endresen 1985, in English). The results of my empirical studies of technological retrogression are presented in two shorter articles (Endresen 1987 and 1988).

1980). Of the GNP in 1977, fisheries constituted only 3 per cent. As regards nutrition, the importance of fish is great because 70 per cent of all animal protein consumed comes from fish (de Mel 1976).

The continental shelf around Sri Lanka is narrow, on average about 25 km. The shelf is very rocky, and the tidal difference is small. Sri Lankan fisheries are coastal, limited by the edge of the shelf. Crude estimates give a total of 750,000 tons of fish, annual increase is estimated to about 250,000 tons, of which two-thirds are pelagic species (Sætersdal and de Bruin 1978). The resources fluctuate according to season. The demersal fish stock is biggest during the Northeast monsoon, whereas the pelagic stock is biggest during the Southwest monsoon. The production was in 1957 estimated at 38,000 tons, and in 1965 it had increased to 127,000 tons (People's Bank 1977). Sri Lanka planned to double the production of fish from 154,000 tons in 1978 to 300,000 tons in 1983.

The seasonal fluctuations of the monsoon climate have up to the age of the mechanized boat been the greatest hindrance for the exploitation of the resources of the sea. During the Southwest monsoon, which is strongest from late May until August/September, the breakers along the coast almost bring artisanal fisheries to an end. The Northeast monsoon creates similar conditions along the Jaffna as well as the Eastern coasts from November to January. This has led to a (limited) migration of fishermen to the East during the Southwest monsoon. There are 969 fishing villages in Sri Lanka. In 1989 the number of inhabitants varied from many thousands to perhaps only 20 families.

Modernization efforts

At Independence in 1948, Sri Lankan fisheries were entirely based on traditional technology, and the nation had to rely on imports of fish from India and the Maldives. Inputs to the fishing industry were locally available raw materials, the boat builders used local timber and the fisherfolk made ropes from coconut fibre. Fishing gear was usually locally made, often by the fishermen themselves. Fish which were not locally marketed were often dried. Private traders, *mudalalis*, controlled the marketing of fish.

State interventions during the past 30 years have resulted in considerable changes (Ministry of Fisheries 1972a, 1972b, 1977, 1980; Ministry of Plan Implementation 1982). The model for the first fishery planners in Ceylon was Japan. The plan made by Japanese experts (Colombo Plan Fisheries Survey Team to Ceylon) in 1958 encompasses every aspect of fisheries development – except the welfare of the fisherfolk. The aim was increased production, which should secure a larger self-sufficiency of fish. This should primarily be obtained by mechanization of the fleet and by the construction of harbours. The latter was especially emphasized because the experts recommended that the country should explore the deep-sea resources of the Indian Ocean. Imports of big, mechanized boats and trawlers were recommended as well as an increase in the capacity of building coastal vessels. Workshops for the modern fleet were also planned, as well as improvements of the existing, and production of new, fishing gear. The two-year plan of 1959 recommended 'progressive mechanization'. The State should finance infrastructure, harbours, freezing plants, workshops and several new mechanized boats. A credit/lease programme granting loans without interest to buy 2-ton boats was introduced. In the following years, several changes were made in this plan.

The Master Plan of the fisheries sector (1978–83) followed in broad terms the guidelines of the previous plans. The plan covers mechanization of the fleet, construction of harbours, improvements of transportation, increased ice production and betterment of infrastructure in fishing villages. The development programme aimed at increased production and consumption of fish, increased income, improved living conditions of the fisherfolk and enhanced employment in the fisheries sector (Ministry of Fisheries 1980). In previous plans, strengthening of the cooperative organizations was considered essential. This plan represents in that respect a shift; in line with the general economic policy at the time emphasis is put on the private sector.

New technology

During the past 200 to 300 years, technological innovations in fisheries have spread from India to Sri Lanka (Alexander 1975b). Of the most important have been the beach seine (*ma-del*) and the outrigger canoe. The fishermen have adapted the techniques according to natural conditions and their own culture. The types of craft vary from coast to coast. Among Tamil fishermen in the north, the common craft is the *vallam*, a carved wooden canoe, and the *catamaram*, a timber raft. The Roman Catholic fishermen on the western coast use a small timber raft with sails, the *teppam*, and the Singhalese Buddhists in the West and South and the Muslims of the South use the outrigger canoe termed *oru*. Before mechanization, the most important methods were hand lining, small nets made from cotton yarn, cast nets and traps. These methods are still used aboard some crafts. During the 1960s the nylon drift gill net has become most important, and this is the dominating gear aboard industrial boats. Long-lining is common, but not as important as gill netting.

The mechanization of the fleet started with the building of a trawler fleet and the introduction of the 2-toner. The trawlers catch little of the total landings, and the 2-toner did not prove feasible. Mechanization gained momentum after the introduction of the 3½-toner in 1960. This is a 28-feet

boat with inboard diesel motor. Experienced fishermen who could deposit
1,000 Sri Lankan rupees could lease a 3½-toner.[2] They had to repay the loans
in five years. This became a success after 1955, when it was possible to get
fishing gear on the same terms. The rate of repayment, however, proved to be
low, which led to increased emphasis on the mechanization of the traditional
fleet by issuing outboard engines. In the late 1960s the glass fibre craft was
introduced. This is 17 feet long and can be dragged ashore. It is, however, too
light to compete with the 3½-toner in high seas during the monsoon season.
In total, Sri Lanka's fleet numbers approximately 25,000 crafts; 2,800 of
these are 3½-toners, 3,900 are glass fibre beach landing crafts and 4,500 are
traditional crafts with outboard engines. The rest, about 15,200 crafts, are
non-mechanized, most of them without sails (Munasinghe et al. 1980).

In 1981, about 60 per cent of the fleet was non-mechanized with a share
of production of about 37 per cent; of this about 5 per cent were caught
with *ma-del*. There is no doubt that the great production increase of the latter
years is caused by the mechanization of the fleet. The fishermen might obtain
loans to buy mechanized boats and fishing gear in the Fisheries Bank, in Asian
Development Bank or in private banks. In addition to state boat subsidies,
some imported inputs were duty free. After 1980 the Fisheries Bank had given
loans to buy non-mechanized crafts as well.

Even before the Second World War, cooperative societies were built among
the Sri Lankan fishermen, on the grounds that private merchants, the *mudalalis*,
exploited the fishermen. Organization of the fishermen was thought to lead to
their liberation from 'the strangle-hold of the middlemen' (Bucksimir 1982).
The most important function of the cooperatives was thus to be an alternative
to the private marketing of fish. The first organizations were small, only 20
of 30 fishermen in each unit (Abeydeera 1980; Fernando and Abeydeera
1980). What motivated the fishermen was first and foremost the ability of
the cooperatives to obtain subsidies to buy mechanized boats. When this
was stopped because of low rates of repayment, response was reduced. The
mudalalis judged the cooperatives to be a threat to their interests and acted
against them. In addition, the fishermen who could not repay their loans again
depended upon their goodwill. But the number of cooperatives increased until
the 1970s. There were then 270 societies functioning with 7,000 fishermen as
members. The cooperatives were united in a mother organization (Ceylon
Fish Sales Union) which should organize marketing of fish. With the change
of government, this organization was in 1970 reorganized into 45 Primary
Societies. Their function was not only marketing of fish but also sales of

---

[2] The value of 1,000 Sri Lankan rupee was about 60 USD in 1981.

fishing gear. The cooperative societies have not lived up to the expectations; according to Goonewardena (1980), this was because of insufficient training of the members, and that too little emphasis had been placed on this aspect of fisheries development. The unification into the Primary Societies may also explain the fishermen's lack of interest in the organization. According to Bucksimir, the fishermen do not consider the societies their own, but as state institutions

> managed by bureaucrats, politicians and their favourites who have become a new class of exploiters of the poor fisherman. (Bucksimir 1982, 10)

Another and perhaps equally important reason may be that cooperative societies are unable to fulfil the *mudalalis'* socioeconomic role.

If the post-war period is seen as a whole, it becomes clear that state developmental plans are only partly implemented. Their aims were unrealistic, especially as regards the building of infrastructure and the reorganization of the marketing system. Although the aim was to give priority to coastal and not ocean fisheries, a lot of the resources of the fisheries industry went to harbour construction. Five Fisheries Training Centres were built, and extension service is available in every district. The fisheries programmes have obtained financial support from, among others, FAO, Asian Development Bank and Japan, Canada and Norway. The aim of increased production was to a large extent fulfilled, first and foremost not only a result of the mechanization of the fleet but also of the introduction of nylon nets and long-lining.

The fisheries of Hambantota

The monsoons divide the year into two seasons for fishermen of the Southern coast. The *season* denotes the time when the Northeast monsoon prevails (September–April). Traditionally, this is considered the fishing *season*. The weather is calm; it seldom rains although the monsoon brings a precipitation peak in October and November. *Off-season* is when the Southwest monsoon prevails (May–September). Mechanized boats are to a lesser extent than artisanal crafts dependent upon weather conditions, especially wind. The off-season is the most important fishing season for the mechanized boats. In 1978, 55 per cent of the catch was landed during this period, compared to 17 per cent before mechanization (Munasinghe et al. 1980). There are lay days for the mechanized boats during off-season, but much fewer than for artisanal crafts. The resources vary according to season. About 5,000 tons of fish are harvested annually on the Hambantota bank, mainly pelagic species (Personal communication, District Fisheries Extension Officer, Tangalle, 1981).

The fishermen of Hambantota differentiate between *inshore* fisheries (out to eight fathoms, about two to three kilometres from the shore) and *deep-sea* fisheries (by the edge of the shelf and beyond). The range of the vessels can be categorized by mode of propulsion, whether oars, sails, or motor. Before mechanization, *ma-del* fisheries and *oru* (the dugout craft with outrigger) were typical on the Southern coast. In addition to *oru* (the most common types of craft on the Hambantota coast) we find the wooden 3½-toner, the glass fibre boat and the mechanized *oru*. The most common methods of fishing are hand lining, trolling (which should not be confused with trawling), different types of drift nets and longlines, rod and line, cast nets and lobster traps. Some of these methods are only used in mechanized boats (like multi-hook trolling, bottom set nets and tuna longline), whereas other methods are used aboard both mechanized and non-mechanized crafts. Drawings of boat types and fishing gear are included in Endresen (1994, Appendix 7).

Marketing of fish on the Hambantota coast is divided into a private and a public sector. Ceylon Fisheries Corporation and Fishermen's Cooperatives market in Kalametiya about 12 per cent of the catch, and in Hambantota 16 per cent (survey figures). The private sector big and small *mudalalis* market the rest.

The *orus* are either owned by *mudalalis* or by fishermen (savings or relatives' joint ownership). Most 3½-toners were financed by bank loans. As in the Malaysian villages, the composition of the crew is decided by the owner of the craft. If the owner is not an active fisherman, the responsibility of the fishing operation rests with a skipper. It is important to get clever and skilled crewmen, but equally important to secure employment for relatives. The latter consideration is limited by the need to spread the risk; not too many from the same family should be aboard the same craft.

The catch is shared according to old customs among artisanal fishermen. For example, the catch on an *oru* with four crewmen will be divided into 1/5 share to *oru* and nets and 4/5 is equally shared between the fishermen. On 3½-toners, fuel and consumption expenses are deducted before the catch is shared (consumption may be food and cigarettes supplied by the owner during the trip). The remaining catch is divided into two, one-half goes to the boat and the rest is equally shared between the fishermen.

The villages of Kalametiya and Hambantota were selected because of the technology mixture they contained. In both villages *oru* without sails was the most widespread craft, 3½-toner came second in absolute numbers, while few *ma-del* were still in use in both villages. A small number of crafts in both villages comprised *oru* with outboard engine and glass fibre boats, while *Oru* with sails was in use only in Hambantota from few fishermen.

Forms of technology

The samples of fishermen are drawn from the active fishermen of the villages. In Kalametiya, 82 fishermen (which gives a 73 per cent sample) were interviewed, in Hambantota 100 (78 per cent sample). The households visited were selected by choosing three houses along the road/path and skipping the fourth. In the analysis, the fishermen are divided into three different groups according to the technique(s) they use. The criterion is type of craft, not method of fishing (except *ma-del*, where craft is not used by all). The most advanced methods were only used aboard industrial boats, partly because of the space required and partly because they are meant to be used far from the shore. Artisanal methods were rarely used aboard industrial boats.

The numbers of the different types of craft in use varied according to the season. During season oru without sails prevailed in absolute numbers, while during off-season 3½-toners were mostly used. This reflects the artisanal crafts' handicap in strong wind. Twenty-one fishermen used *oru* without sails during off-season in Hambantota, in contrast to only seven in Kalametiya, where there is no protective bay. The fishermen who used *oru* during off-season could, however, do this only for a limited time, from two weeks to maximum two months. During season 3½-toners are less frequently used than during off-season. The fishermen's explanation for the lay days was that resources were lacking. None had less than three months of fishing. During season, the crew was in some cases less than four skilled fishermen. Youngsters have a chance to get experience on these boats during season. The lengths of season and off-season vary. Mechanization of the fleet may double the fishing days per year, not only because mechanized boats go fishing during off-season but also because they can be used when artisanal crafts have lay days when there is a strong wind in season.

When classified according to the industrial/artisanal dimension, *mode of propulsion* is the basic classification criterion. A *three-fold* division is apparent. Some fishermen used artisanal crafts only, others used industrial, whereas a third group, the combination fishermen, *combined* the two. Some of them used artisanal during season, industrial during off-season and others combined the techniques during season as well. In 1981, the share of fishermen who used only artisanal technology in Kalametiya and Hambantota was 31 and 34 per cent, respectively, industrial 40 and 34 per cent and combination 29 and 32 per cent.

Forms of technology and age

If a form of technology has a young population, vitality is indicated, and reverse, it is a sign of weakness if the population consists of old men. In both villages, the artisanal form of technology has an aged population (many fishermen are over 40 years old). In Kalametiya the artisanal form of technology has only 14 per cent of the fishermen in the age group 21 to 30 years, whereas this form of technology has a somewhat higher percentage in Hambantota (22 per cent). The share of the next age group is equal in the villages, whereas Kalametiya has a relatively higher share of the group 41 to 50 years (44 per cent as compared to 25 per cent in Hambantota). What makes the artisanal form of technology different from the other forms is, however, the large share of older fishermen. In Kalametiya, the artisanal form of technology has 61 per cent of the fishermen over 50 years, and in Hambantota 81 per cent. Thus, the artisanal form of technology has fewer new recruits than the other forms. Young fishermen are more attracted to the industrial form of technology or to combination. In the light of the diffusionist model, this supports the hypothesis that artisanal fisheries would die with the old users.

What also supports the hypothesis is that the industrial form of technology has a relatively large share of fishermen below 40 years. The figures for the age group 21 to 30 years are 41 per cent and 32 per cent in Kalametiya and Hambantota, respectively. Of fishermen over 50 years of age, the industrial form of technology has relatively many in Kalametiya. The share of young men is much higher than it was in the artisanal form of technology. But it is not possible to argue that the industrial form of technology attracts the young fishermen the most. This is because of the large share of young fishermen who use the combination form of technology. The difference between the share of young fishermen in the combination and the industrial form of technology is *insignificant*. Both attract the young, but the combination form has slightly more in the age group 21 to 30 years. The shares of the age group 41 to 50 are equal. The young are mostly attracted (and equally strong) to the industrial and combination forms of technology in both villages, and these forms of technology have a small share of old fishermen. In conclusion, the strong position of the combination form of technology as regards recruitment of young fishermen serves to modify the picture of the dying artisanal fisheries.

Reconstruction of technological change

The solid recruitment to the combination form of technology demonstrated cannot be explained by examining data of current forms of technology. To find out whether this is an adjustment typical of the transition phase of the ideal spread of modern technology, the recruitment to and growth of the combination form of technology should be examined. To compare with the other forms of technology, a reconstruction of the process is necessary. To do this by means of individual work histories makes a reconstruction of change at both individual and village levels possible. Since employment statistics which differentiate between artisanal and industrial fishermen do not exist, this is the only possibility. Production statistics are also useless because they do not differentiate between types of craft.

Changes within artisanal fisheries

By means of the work histories, the relative distribution of labour using artisanal technology through time is reconstructed. In the beginning, mechanization of the fleet led to a transfer of labour from artisanal to industrial fisheries in both villages. This had effects on the *internal* distribution of labour within artisanal fisheries, that is, the relative weight on the techniques *oru* with sails, *oru* without sails and *ma-del*. The figures of those using *oru* with sails include fishermen who combine with 3½-toners in the 1970s. This can be done since nobody combines any other artisanal technique with industrial fisheries. As becomes apparent when the point of departure is the present situation, there has been *a radical shift of weight on the different techniques within artisanal fisheries*. The share of *ma-del* has been low in both villages during this period, with a noticeable increase between 1960 and 1970. There is a distinct decrease of the proportion of *oru* with sails during the whole period, clearly to the advantage of *oru* without sails.

All over Sri Lanka, *ma-del* is a dying method of fishing. The reasons for this are many and are not only related to the new opportunities which came with modern technology. The technique is labour intensive and has shown decreasing output (Munasinghe et al. 1980). Fishermen in both villages contended that the increase of *oru* without sails has led to increased exploitation of inshore resources. *Ma-del*, which exploits these resources, is sensitive to this. There is therefore reason to believe that the decrease of *ma-del* production is caused by the gill net fishing of *oru* without sails. The decrease of *ma-del*, however, started before there was a marked tendency to change to *oru* without sails; it is therefore not probable that the reduction is caused solely by this. In addition, because of annual fluctuation of resources, it is difficult to state the effects of technological innovations just by examining production statistics. Overfishing in one area can go far beyond the limit of biological reproduction, but the effects are maybe felt years thereafter – and maybe far away. The temporary increase in those using *ma-del* was caused by the rich prawn fishery in the Kalametiya Lagoon, which ended because of overexploitation.

The most marked change within artisanal fisheries is the *increase of oru without sails, and the corresponding decrease in oru with sails.* At the time of the investigation, only a few fishermen use sails in Hambantota, and nobody in Kalametiya. In 1950, about 70 per cent of the fishermen in Kalametiya and 50 per cent in Hambantota used *oru* with sails. The rest was equally divided between *oru* without sails and *ma-del*. The decrease is evident from about 1960 in both villages and is followed by a corresponding increase in *oru* without sails. The course of events is the same in both villages, but the changes seem to occur somewhat later in Hambantota (Figures 11 and 12).

The reduced importance of sailing crafts and the introduction of mechanized boats occur simultaneously. An explanation may be that *oru* with sails go further out than *oru* without sails. This requires greater navigation and sailing skills, qualities which also were needed aboard the new, mechanized

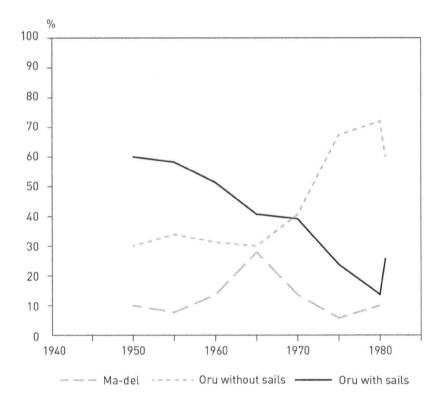

Figure 11 Changes within artisanal fisheries 1950–81 Hambantota.

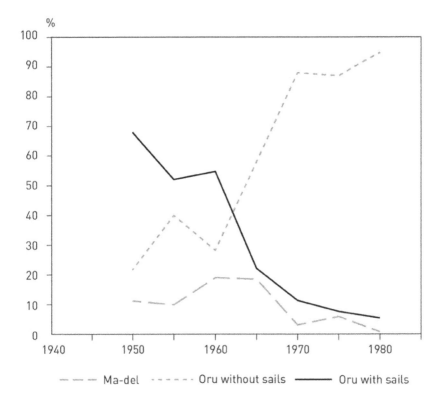

Figure 12 Changes within artisanal fisheries 1950–81 Kalametiya.

boats. Therefore, fishermen of the *orus* with sails may have been preferred as crewmen. This is underlined in the criteria for obtaining state loans: the fishermen shall have experience from deep sea fisheries. When the best skilled fishermen change to industrial fisheries, the others have three choices: to learn how to sail, to change to *ma-del* and to *oru* without sails.

The hypothesis that fishermen with experience from *oru* with sails are preferred and therefore change firstly (when industrial fisheries cannot absorb all) can be tested by examining individual careers. When the last job before mechanized fisheries is examined, the hypothesis is strengthened, since in Kalametiya, 38 per cent came to mechanized boats directly from *oru* with sails, and 26 per cent came from *oru* without sails. Nine per cent came from *ma-del*, and the rest had no experience at all. In Hambantota, the picture is somewhat different, as 30 per cent came directly from *oru* with sails and as many as 50 per cent came from *oru* without sails (of these, 10 per cent had sailing experience). Twenty per cent had no experience from fisheries. The hypothesis is also strengthened when examining where fishermen with experience from sailing crafts work in 1981. It appears that 68 per cent are found within industrial fisheries in Hambantota. The figure from Kalametiya is 90 per cent. Those with experience from sailing craft who were left in artisanal fisheries go to *oru* without sails. In Hambantota, half of them stay on aboard sailing crafts, the other half join *orus* without sails.

We observe polarization: Mechanization has the unexpected result that traditional fisheries become less advanced, the most advanced type of craft loose terrain.

The transition

So far, the relative strength of the different artisanal techniques as modern technology was introduced has been examined. *The general picture* of the process of technological change must now be established by viewing the three forms of technology simultaneously. The result is illustrated in Figures 13 and 14. The graphs show the relative shares of the artisanal, the industrial and the combination forms of technology. Firstly, the relationship between artisanal and industrial technology is treated and later combination of artisanal and industrial technology. For both villages, technological modernization, defined as transfer of labour to the (exclusively) industrial form of technology, appears to have *stagnated*. As regards the long-term movement of labour, it appears that there is a continuous transfer of fishermen to industrial fisheries in Kalametiya. The share of artisanal fisheries reduced from 100 per cent in 1955 to 54 per cent in 1961. From 1963, the share of industrial fisheries is greatest, and then, the relative strength of the two forms of technology does not change significantly unto 1981. The share of the industrial form of technology is then 40 per cent, artisanal has a share of 31 per cent and combination 29 per cent. The changes in Hambantota were similar. The share of artisanal technology decreased from 100 per cent in 1955 to 35 per cent in 1981. The same year, the share of the industrial form of technology is 33 per cent while combination has 32 per cent. In this village, most of the fishermen have used artisanal technology the whole period. From the middle 1970s, the relative strength is however weakened, and *the three forms of technology are equally important*.

Except for the rise of the combination form of technology, the process of technological modernization at village level has been *stable* for two decades. This *stability at village level disguises variation at individual level*. When the *career paths* of artisanal fishermen are examined, a picture of the unstable *technological pasts* of the fishermen emerges. Of the industrial fishermen in Kalametiya, 24 per cent had this as their first job. Most of them got a job aboard their father's mechanized boat. Most of the fishermen, however, had experience from artisanal fisheries. The figures from Hambantota show the same tendency.

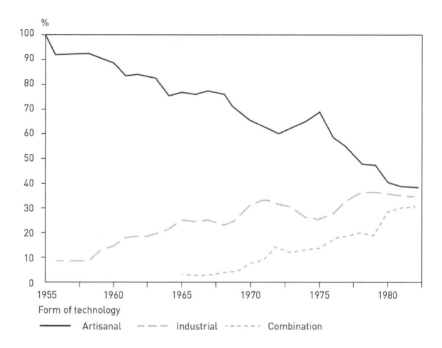

Figure 13 Technological change in Hambantota 1955–81.

Examining the career paths, an unexpected pattern emerges, *about half of the artisanal fishermen in Kalametiya were earlier industrial fishermen who have returned to artisanal fisheries, indicating a pattern of technological retrogression.* In Hambantota, the career paths of artisanal fishermen indicate far greater stability than in the other village, but here too, 26 per cent of the artisanal fishermen had earlier worked aboard industrial boats.

The return to artisanal fisheries is a relatively *new* phenomenon. From a few occurrences towards the end of the 1960s, it becomes a clear tendency from about 1975. In Kalametiya, 58 per cent of the returns occur after 1975, in Hambantota the percentage is 69. Between 1970 and 1975, 28 per cent and 23 per cent (respectively) of the returns occur. Compared to Kalametiya, there are fewer in Hambantota who return to artisanal fisheries. The reason may be scarcity of artisanal crafts in this village.

The fishermen's own reasons for changing techniques are registered in the *work history* matrix. In this discussion, it is important to note that the samples are small. The most frequent reason stated for adopting industrial technology is that they think the catches will be bigger (68 per cent in Kalametiya, 53 per cent in Hambantota). The reason 'easier work' is second in importance (15 per cent and 20 per cent respectively). It is evident that insufficient and

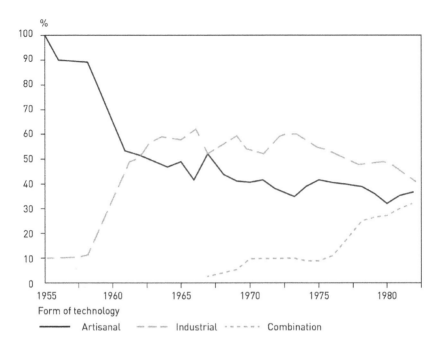

Figure 14 Technological change in Kalametiya 1955–81.

irregular incomes aboard industrial boats are the most important reasons for returning to artisanal fisheries. Negative, traditional attitudes towards industrial technology seemed irrelevant when discussing change of technology. The problems of repairs and maintenance of the boats are stated as reason for change, as are increased oil prices (a reason stated by crewmen as well as owners). Another indicator of the dependence upon oil prices is that some of the mechanized boats have started to use sails in addition to motor to save fuel. The 12 owners in Kalametiya started to do this during the last five years. None of the mechanized boats in Hambantota used sails probably because this village is located closer to the richer part of the bank. Disagreements between owners and crewmen, which were stated as causes in many cases, also originated in disagreements on income: the crewmen found that the shares of boat and owner were too high.

Fewer owners than crewmen return to artisanal fisheries. Four owners had done so, but later returned to 3½-toners. Of the 20 crewmen that gave up industrial fisheries, three had owned an *oru* previously and still own the craft they work on. This may indicate that they kept the craft to secure a possible withdrawal. In Hambantota, the returned fishermen owned crafts neither before nor after they retrograded. There are, however, two exceptions: two fishermen bought their own *oru* from savings after having worked aboard 3½-toners. In Kalametiya, four fishermen did this. Such target workers are therefore rare.

Irrespective of motivation stated by the fishermen themselves, there is reason to expect that those who return to *oru* are *old* fishermen who cannot manage hard work. This is what should be the case according to the modernization hypothesis. *But fishermen who return to artisanal fisheries are relatively young.* My findings testify an overrepresentation of younger fishermen among the group of retrogressed fishermen: 54 per cent in Kalametiya and 46 per cent in Hambantota were below 30 years old at the time of retrogression. (The figures include everybody who has at one time during their careers returned to artisanal from industrial fisheries. I have not controlled for the age distribution of the sample each year. This weakness is, however, regarded insignificant.) The hypothesis of old age as an explanation of retrogression is thus falsified. There is greater reason to believe that artisanal fisheries became more competitive in the 1970s as a result of increased cost of inputs to industrial fisheries.

Combination

In the late 1960s, some fishermen started to combine industrial fisheries during off-season with artisanal fisheries during season. The very first case is recorded in Hambantota in 1964 and in Kalametiya in 1967. These are cases of unstable careers, that is, fishermen who frequently change craft. In the beginning of the 1970s *many* start to combine, and their career paths show that *combination of artisanal and industrial technology cannot be explained by labour instability.*

The graphs showing the combination form of technology in Figures 13 and 14 show a gradual increase from 1969 until 1981. Comparing the two villages, the similarity is striking, and the result in 1981 is identical. Twenty-nine per cent of the fishermen in Kalametiya and 32 per cent of the Hambantota fishermen combine artisanal and industrial technology. The *career paths* of the combination fishermen are different in the two villages: Most of the Kalametiya combination fishermen have experience from both artisanal and industrial fisheries as they start to combine. Many have an exclusively industrial background in this village. In Hambantota, none of the combination fishermen have so, which reflects that very few fishermen have an exclusively industrial background in this village. It seems that the adjustment which the combination form of technology represents has gone further in Hambantota than in Kalametiya, since many fishermen who combine artisanal and industrial technology here have always done so. Most of the fishermen who turn to combination form of technology are crewmen, not owners.

It is interesting to note that the innovation of combination is firstly accepted by crewmen, then by owners of artisanal crafts and in the end by owners of industrial boats. According to the modernization hypothesis, combination should be a phenomenon of the transition period, for instance when fishermen who work aboard artisanal crafts take jobs aboard industrial boats during off-season to gain experience, for later to become fully industrial. If this is correct, the *career paths* of the combination fishermen should firstly show a change from artisanal craft to combination, and then to industrial. According to the retrogression hypothesis, however, combination results from industrial fishermen turning or returning to artisanal fisheries. The career paths expected are then from industrial to combination. It is earlier shown that there are both artisanal and industrial technologies in the combination fishermen's technological pasts. To find out which *direction* is the most common, these fishermen's last job before they started to combine must be examined. In Kalametiya 15 combination fishermen came directly from industrial fisheries, while nine came from artisanal. In Hambantota eight came from industrial, 15 from artisanal, while nine had always combined.

As regards Kalametiya, it can be concluded that both hypotheses have power of explanation, but that the retrogression hypothesis stands the strongest. It is more difficult to interpret the results from Hambantota. About half of the fishermen came directly from artisanal crafts, whereas only eight came from industrial fisheries. However, here it appears that young fishermen increasingly go for combination. According to the modernization hypothesis, the young should increasingly go directly for *modern* fisheries. Thus, the results from Hambantota as well strengthen the retrogression hypothesis.

If the seasonality of fisheries previously described is compared to what has emerged after the mechanization of the fleet started, some most interesting changes appear. It was earlier possible to go fishing during season mainly, and the fishermen had to save enough money to manage livelihood expenses through off-season. Mechanized fisheries have the advantage that fishing can be done throughout the year, except in the roughest weather. From the artisanal fishermen's point of view, the combination form of technology opens the chance to have incomes in a period when they earlier had none. It is more difficult to explain why fishermen aboard industrial boats are attracted to this form of technology. Their own explanations were in Kalametiya, '*not enough income aboard the industrial boats*' (18 out of 24 fishermen), and '*the unjust share system*' (the rest). In Hambantota, 18 out of 32 claimed that they changed because of insufficient incomes, which also underlies the reason given by the rest of the fishermen: nine told that they changed because the oil prices were too high, and five were dissatisfied with the share system. The fishermen who combine artisanal and industrial fisheries were asked to state their most important source of income. They were reluctant to do so, they usually answered that '*oru is most important during season and the 3 ½-toner during off-season*'. This indicates that they have difficulties in saving money from one season to the other, as the old seasonality of fisheries required.

There may be several reasons why the fishermen find it necessary to have incomes throughout the year. One of these is that they see the chance to *improve* their standard of living. Another is that they are forced to do so to *keep up* their standard of living. It is no longer possible to survive on what can be earned during one season. The combination fishermen's standard of living (see below) indicates that the latter cause is the more plausible. Inflation and increased oil prices in the 1970s point in the same direction.

So far, the combination form of technology can be considered an end stage, a permanent adjustment for many fishermen. In Kalametiya one fisherman only has given up combination. He combined *oru* with 3 ½-toner from 1974 to 1979, when he got an outboard engine on his *oru* and turned industrial. In Hambantota as well, one case is registered. This fisherman used *oru* with sails for 18 years, then worked five years aboard a 3 ½-toner until he started to combine. In 1981, the circle was completed, as he returned to his old *oru* with sails.

There is reason to believe that the share of the combination form of technology may increase in the years to come. During the interviews, 15 fishermen from Hambantota said that they would start to combine if they got the chance. Ten of them were crewmen aboard industrial boats, who did not dare to take a job during season aboard an *oru*, fearing that they thereby would jeopardize their off-season jobs. The artisanal fishermen who would prefer to combine claimed that there were not enough 3 ½-toners to make this possible.

Summing up the reconstruction

The model of the ideal spread of modern technology presented in the introduction shows three distinct phases: traditional dominance, transitional phase, and modern dominance. During the latter, artisanal technology should have become a dying remnant. The experience from Kalametiya and Hambantota suggests a process in which the last phase is not modern dominance, but a phase where the three forms of technology are equally important. The contours of a transitional phase are, however, clearly visible. In Kalametiya this is visible from 1963 onwards, in Hambantota from the mid-1970s. In both villages, the 1970s are characterized by the rise of the combination form of technology. From a weak beginning at the end of the 1960s, it counts for about one-third of the active fishermen in 1981. In the last phase, the stagnation tendency of the diffusion of industrial technology, which this indicates, is reinforced. In addition, artisanal fisheries are reproduced through the return from industrial to artisanal fisheries.

Within artisanal fisheries, there has been a radical shift. The share of *ma-del* was reduced after a short flourishing period. The most conspicuous changes, however, are those caused by the mechanization of the fleet: The importance of *oru* without sails rises, corresponding to the decreased importance of the sailing *oru*, probably caused by the selective recruitment of skilled fishermen to industrial fisheries. This has led to a *weakening* of artisanal fisheries in the competition for resources and increases the danger of inshore crowding of crafts and overexploitation of demersal resources.

When discussing effects of mechanization of the Sri Lankan fleet, Alexander found that the introduction of industrial boats has led to '*drastic reductions in the non-mechanized section of the industry*' (Alexander 1975b, 7, emphasis in the original). His argument is that the proportion of *orus* with sails has decreased severely from 1950 to 1975 on the Southern coast. This again, he claims, led to a reduced number of artisanal fishermen. Based on the experience from Kalametiya and Hambantota, this seems to be wrong. Mechanization did lead to transfers of labour from sailing *orus* to industrial boats. But this again led to an upswing of *orus* without sails.

According to the modernization hypothesis, the artisanal form of technology was expected to consist of older fishermen, unwilling to change. This hypothesis is *strengthened* in both villages as the *exclusively* artisanal form of technology has an old population. The hypothesis, however, is *weakened* by the fact that this form of technology also comprises younger fishermen who have returned to artisanal crafts. Artisanal fisheries are also reproduced because some fishermen who earlier worked aboard industrial boats now combine artisanal and industrial technology. The fact that many young fishermen have *always* combined is also an indication of a strengthening of artisanal fisheries.

Industrial fisheries show no signs of becoming dominant. Technological modernization, defined as transfer of labour to the exclusively industrial form of technology, has stagnated. From the mid-1970s the stagnation is caused not only by lower recruitment of young fishermen but also by fishermen returning to artisanal fisheries. For artisanal fishermen who changed to the combination form of technology, this can be regarded as a technological modernization and represents therefore a strengthening of industrial fisheries. These fishermen may be in a stage of transition; combination may be the first step to industrial fisheries. I find this explanation of the combination phenomenon improbable. The fishermen in the 1950s and 1960s needed no adjustment time, it is therefore no reason to believe that the fishermen in the 1970s suddenly should need so. On the contrary, the technology has been the same all the time, and it is therefore probable that technical and other uncertainties should be *fewer*. There is greater reason to assume that many of those turning to combination in the 1970s under different conditions *would have changed to industrial fisheries*. In this perspective, the combination form of technology indicates a weakening of industrial fisheries. However, young fishermen are still recruited to the industrial form of technology; the young are attracted both to the combination and the industrial form of technology. These forms have the lowest proportion of old fishermen, and thereby show a greater vitality than the artisanal form of technology. As regards recruitment, there is reason to believe that young fishermen are preferred because of their physical strength rather than their education.

The innovation combination is spread firstly to crewmen, who constitute the main recruitment, then come owners of artisanal crafts. Last, as well as least, come owners of industrial boats. Summing up the reasons given for the return to artisanal technology and the change to combination, it seems clear that artisanal fisheries (as compared to industrial) are more competitive for labour in the 1970s because of the increase in fuel costs. The main single factor of explanation is undoubtedly the increasing price of oil, which also has led to attempts of saving fuel by using sails aboard industrial boats. For the fishermen who earlier worked aboard artisanal crafts only, combining this with work aboard industrial boats has increased the time they can go fishing annually. This is an important improvement. Earlier, many survived during off-season by borrowing money from moneylenders, *mudalalis* or relatives. This way out is now insufficient. A probable cause is the decreasing real wages in the 1970s. The hypothesis that the combination form of technology is and adjustment to the economic recession is strengthened by the fact that many households have been searching for additional income during this period.

Standard of living

Sri Lankan authorities characterize a large part of the fisherfolk as poor, and many families in both villages received monthly food stamps. In Kalametiya, over 30 per cent of the households visited (in Hambantota over 40 per cent) claimed that shortage of food was their biggest problem. Most of them, however, explained that food was insufficient in periods only. Many claimed that their biggest problems were an uncertain future, education of children and a low standard of their houses. The fishermen were asked how they survived during their longest period without work (seasonal variations in fisheries excluded). A few fishermen reported to have starved during periods of illness, but most families relied upon the *mudalali* in times of crisis. The security net second in importance was loans from relatives and friends. Much fewer households here could rely on their savings compared with the Malaysian village studied, which reflects a generally higher living standard in Malaysia. My findings from both villages showed that, contrary to my expectation, households in which the fisherman has many dependents were not worse off than small fishing families. As shown in Chapter 5, this was the case in the Malaysian fishing village as well. Neither was there any correlation between the length of the fisherman's career and his household's standard of living.

The hypothesis that the combination form of technology is an adjustment to worsened living conditions in general in Sri Lanka in the 1970s is strengthened: many fishing households try to supplement incomes from fisheries with various kinds of other work. In total, 38 of the fishing households in Kalametiya had tried to get additional income outside the fishing industry and 15 in Hambantota. This is a *new* tendency, pronounced in the latter part of the 1970s, which should not be considered an indication of fisheries losing importance in these communities. For most of the households in question, additional incomes are small compared to the fishermen's income from fisheries and may come from gardening, working in paddy farming or other casual work. In Kalametiya there is a correlation between additional incomes and standard of living, since the rich are overrepresented in the category which comprises those with additional incomes. It is, however, not possible based on my material to state whether an additional income leads to prosperity or if prosperity increases the chance to get additional incomes.

Ownership and standard of living

There is all reason to believe that owners of boats have higher incomes than crewmen. The catch is equally shared among the fishermen who take part in the operation, but it is shared after the deduction of the owner's share. The share of the boat is supposed to cover running and capital costs. These expenses may, however, be smaller than the share of the boat. The difference will be the owner's profits. When investigating the relationship between ownership of craft and standard of living, all the fishermen who own (or during their careers have owned) a craft are contrasted to those who never have owned a craft. Ownership of both artisanal and industrial crafts is included, and the length of the ownership period is not considered. The findings therefore give a simplified picture. As expected, however, ownership of craft seems to be an important factor of explanation when the fishing households' standard of living is analysed. More than 30 per cent of craft owners can be included among the rich and 10 per cent among the poor in both villages. The rest belong to the middle stratum of society. In contrast, among the crewmen 8 per cent are rich in Kalametiya and 20 per cent in Hambantota. The share of poor that are crewmen is 42 per cent in Kalametiya and 25 per cent in Hambantota. The rest 50 to 55 per cent are to be found among the middle societal layer. The correlation between ownership of craft and standard of living is clear, but there are interesting nuances: It *is* possible to have owned a craft and be poor, or to be rich without having owned a craft. It remains, however, to find out whether it is ownership of artisanal or industrial craft which have this effect.

Alexander (1975a) claims that the profitability of industrial boats is limited because of the share system. This system is regarded as a traditional remnant which is not functional in modern fisheries since a higher rate of depreciation and higher running costs are not taken sufficiently into account. According to this line of argument, ownership of industrial boats should not lead to a considerably better living standard, and therefore, artisanal crafts should produce the effect demonstrated. But in Kalametiya, it is ownership of industrial boats which to a greater extent than ownership of artisanal crafts leads to prosperity. Ownership of industrial boats does not, however, represent any guarantee against poverty. In Hambantota, ownership of artisanal crafts gives a higher profitability. This may result in a preference among the fishermen to own such crafts rather than to work as crewmen aboard industrial boats.

Forms of technology and standard of living

The investigation of the relationship between the form of technology and standard of living resulted in some interesting findings. In Kalametiya, the expected tendency is found: It pays to use modern technology as compared to artisanal. Industrial fishermen have the highest percentage of rich, 33 per cent, and only 15 per cent among the poor, whereas artisanal fishermen are to be found among only 4 per cent of the rich and 24 per cent among the poor. There are, however, nuances: artisanal fishermen have a higher share of the middle group and a lower proportion of poor than expected. It is also noteworthy that the probability of finding a rich artisanal fisherman is lower than finding a poor industrial one. At last, it is striking that the combination form of technology shows the highest proportion of poor, 33 per cent. In Hambantota, the results are somewhat different. The artisanal form of technology has a higher proportion of rich than of poor (24 and 15 per cent respectively). In fact, among artisanal fishermen in Hambantota, we find the lowest share of poor. The industrial fishermen have equal proportions of rich and poor. Here too, the combination form of technology shows the highest proportion of poor.

Technological pasts and standard of living

A premise of stabile careers, underlying the above computations, cannot be accepted when the importance of form of technology for living conditions is analysed. The fishermen's technological pasts should be analysed as well. As demonstrated above, some fishermen have stable careers whereas other fishermen change technology several times. How careers can be summed up in terms of form of technology is demonstrated in the treatment of the Malaysian data. The sample size of the Sri Lankan material is too small to undertake a detailed analysis of each form of technology. The share of industrial fisheries in the fishermen's careers can, however, be correlated with their households' living standard. There is a clear correlation. Of those with least proportion of industrial technology in their careers, only 4 per cent are rich, many are found in the middle group and 21 per cent are poor. Of the intermediate group, the proportion of rich is high, fewer are in the middle group and few are poor. For the most industrial fishermen, it appears that some are rich, some are found in the middle group and many are poor. Although a high proportion of artisanal technology in the career gives lowest proportion of rich, it is striking that the group with the highest share of industrial form of technology in career has the largest proportion of poor.

The picture in Hambantota is somewhat different. The correlation between the variables is not significant here. The proportion of rich in the group with the largest proportion of artisanal technology is 23 per cent and the proportion of poor is also relatively high in this group, 26 per cent. The chance of becoming rich does not increase significantly with higher share of industrial technology in the career. However, the chance of staying poor decreases. There were no poor fishermen among those with the highest share of industrial technology in their careers.

It is possible to examine the relationship between form of technology and *degree of equality* based on this investigation. One could argue that the lesser the spread, that is, the more who belong to *one* level of living groups (irrespective of which), the greater the equality within the group. And vice versa: the greater the spread, the greater the inequality within the group. In Kalametiya, the group with the greatest share of artisanal technology shows the greatest equality (as was the case in the Malaysian village), and inequality increases with rising share of industrial form of technology in career. In Hambantota, the opposite is the case.

Two fishermen with the same share of industrial form of technology in their careers may have from 3 up to 30 years of experience from the fishing industry. It was, however, concluded above that there is no correlation between career length and living standard. It *might* be that fishermen who have worked aboard artisanal crafts for 10 years or more are just as poor as when they started. This *might not* be the case for industrial fishermen. To test this hypothesis, the statistical basis is insufficient. But an indirect route can be tried out: the absolute number of years in industrial fisheries can be correlated with standard of living. The results show that in Hambantota, fishermen with 10 or more years in industrial fisheries have the largest share of rich, none among the poor, while 53 per cent are in the middle societal layer. The expected tendency is thus evident in Hambantota. In Kalametiya, however, the proportion of poor among fishermen with long careers in industrial fisheries is unexpectedly high, 24 per cent. In Kalametiya the increase of total number of years in industrial fisheries seems to influence the upward mobility of the middle societal layer, while the number of poor remains unaltered. This deviation is treated below, where differences between the villages are discussed. It should be concluded that the chance to improve living conditions increased with more years in industrial fisheries.

Summary

The aim of the analysis is to clarify the relationship between form of technology and the households' standard of living. To do so, it has been necessary to examine the relationship between living standard and a selection of variables thought to be of importance. As will be shown in the next chapter, in the Malaysian as well as the Sri Lankan case, the hypothesis *the bigger the household, the lower the standard of living* is falsified. The general hypothesis of career length positively affecting living standard is also rejected. Those who have worked long aboard an industrial boat have, however, managed to improve their lot. Furthermore, additional incomes seem to be of little significance to the households' standard of living.

The analysis of the relationship between form of technology and living standard is intricate both due to small sample sizes and because technological pasts are difficult to categorize. However, the following results seem reasonable: In line with what was expected according to the modernization hypothesis, artisanal fishermen in Kalametiya are rarely rich. But it also appears that many poor fishermen are found within the industrial form of technology. To have worked long aboard an industrial boat will increase the chance to improve the living conditions but will not remove the chance of staying poor. In Hambantota, the chance to improve living standard will not increase much with a change to industrial fisheries. But here too, the chances increase with time.

It is evident in both villages that ownership of means of production magnifies the possibility to become prosperous. In Kalametiya, this is clear when it comes to industrial boats. In Hambantota, ownership of artisanal crafts best produces this effect. This reflects the fact that artisanal fisheries seem to be more profitable in this village.

The crewmen aboard the industrial boats are hit hard by increased costs of fuel because of the share system. Through this mechanism the boat owners are 'insured' and some of the risk is transferred to the crew. For the owners too, there is of course a profitability threshold, reflected in their recent interest in the combination form of technology.

The most distinct differences between the villages as regards the relationship between form of technology and standard of living are *firstly* that artisanal fisheries are more profitable in Hambantota than in Kalametiya. The chance for artisanal fishermen in Kalametiya to be included in the category rich is small. *Secondly*, it appears that industrial technology brings a greater chance of poverty in Kalametiya than in Hambantota. These differences could be subscribed to the villages' different locations. As the fish resources get richer towards the East and within the range of artisanal crafts in Hambantota, these crafts can better compete in profitability with industrial boats. In addition, the Hambantota bay gives protection in bad weather, a protection which Kalametiya fishermen do not have. In addition, the running costs of the industrial boats in Hambantota are, due to the location, probably less than in Kalametiya. The risk of poverty for industrial fishermen is therefore less in Hambantota than in Kalametiya.

In the analysis of technological change, it was argued that the combination form of technology originates as one of the adjustments to the national economic setback in the 1970s. The fishermen who combine artisanal and industrial technology have been doing this for a too short period to make a discussion of the profitability feasible. There is, however, reason to assume that the combination fishermen's standard of living will reflect the households' point of departure as the fishermen decided to try out this form of technology. Combination fishermen are found in the middle group and among the poor, indicating that these households' living standard may have been decisive for the choice: Combination of artisanal and industrial technology is an attempt to maintain the accustomed standard of living in a period with decreasing real incomes.

Chapter 5

EMPIRICAL EVIDENCE OF TECHNOLOGICAL RETROGRESSION: THE MALAYSIAN CASE

Poverty and inequality

My second empirical investigation of technological retrogression is presented in this chapter. Malaysia was selected after I studied (in the FAO library in Rome) descriptions of fishing societies and boat statistics of several Asian countries. Other candidates were India, Indonesia and The Philippines. Considerable 'traditional sectors' were found in all contexts, but no evidence of technological retrogression could be traced. This did not deter me; the process is invisible in statistics. Thus, the danger of zero case was there when I started fieldwork. Among Malaysian scholars and in the ministries, there were no awareness to this phenomenon, so moving from Kuala Lumpur to Kedah was a journey into the unknown! As with the Sri Lankan case, I should warn you that the empirical material has been abbreviated, and nuances and details are lost. A full description can be found in Endresen (1995). I will stress once more that the work history method is labour intensive; this fieldwork as well lasted about a year. I did not update this study either but moved on to explore different contexts and problems. This Malaysian snapshot is thus more than 30 years of age.

The empirical investigation of technological change in Malaysian fisheries was undertaken in the late 1980s. Already, at that time, substantial economic growth due to a flourishing manufacturing industry had placed Malaysia among the Newly Industrializing Countries. But fisheries were considered a backward sector by Malaysian social scientists, who pointed at a high incidence of poverty and great income inequalities (Yahaya 1978; Munro and Chee 1978; Ling 1978a; Fredericks and Wells 1980; Yahaya and Wells 1982; Jomo 1991). Poverty in Malaysia was mainly a rural phenomenon, and the four northern states (of which Kedah is one) had above average incidence of poverty (Anand 1983). Poor fishing households were the fifth largest poverty group in Malaysia after rubber smallholders, paddy farmers, agricultural labourers and estate workers (Jomo 1991).[1] Although technological modernization led to economic growth in fishing villages, the subsequent gains were distributed unevenly. Widened income differential between the West Coast trawler fishermen and traditional artisanal fishermen was also found by Fredericks and Wells (1980). A survey by The Malaysian Fishermen's Network concluded that nearly 73 per cent of the coastal fishermen were poor (Yusuf 1988).

Malaysian society is multi-ethnic, comprising besides the indigenous Malays and Orang Asli, Indians and Chinese. The proportion of Malays in traditional rural economic activities such as farming and fishing has been high throughout the twentieth century, especially on the East coast. Fredericks and Wells (1980, 9) point at the 'ethnically dualistic structure of fisheries' and tends to identify poverty with ethnicity: They maintain that the weaker position of Malays as compared to Chinese is due to the greater involvement of the latter in modern fisheries for a long period of time.[2] I find 'rich Chinese, poor Malay' too simplistic a conception. In terms of standard of living, there are great inequalities *within* Malay fishing communities, as there are within Chinese. Jomo (1991) maintains that to explain poverty and inequality in fishing societies one should rather study occupational and regional differences, and access to gear and boat ownership. It is thus more fruitful to study poverty and inequality in terms of class. In Malaysian fishing communities, some groups have greater access to resources of various kinds (including means of production and power) than other groups, irrespective of ethnicity. This is supported by the findings of Fredericks et al. who found that on

> the basis of ethnic group, Chinese households had a marginally higher degree of income disparity than Malay households [...] policy guidelines must be based upon a differentiated approach rather than on

---

[1] Official estimates of the incidence of poverty in fishing societies were confusing due to varying poverty line definitions. Jomo (1991) pointed at this difficulty by giving a few examples: In 1983, 18,100 fishing households (45 per cent) lived in poverty. By 1984, the official estimate was 9,500, which is 28 per cent only. This reduction is unlikely; and although I cannot substantiate it statistically, I also find the decline from 73 per cent in 1970 (63 per cent in 1975) to 28 per cent in 1984 (and even to 45 per cent in 1983) too dramatic, based on the study of living standard in the two fishing villages. Statistics or analyses which could clarify these problems are unavailable.

[2] In 1973, only 10 per cent of the Chinese fishing households earned less than M$ 150 per month as compared to 45 per cent of the Malay households; 19 per cent of the Chinese households earned more than M$ 500, whereas only 5 per cent of the Malay households had such high incomes (Jomo 1991).

the presumption that the fishing population is a homogeneous group. (Fredericks et al. 1985, 54)

By planners and some researchers, development problems such as poverty in fishing villages are often expressed in terms of *surplus labour*. The number of 'surplus fishermen' is calculated by estimating the optimum crew sizes for each boat type, and the number of men exceeding this is considered superfluous. In 1970, the official estimate of the Second Malaysia Plan was 19,300 'surplus fishermen' (Ministry of Agriculture and Co-operatives 1970), and in 1986, the number had increased to about 30,000.[3] Then, what do 'surplus fishermen' do? Are they unemployed, or perhaps underemployed? My hypothesis, supported by other researchers, is that they do what fishermen normally do, they go fishing. I do not question that the technologies introduced were labour displacing, but nobody is getting any wiser by terming half of the active fishermen superfluous. A more probable hypothesis is that both industrial and artisanal fishermen were trapped in a situation with diminishing returns and few alternatives. In discussions of the surplus labour, technology choice is often taken as given; the introduction of labour displacing modern technology seems an inevitable fate to which the inhabitants of the fishing villages must adapt. A suggested adaptation, often the only suggestion, is the reduction of the fishing population.

Reduction of the 'surplus labour' may result from the absorption of labour by growth of other sectors elsewhere, from population decline or from investments in alternative employment within the villages. To raise the standard of living of the fisherfolk, the development plans recommend government efforts to create non-fishing employment as well as more intensive labour utilization in the fishing households. However, governments' attempts to create outlets by investing in Land Development Schemes have given meagre results for the fisherfolk, they queue up behind other rural dwellers. There is no evidence that surplus labour in fishing societies is due to fisherfolk's reluctance to resettle to find alternative employment, but rather their immobility seems to be a condition externally imposed (Ling 1978b, 296). Thus, poverty eradication and resource conservation remain major policy challenges.

As stressed by other researchers the phenomenon of 'surplus labour' is a sort of disguised unemployment due 'in essence to problems in the allocation of productive resources, both within the fishing sector and between the fishing sector and other parts of the economy' (Munro and Chee 1978, 1). They conclude that it is the *trawler fisheries* which have reached the stage of overfishing and that unless a major change of technology occurs, no further

---

[3] Personal information, Majuikan official, September 1986.

expansion should be allowed. By adding the obvious, that fisheries are linked to the wider economy, they stress what is frequently overlooked: Overexploitation in fisheries cannot be viewed a type of resource allocation problem which can be solved through *regulation of the access to resources* only. If labour is continuously transferred from low- to high-productive technologies, it obviously requires an ever-increasing resource base *if no labour exits the industry*. If the producers stay on, they are met with a situation of ever-diminishing returns. Then, to avoid 'technological unemployment' (Standing 1984), technological modernization in primary production must parallel the building of secondary and tertiary industries. In the fishing societies of industrial countries, technological modernization resulted in a relative exit.

The policy predicament arising from the above argumentation is severe. In order to avoid overexploitation of resources the fishing fleet and the labour force should be subject to contraction, but if under the existing conditions, this would simply lead to displaced, unemployed fishermen, the argument for contraction becomes seriously weakened (Munro and Chee 1978).

The fisheries

Technological change was reconstructed in two villages in Kedah state, Kuala Kedah and Kuala Jerlun on the West Coast of Peninsular Malaysia. Here, fish is a major source of animal protein, and fisheries are important for employment in the coastal settlements. At the time of the study, Malaysian fisheries were mainly costal, in the Straits of Malacca in the West and off the East Coast in the South China Sea. In the text, inshore fisheries refer to fishing from the shore up to about 10 miles; offshore fisheries are undertaken in deeper waters up to 50 or 60 miles away.

Many researchers (Yahaya 1978; Ling 1978a; Fredericks and Wells 1980; Jomo 1991) pointed at the severe overexploitation of resources in Malaysian waters. Fishery resources are common property resources over which specific property rights have not been established. Consequently, the individual fisherman has, according to Fredericks and Wells (1980), almost no incentives to exercise restraint, as the resources left unexploited by one will be caught by another later. Fish landings doubled in the 1970s, but then declined. Whereas annual growth rate in the period 1961–71 was about 7.8 per cent, the period 1981 to 1985 shows a negative growth rate of 6.3 per cent. The decline in production indicates overexploitation of resources; what is harvested exceeds maximum sustainable yield.[4] Jomo (1991) maintains that since 1971, there were

---

[4] Maximum sustainable yield may be defined as 'the maximum resources of fish obtainable and utilized in a way in which the productivity of the fish resource is sustained' (Yahaya

125 per cent overfishing on the West Coast. During this period, authorities were increasingly concerned about the amount of trash fish captured.

Although property rights in the strict sense are most unusual in fishing societies, there may be both customary regulation systems and state systems controlling resource exploitation. However, attempts to bar entry proved ineffective in Kuala Kedah. Major regulation instruments were licensing of crafts, limits to mesh size of the gear and the creation of fishing zones, that is, trawling is outlawed inside the 0–7 miles limit. Penalties have been non-renewal or withdrawal of licenses as well as fines (Ling 1978a). However, regulation of entry by means of licenses was a failure. When licenses were issued to the bigger trawlers, protests from artisanal fishermen were checked by increasing the number of licenses given to small trawlers. Licenses were to be given to fishermen who were members of cooperative societies only, resulting in the formation of many societies. Overinvestment and overexploitation of resources were the consequences.

The effects of the Malaysian regulation policy are disputed. Reserving the zone close to the shores to small-scale fisheries gives a limited protection of these resources. At the time of the study, illegal trawling persisted. As a trawler fisherman put it, 'we share the fines as we share the catch. The crew takes part in the decision to fish illegally' (Fisherman, Kuala Kedah). Yahaya (1976) advocated another solution: if renewal of licenses was refused, this would force owners of trawlers to use less efficient gear. This means moving backwards in terms of technological advancement for the sake of preservation of fishery resources. As will be shown, this did not occur in the study villages. The owners kept their trawl nets, and when catches decreased, they stayed in business by exploiting labour more severely. Fredericks and Wells (1980) maintained at the time that the solution was stricter regulation and the encouragement of artisanal fisheries. According to them, traditional fishing methods should be preferred to safeguard future employment and conserve resources. These researchers in fact advocate technological retrogression; in the one case a minor retrogression, in the other a radical one.

To some extent, employment figures over time correspond to the ups and downs of fish production: In 1949 there were 76,100 registered fishermen in Malaysia. Thereafter their number fluctuated and eventually reached a high of 88,972 fishermen in 1980. The estimated number of fishermen declined in the 1980s and in 1987 it fell to 60,569. The average yearly rate of decline

---

1976, 7). The future reproductive capability of a stock of a species depends on harvested volume and composition of the catch (removal of young and breeding fish may be particularly harmful). Reproduction is, of course, influenced by *natural* changes in the habitat of the species as well.

between 1980 and 1987 was 5.3 per cent, which is substantial. The reliability of employment statistics is, however, questionable. This is evident when studying early periods, but there may also be a *statistical bias against artisanal fishermen* who are fishing in unlicensed or illegal vessels. The peak in 1980 no doubt reflects an increase in industrial fisheries during the 1970s, but to what extent the industrial fishermen who turn to artisanal fisheries during the 1980s *re-enter* fisheries *statistics* is an open question. It is possible that these figures mainly reflect changes in modern fisheries. There may be a relative exit of fishermen from modern boats, but not from the fisheries industry: What appears as modernization may hide retrogression.

It is sometimes argued that the diffusion of modern fisheries technology was mainly due to the fishermen's own initiatives, a willingness to adopt new ideas. However, the overall policy has been to allow and promote the use of more capital-intensive technology rather than encouraging small-scale fisheries. A Western model is easily traced in the planning of fisheries development in Malaysia; there were considerable state investments in trawlers. The aims of development planning in fisheries were to increase fish production, generate employment, upgrade the socioeconomic status of fishermen and reduce economic inequalities among them. A rural development approach was tried out. By defining Fisheries Development Areas, the hope was to achieve greater participation of fishermen, mobilize the grassroots level to identify needs as well as appropriate assistance from the Government.

Four major phases in the modernization process can be discerned. During the early twentieth century, purse seine gear was to some extent used to harvest pelagic species. Powered engines were introduced from the 1930s, and synthetic materials for nets were in use from the 1950s. Modernization accelerated when trawls for capturing demersal fish and prawns were introduced a decade later. Trawling and large-scale purse seining were during the time of the study most important, and by planners considered the only modern technologies, the rest was termed *traditional*. These traditional types of gear are drift net, lines, bag net, lift net and other old, low-productive methods. In the years 1968, 1974 and 1981, the respective proportion of the different types of gears in operation was: Trawl 9, 29 and 14 per cent, seine net 13, 11 and 7 per cent, while the *traditional* gears 78, 59 and 79 per cent. The importance of the various types of gear is better understood when taking landings according to gear into account. In 1985 the trawlers constituted 16 per cent of gear in operation but contributed to 41 per cent of landings. Traditional fisheries are losing terrain in terms of production volume, but the reduced importance for employment is less dramatic.

Instead of drawing the bulk of fishing activity to the offshore sector, the expansion of trawling in the early 1970s only exacerbated the depressed conditions in the inshore sectors and contributed to widespread hostilities between artisanal and industrial fishermen along the coast, as discussed in the case of Penang waters by Ooi (1970). Artisanal fishermen considered decreasing resources not an outcome of crowding of crafts in inshore waters, but a result of the increase in the trawler fleet. The trawler fishermen, on the other hand, protested fiercely at attempts to regulate their activities.

The government's interest in small-scale fisheries had results. After the decline in the 1960s and early 1970s came a revival during the 1980s with the conversion of many rowing crafts to mechanized ones: the installation of outboard engines. Capital intensity increased, inboard engines on the bigger boats became ever more powerful. Mechanization of traditional crafts was slower. It should be noted that the category *artisanal crafts* in the village study includes crafts with an outboard engine. This corresponds closely to what the Fisheries Department (1984) terms *traditional*. This means that the types of boats classified as modern in the case study include only trawlers and purse seiners which in 1987 accounted for 19 and 3 per cent of the total number of crafts, respectively.

Forms of technology in Kuala Kedah

The village

Kuala Kedah is located about 8 km west of Alor Setar, the capital of Kedah State. It is a typical river-mouth (*kuala*) fishing settlement, densely populated on both banks of the Sungai Kedah. In the mid-1980s, the population of Kuala Kedah was about 12,200.[5] The number of fishermen was 3,029; of these, 640 were Chinese. Kuala Kedah is the biggest fishing village of Kedah State, which has about 8,200 fishermen (Fisheries Department 1984). The sample was drawn among the active fishermen: those who take part in fishing operations at sea. Boat owners who are investors only (absentee owners) and retired fishermen were not included. However, two old and retired fishermen were included to get information on the technologies in the 1930s and 1940s. In addition to formal interviews, I had discussions with older people to gain knowledge on technologies of the past and socio-economic changes they have experienced.

Only fishermen who have a fishing license are registered by the authorities; therefore, no reliable register of the fishermen existed at the time. The sample

---

[5] In official statistics, population size and number of fishermen vary; I have judged the numbers given in LKIM (1985), which is based on a comprehensive base line study, the best.

was drawn by choosing every 5th fisherman's house, after mapping the *kampongs* where the Malay fisherfolk live. Of the total of 2,389 Malay fishermen, 216 were interviewed (9 per cent). This number constitutes 'the contemporary sample' of the analysis; as explained above, the size of the sample is reduced when one moves back in time. Thus, the size of the sample from 1931, when the oldest fisherman started his career, to 1987, increases from 1 to 216. Attempts were made to find out whether there have been periods of substantial out-migration which could influence the investigation. Old fishermen of the village could recall no such periods. A few cases of migration to East Johore by purse seine crewmen had, however, occurred in the 1960s. This corresponds to the findings of Ling (1978b) who points at a low geographical mobility of the fishing population in Malaysia. There is evidence in the sample of the fishermen's work histories of such labour migration. The representativity of my sample is controlled by comparing my data findings with the data from an official survey conducted by Majuikan (1983) comprising 1,762 fishing households. The correspondence proved good.

Discovering hidden variation

Technological changes in fisheries are normally studied by figuring out the number of modern versus traditional crafts, ending up with the rate of acceptance of modern technology in an area. But then, any hidden variation, such as the intra-industry mobility of labour between different technologies, remains undisclosed. The inadequacy of boat statistics, both as regards reliability and also as regards the 'missing link' to the standard of living of the households, has put me on the trail of unexpected technological changes.

The *work history* method has many shortcomings; people's memories were, however, better than I thought they would be. The change from one technology to another is an important event in every fisherman's life. The most important limitation of the method therefore is the decreasing size of the sample as one goes back in time. This can only to some extent be made up for by increasing the size of the sample. The greatest objection is perhaps that the research method is very labour intensive. During fieldwork, old technologies must be reconstructed, everything must be controlled and nothing can be left to assistants. The data puzzle to be created, based on the producers' choices of technology, is a challenge to one's patience. But where I undertook the investigations there are no alternatives to this method, if individual adaptations implying technological retrogression are to be found.

Forms of technology

The fishing technologies of the Kedah coast are classified into three major categories. These are *low, intermediate* and *high forms of technology*. The basic classification criterion is *labour productivity*. I assume a positive correlation of labour productivity to capital intensity, as stated in the above definition of *artisanal* and *industrial* fisheries.[6] Labour productivity can for instance be measured as quantity of fish produced per hour. In most social studies of small-scale fisheries, the difference in labour productivity between what is termed traditional or small-scale and modern or large-scale fisheries is taken for granted. It is, however, difficult to substantiate this without any cost–benefit analysis. Such analyses are extremely complex, labour productivity in fisheries may vary from trip to trip, due to resource fluctuation and climatic conditions, production must be carefully monitored over time. Figure 15 shows the classification and how the technologies are visualized in a career path graph. This is an attempt to visualize the differences which should not be considered accurate: The difference in labour productivity between, for instance, a C-trawler crewman and the clam gatherer is much greater than can be read from the graph. The three forms of technology in Kuala Kedah all consist of three or four different technologies each. Type of craft is used to define form of technology. This classification criterion brings with it no serious problems as regards high and intermediate technology. But it is obvious that difficulties may arise as regards the category low form of technology, since a wide variety of fishing methods is used in *sampans* and *perahus*. Gathering of clams does not require the use of a craft.

The high form of technology consists of trawlers of different sizes. The range of operation of these trawlers is regulated by law.[7] In the high–low technology dimension, the trawlers are categorized according to size, the A lowest, the C highest.

---

[6] Carefully avoiding tautological reasoning, I will argue that when in the analysis of living standard I find that fishermen who have used hand lining for many years are much poorer than fishermen who have been working aboard the trawlers for many years, this can only be explained in two ways: If increase in labour productivity does NOT explain improved living standards with technological modernization, then the *share system* must explain it: Maybe industrial fishermen produce just as little as artisanal fishermen, but they get more of the catch value? The opposite is true: The share system within artisanal fisheries is more egalitarian. The explanation of higher standard of living among industrial fishermen is increased value formation with technological modernization. This is not disputed in the literature.

[7] The trawlers are classified according to size, which is related to the zone where they can operate: A-trawlers 5–25 t Zone A, 1–5 miles, *inshore*. B-trawlers 26–40 t Zone B, 6–12 miles, *offshore*. C-trawlers 41–69 t Zone C, 13–30 miles, *offshore*. Trawlers 70 ton and over, fishing in Zone D, *deep sea*, are not found in Kuala Kedah.

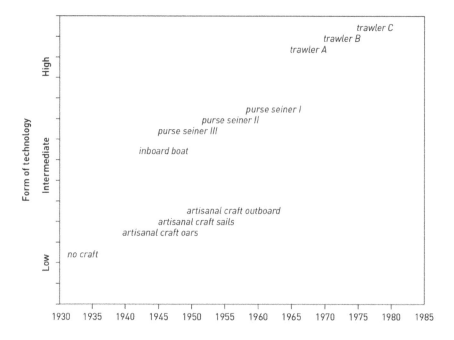

Figure 15 Forms of technology in Kuala Kedah.

The intermediate form of technology consists of two different types of technology, namely 20 to 30 feet boats with inboard motor, which appeared on the scene in the 1960s. Various types of nets were used from these boats. The second type is purse seining. These large boats dominated the scene from the late 1950s until the 1970s. Three different types of purse seining have been used in this area. The first type was one with a big mother vessel and two rowing crafts, the second type had only one rowing craft and the third does not mix elements of technologies at different productivity levels. In the high–low technology dimension, these technologies are placed according to year of introduction.

The low form of technology consists of crafts in which many different methods of fishing are used. The different crafts are categorized in a high–low technology dimension according to mode of propulsion: *Sampans* and *perahus* in which only oars are used are considered lower than the same boats with sails (the range increases radically). The use of outboard engine in the same crafts places them higher. However, this could be disputed, since then you may sail further away than what is advisable to venture with only an outboard engine; and just as fast – on a windy day. Technologies which do not require the use of a craft are considered at the lowest productivity level. Examples are the gathering of clams, rod and line fishing from the shore and casting with nets. In general, artisanal crafts are more dependent upon weather conditions than the bigger vessels.[8]

My classification was the object of criticism by various fishermen. Sometimes the men could not agree on which technology should be considered the most advanced. It appeared that they often mixed the concept *profitability* with the concept of labour *productivity*. Fishermen with experience from many types of crafts tended to value the one aboard which they had earned the most as the best, and therefore as the highest technology. When I explained that it is a question of *quantity of fish produced* in relation to *the number of fishermen* working aboard the craft, there was a near total consensus on the classification.

Although *time* is represented in the X-axis of Figure 15, it neither gives a correct picture of the time of introduction of the various technologies to the village nor the time when the various forms dominated the scene. It represents, however, an illustration of a *hypothesis* on the introduction of the technologies: The least advanced technology appears firstly, followed by the more advanced. To validate this statement, some modifications are needed. Firstly, crafts like *sampan* or *perahu* with oars or sails are indigenous to the area, and it is evident that low technology therefore should appear first. Likewise, the first purse seiner came before the first trawler. *But the least advanced technology, gathering of clams as a full-time occupation (artisanal with no use of craft), appears in 1980, long after the introduction of the C-trawlers. Secondly, the more advanced forms of technology do not simply replace the less advanced; the technologies exist simultaneously.*

Starting from the technologically highest type of craft and moving down the scale, the different technologies were introduced in the following points of time: C-trawler in 1962, B-trawler in 1957, A-trawler in 1954, Purse seiner I in 1961, Purse seiner II in 1944, Purse seiner III in 1939, Inboard boat in 1940, Artisanal outboard in 1948, Artisanal no craft in 1980.

---

[8] According to Kedah fishermen, three different seasons determine the weather conditions of the north-western coast of Peninsular Malaysia. The *Musim Timor*, the Eastern or dry season, is from November to March. The dominant wind comes from the east. Seas are calm and the weather is dry. In April the season changes, the wind comes from the South. This season, which is called the *Musim Barat Muda*, brings calm seas, small waves and little rain. These weather conditions may last about two months. June brings another change, the time of the *Musim Barat Tua*, the rainy season. Storms, rain and rough seas are common until October. In this period, the north-west monsoon is dominant. However, this is a general picture; weather conditions may vary year by year. Several fishermen even maintained that the climate was changing. The coming of the rainy season the last few years could not be predicted, and violent storms had occurred during the calm season.

Technological change in Kuala Kedah

Based on the fishermen's work histories, I have reconstructed the process of technological change. It is important again to stress that when using this method, the analysis is based on estimated employment figures. When the work history method is used, all figures should be treated with caution, since they only *indicate* the size of real figures. Before a comparison of the model transition with the empirical findings from Kuala Kedah is made, attention is directed to some technology changes within artisanal fisheries.

Changes within artisanal fisheries

Technological polarization was observed *within* the artisanal form of technology during the period when purse seiners and trawlers were introduced. While the sailing crafts almost disappear, outboard engine crafts increase in importance. The artisanal fleet now consists of rowing crafts and crafts with outboard engines. In Figure 16 mechanized crafts are excluded to demonstrate how the reduction in sailing crafts corresponds to the increase in rowing crafts.

Mechanization led to the extinction of sailing crafts, both because of the gradual technological modernization within the form of technology and also

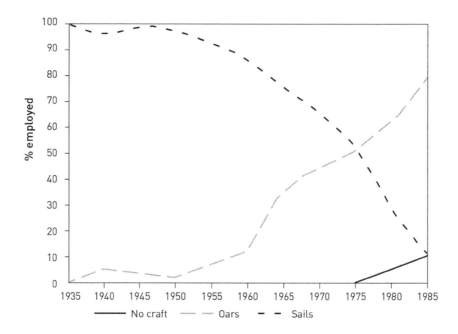

Figure 16 From sails to oars in Kuala Kedah.

because there has been a drain of skilled labour from low to intermediate and high form of technology: Most fishermen who had experience from artisanal technology before being recruited to industrial boats came from sailing crafts. The last job before purse seiners shows that more than half of them came directly from sailing crafts, many came from crafts with an outboard engine and only 8 per cent came from a rowing craft.

A more thorough discussion on the fishermen's career paths is included below; the point made here is that there has been a *selective recruitment* to industrial fisheries, involving a drain of sailing and navigation skills from artisanal fisheries, just like in the Sri Lankan case. What this implies is that when industrial fishermen return to artisanal fisheries, they do not return to the fisheries they left; it has radically changed through technological modernization and retrogression of tools (from sails to oars). It is also worth noting that the least advanced technology, where no craft is used at all, appears late in the history of technological change, as commented on above. Few fishermen have, however, taken up this technology so far.

The transition

Technological change normally implies a movement of labour from one productivity level to another. In the present context, it should be stressed that *the concept of change is direction neutral*: It either denotes a movement from a less advanced to a more advanced level (technological modernization) or from a more advanced to a less advanced level (technological retrogression). When no change occurs, a period of *stagnation* is identified.

In Kuala Kedah, technological modernization was first rapid, then stagnated: The low form of technology decreased in importance until the 1970s, but the decrease came to a standstill in the middle of the 1980s. By then, high technology took over the position that intermediate had earlier. At the time of the study, nearly half of the fishermen worked aboard trawlers.

In 1950, lift nets and purse seiners were in use in Kuala Kedah, resulting in over 30 per cent of the workforce on industrial boats. These boats are intermediate technology only in hindsight; that is, compared to the trawlers of today. In those days, they were high technology compared to sailing and rowing crafts, which dominated. From 1950 onwards, the purse seiners gained in importance. Their highest share of the workforce was 59 per cent (1965). In the late 1970s the share of intermediate technology was only about 20 per cent. Trawlers then dominated with their share of the labour force steadily increasing; from 4 per cent in 1960 to 17 per cent in 1970. It reached a top of 46 per cent in 1985. The low form of technology, which started with the whole labour force in the 1930s, has experienced a steady decrease until 1970, when

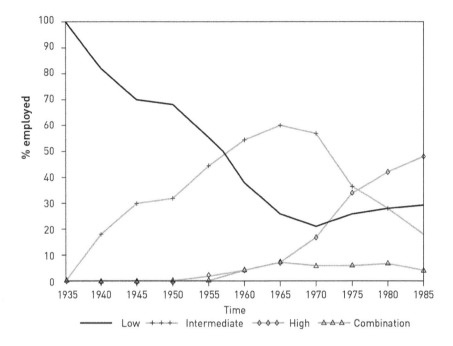

Figure 17 Technological change in Kuala Kedah 1931–86.

the share was about 22 per cent. During the last 20 years its share has been stable; between 20 and 30 per cent. Today, the share is 29 per cent.[9] The share of the labour force which combines technologies at different productivity levels is low for the whole period.

As shown in Figure 17, the low form of technology decreases steadily in importance, intermediate and high increase accordingly. However, in the 1970s it becomes evident that the transition is incomplete: Rather than the disappearance of low forms of technology, the curve flattens out. There is no S-curve of acceptance of modern technology. A complete transition, if it ever comes, is delayed. This is visible when the most advanced forms of technology (high and intermediate) are added up and contrasted to the low form of technology (Figure 18).[10]

---

[9] If my figures are compared to the boat statistics of the Perspective Plan my figures for low technology has a much higher share, 29 per cent as compared to about 17 per cent (LKIM 1985, 18, table XV). This is probably due to an underestimation of the number of artisanal crafts. Only licensed boats are counted. This is an illustration of the low quality of official statistics earlier pointed out.

[10] To some extent, this corresponds to the artisanal/industrial distinction made in the Sri Lankan case. An important qualification must, however, be made: In the Malaysian

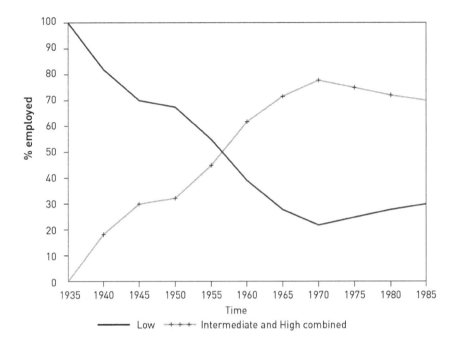

Figure 18 Low form of technology versus intermediate and high combined.

The contours of an ideal spread of modern technology (Figure 2) are visible until about 1970. The most interesting period to explain is thus from then until today. Although an upturn of the low technology curve is visible, I am reluctant to claim, based on 7 per cent increase between 1970 and 1986, that this should be interpreted as anything more than a slowdown of modernization, a *technological retardation*. To claim that technological retrogression is a reality *at village level* at present would be to ignore the upturn of the curve describing high technology (see Figure 17), and perhaps to overestimate the significance of the actions of industrial fishermen who in this period turned to artisanal technology for survival. However, as shown below, where variations at the individual level are described, this tendency increases. *Thus, instead of dying out, the strength of artisanal as compared to industrial fisheries increases during the later decades.* This does not necessarily imply that the low form of technology is

---

case classification are included in the low form of technology, modern elements such as outboard engines attached to artisanal crafts. To stress relativity: Malaysian sampans with outboard engines are low fishing technology compared to trawlers and purse seiners. The same craft would have been classified as industrial in the Sri Lankan case study.

vigorous, which can only be established by studying its age structure today and future recruitment. A stable recruitment to the low form of technology may be secured for years if industrial fishermen use artisanal fisheries as retirement. They may be unable to cope with the speed in industrial fisheries when they grow older. If the low form of technology consists solely of old people, and if it is not used as retirement, one should expect artisanal fisheries to vanish with the old users.

Low form of technology has the highest share among the fishermen above 50 years, whereas the high form has a larger share of the sample's young fishermen. The fishermen within the intermediate form of technology are evenly distributed. The share of low technology of the sample's fishermen below 30 years shows that young men still are recruited to artisanal fisheries, and more so now than a decade earlier. Twenty-eight per cent of the artisanal fishermen are younger than 41 years and 43 per cent are below 46 years. The figures for the intermediate form of technology are 40 per cent and 55 per cent respectively, whereas the high form of technology has a younger population: 53 per cent are below 41, and 75 per cent are below 46. A more thorough analysis of the age structure is not possible, since the sample includes only 21 fishermen in their twenties.

Whether the higher share of artisanal fishermen consists of fishermen who have been pushed out when they grow old or of fishermen who have been artisanal all their lives will be analysed further below. If industrial fishermen use low technology as retirement, then those who are pushed out (or voluntarily retrograded) to artisanal fisheries from the intermediate or high form of technology should be old fishermen. They are *not* (see Technological retrogression below).

Expectations and reality

Expected career paths

I will first address the oft-quoted assumption that the major cause of 'the economic retardation of the Malays' is their attitude toward economic development; that is, resistance to economic change which is part of a broader resistance to change in general and reluctance to accept innovations which require radical change in *kampung* life' (Snodgrass 1980, 114).

In my study, I have not found any evidence of unwillingness to accept technological innovations which change society radically. To the contrary, either this was never true or it was valid earlier. Cultural traits of such fundamental character cannot vanish fast. I therefore hold the view that this is a prejudice. It is interesting to note that of 206 fishermen, only 19 had never

Work history

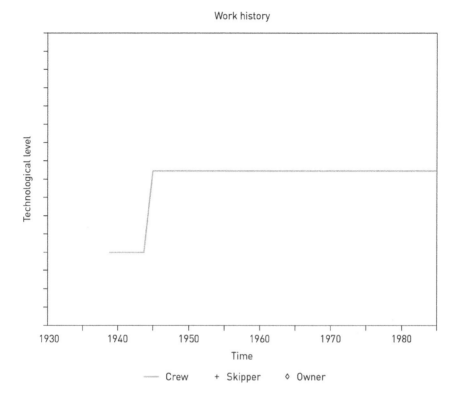

Figure 19 From low to intermediate.

experienced any change of technology: 15 of these were industrial fishermen, six of whom had just started their careers; the others were in their forties and fifties. Then we are left with only four immobile artisanal fishermen, two below 41 years and two above. There are thus few stubborn traditionalists. And the Kedah fishermen are more technologically mobile than I expected. In fact, since the *conservatives* are nearly absent, I wonder if some of them would have preferred to stay aboard the craft they first chose, but that they were *forced* to change.

The approach to the analysis of career paths which I have chosen is first to present career paths which correspond to the ideal spread of modern technology. Afterwards, the ideals are compared to reality. What I present as expectations becomes hypotheses to be tested in the next section. Instead of presenting purely theoretical constructs, I selected real fishermen's career paths which correspond to such expectations. Two of the fishermen who are selected use intermediate technology, two use high technology and three use low technology. In addition, I present a fisherman who combines different technologies, and another who is chosen to illustrate career instability. In the first phase of technological modernization, one should expect that the career paths of those who become industrial resemble the career path presented in Figure 19. This fisherman moves from a sailing craft to the highest form of technology available at that time, a purse seiner.

As time goes by, one should expect that the owners of purse seiners start to recruit (promising) young men without any previous experience from fisheries, resulting in the career path type which is presented in Figure 20.

The career paths of the fishermen who use the most productive technologies should be expected to be like the ones presented above. It is, however, likely that fishermen with previous experience from industrial fisheries were preferred as labour on the trawlers when they were introduced. Therefore, the first career path which shows a move to the top (Figure 21) shows a movement from the intermediate form to the high form of technology.

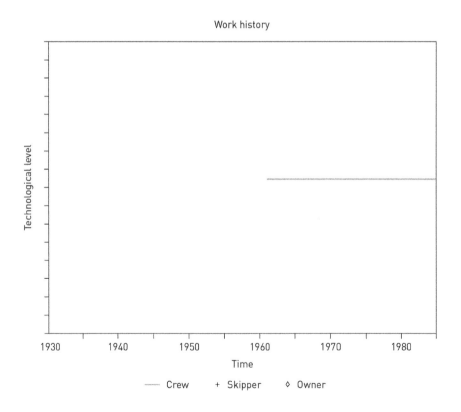

Figure 20 Only intermediate.

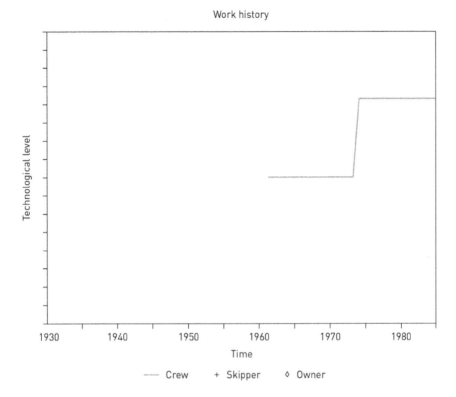

Figure 21 From intermediate to high.

The next career path presented (Figure 22) looks quite dramatic. This fisherman left his sailing craft only a year after he had invested in an outboard engine, to become a crewman aboard the biggest trawler in the village. He thereby lost his status as craft owner. According to modernization theory, fishermen who have been willing to jeopardize the safety of tradition should be rewarded by experiencing considerable improvements in their living conditions. Then, tempted by the performance of the innovators, other enterprising fishermen would leave artisanal technology behind.

In a very late phase of technological modernization when, according to the ideal model, the advanced modern technologies have taken over and all the other technologies are dead, all career paths will finally follow a horizontal line along the high technology level (Figure 23). To follow the predictions of the diffusionists, the most advanced technology will probably be the only technology in the village for some time – until even more advanced technologies are introduced. On the other side of the scale we expect to have

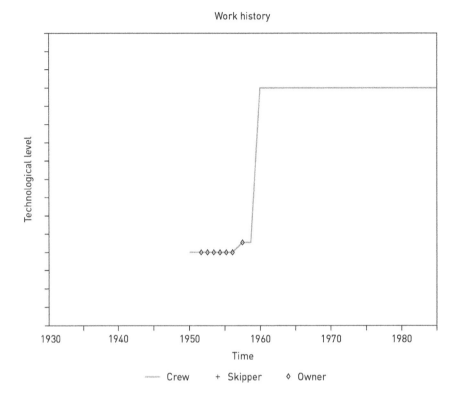

Figure 22 From low to high.

the conservative traditionalists, those who stubbornly remain artisanal. Their career paths should also follow a horizontal line, along the level of low form of technology (Figure 24).

It is probable that some fishermen who tried to work aboard industrial crafts could not make it and had to return. Two such examples are presented here. Figure 25 shows the career path of a fisherman who earlier had his own small craft. He tried his luck as crewman aboard a purse seiner but decided to return to artisanal fisheries after only two years. The other fisherman, whose career path is shown in Figure 26, stayed a little longer on the top, before returning to artisanal fisheries.

In general, artisanal fishermen should be expected to be older than the average. It may be harder to adjust to new technology as one gets older, and besides, in a physically hard occupation such as fisheries, the young and strong are probably preferred as labour aboard modern boats.

In an early phase of technological modernization, the fishermen are probably uncertain whether the new technology will bring them any profit. They may therefore be reluctant to burn the bridges to artisanal fisheries. The fisherman whose career path is presented in Figure 22 kept his *sampan* while he was working aboard the purse seiner. He did not use it; he just kept it as a retirement possibility. Another way to create a safety net is to *combine* artisanal and industrial technology. Figure 27 shows the career path of a fisherman who did not put all his eggs in one basket before he was sure that he could carry them safely. During the 1960s, he had one leg aboard a *sampan* and the other aboard a purse seiner, thus combining two forms of technology by season. He was able to try out something new without giving up the old, which seems a wise decision, since he ends up where many enterprising fishermen want to be, as the skipper aboard a big trawler. This combination fisherman seemed to have planned his career, but there are some people who never can steer a steady course. The career path shown in Figure 28 is a case in point. This fisherman has tried many different occupations. From the time he moved from Penang to buy a *sampan*, only 17 years old, until he ends up the same, he has tried both purse seiners and trawlers. The broken lines indicate that he has been engaged in work outside fish production: The explanation of the first open space is that he joined the police force during the Japanese invasion. During the next intermission he sold food at the market. The last period he was ill for some time and then worked at the market again. Within every occupation – any time, any place – one can find people with unstable careers such as this one. They should, however, be expected to be very few, in comparison with common security maximizers.

Four fishermen's careers

As an introduction to the overall picture, I first present four fishermen who have different career paths. I refer to the reasons they have stated for their choices of technology and put some flesh and blood on their technological pasts by describing their living conditions and the families they provide for. They are not *typical*, that is, selected to illustrate common career paths of the village, but represent examples of the types of expected career paths presented above.

The labels I have used to characterize these fishermen are of my own making – but clearly inspired by prejudices which are not by me. Here you can meet with a *progressive entrepreneur* and a *reactionary traditionalist*, an *aimlessly wavering* man – and a man who at first sight looks the *complete failure*. They are presented to demonstrate that by appearance, career paths may conform to prejudices inherited from modernization theory, but when the context of their

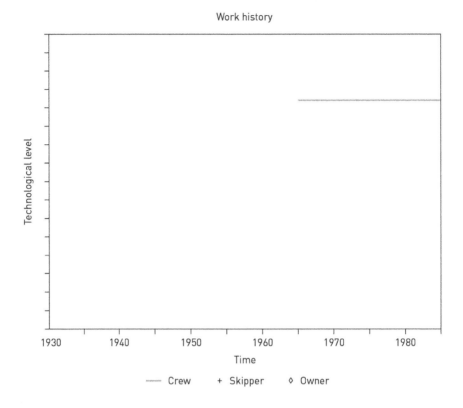

Figure 23 Only high.

choices is added, the pattern becomes far more complex, and the inadequacy of modernization theory becomes evident. I could, and perhaps should, be accused of digging up dead dogs when, in this context, I refer to the works of modernization theorists who are no longer central in development theory. Suppositions on the importance of personality differences are no longer central, but they are, however, by no means dead in development thought, which theorists share with planners and ordinary people: We *still* do make suppositions about how such differences affect economic development; and we *are* inspired by modernization theorists, probably because nobody has described this more explicitly. Who has described entrepreneurs better than Schumpeter – or has his description formed our perception to the extent that we see only his type examples, not reality?

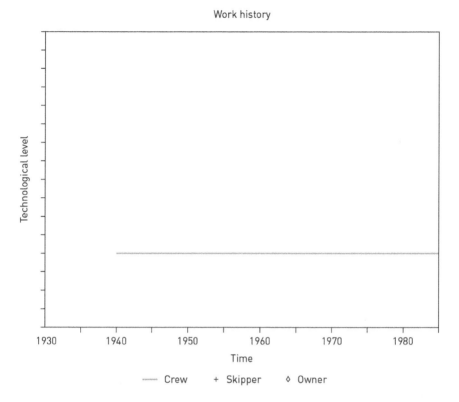

Figure 24 Only low.

A progressive entrepreneur?

The fisherman whose career path is presented in Figure 29 has steadily moved upwards, from low form of technology, via intermediate, ending up in the high form of technology category. His career path reflects social mobility as well, since he started as an ordinary crewman, then became skipper and, in the end, he owns a boat.

He started to go fishing with his father aboard a *perahu* with sails, becoming a fulltime crewman in 1954, when he was 15 years old. Twenty years old, he left his father's craft to become one of four crewmen aboard an inboard boat. For seven years he had this job, until he got the chance to work aboard a purse seiner, where he advanced to skipper in 1972. All through the 1970s, he worked aboard the purse seiner and was during that time able to save enough to get his own small trawler in 1985. He was 47 years old at the time of the study. Every change of technology he made to increase his income, he claimed.

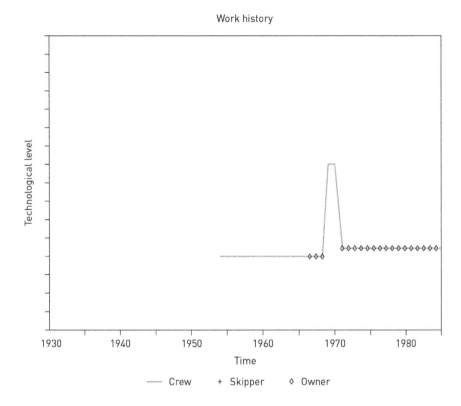

Figure 25 Trial and failure I?

He lives with his large family, consisting of wife and 10 children aged from 23 to 2 years, in a relatively large house, badly maintained, quite empty of furniture and consumer durables. None of his children contribute to the family income. The eldest boy has moved to Mersing with a friend to try to get work, another son earned a little last year working for a fish merchant. He and his wife got only 5 years each of (irregular) schooling, but all his children have gone regularly to school.

During his career, this fisherman's health has been quite good, he has had no long period without income from fishing; in fact, he has never tried other work. He claims that this is what he wants to do. Besides, he wants to live in Kuala Kedah, where he was born. He wants his children to get a good education, and only if they find no other opportunities, they should go into fisheries. This relative reluctance to advise the youth to become fishermen reveals uncertainty about the future. When confronted with the (apparent) inconsistency that he is uncertain of the future of fisheries, but has recently

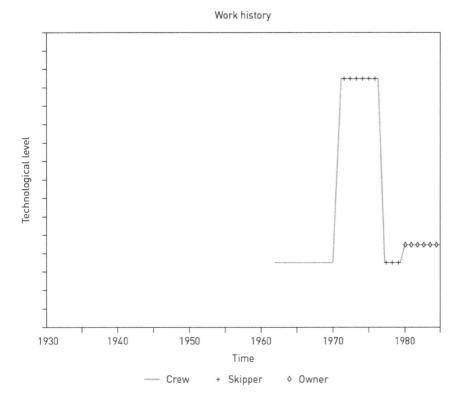

Figure 26 Trial and failure II?

bought a trawler, he tells me that right *now* he is optimistic, but it varies; he is often worried about the decrease in fish resources. As regards the short-term view on fisheries, his own future, he is optimistic, but less so as regards the long-term prospects, his children's future.

A reactionary traditionalist?

As regards technological as well as social mobility, the career path presented in Figure 30 is less impressive than that of the above entrepreneur. Day by day, year by year, decade by decade he has used the same type of technology, hand lining from a *sampan* with sails and oars.

Born in 1919, he started to work when he was 12 years old when he finished school. In the later years he has been working less than before, but still he was seen on the banks of the river, mending his fishing gear. Sometimes he worked together with his son, but most often he went to sea alone. During

Work history

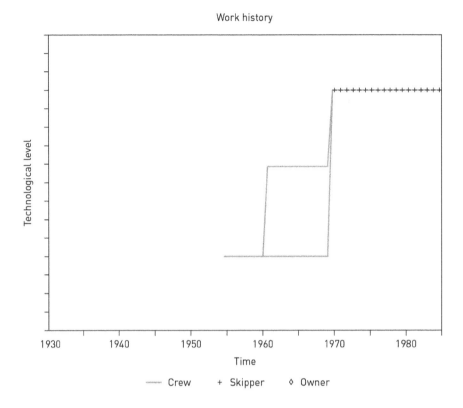

Figure 27 Early combination.

this long career, at least ten major new technologies have been introduced, but he has tried none of them: Is this a traditionalist, unable to make use of new opportunities created in the village, and who instead clings to what he has learned from his forefathers?

I discussed advantages and disadvantages of the use of sails compared to the use of outboard engines with this fisherman. He held the view that a return to sails, such as I had observed in Sri Lanka, was impossible in Kuala Kedah. He meant that the youth now lack the skills, they have never learned sailing; and besides, 'they want the engines, they are more modern'. To my surprise he added that, in fact, he would have bought an outboard engine himself a long time ago, but he could never afford it. If he had an engine, he would go fishing even in the rainy season. Since he puts forward rational arguments *for* modern technology (he was not even asked), one cannot claim that he asserts a 'persistent preference for the traditional' (Hirschman 1958, 127), which might have prevented him from becoming modern.

Work history

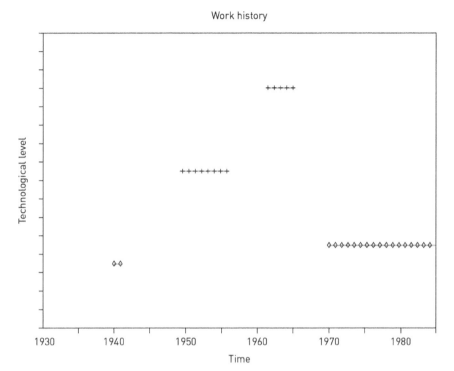

Figure 28 Instability.

But he sees the technical advantages of modern technology, and he is unwilling to buy the whole package. His attitude towards *credit*, for instance, must be classified as traditional: He never, by principle, borrows any money. Vividly describing the grip of the middlemen, in which he perceives his fellow fishermen to be, he praised the virtue of independence. Besides, he never applied for a subsidy, which he claimed that he would not get 'for political reasons'. Neither would he want to live at the mercy of any bank. The first craft this fisherman used, he had inherited, and later he had saved the money to buy another. During the few periods he had been unable, due to illness, to go fishing, he had got money to support his family by mortgaging jewellery. Due to old age, he was unable to support his wife and himself. They relied upon gifts from some of his 18 children (he now lived with his third wife). The house was empty of consumer durables; the couple's major problem was, however, that in the rainy season, the roof of the house was leaking.

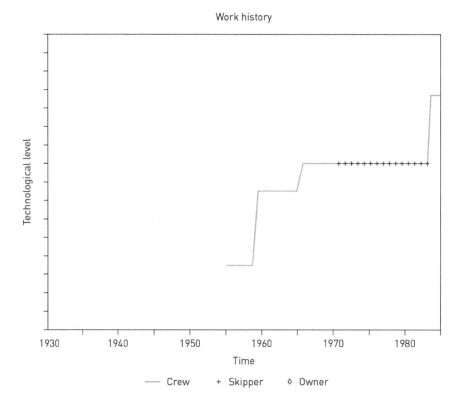

Figure 29 A progressive entrepreneur?

As regards the future of the village, this fisherman was quite worried, blaming the trawlers for the resource crisis: 'They take the young fish as well.' But still he would encourage the youth to go into fisheries: 'They should *do* something. It is bad for them just to walk around all day.' In his youth, healthy 16-year-old men were never idle.

An aimlessly wavering man?

The next career path (Figure 31) looks like the career path of an unstable person, unable to make up his mind – or has he been unable to keep a job? Apparently without a goal in life, he moves from one type of technology to the other.

This trail can hardly be predicted by any theory. His own explanation of the choices is as follows:

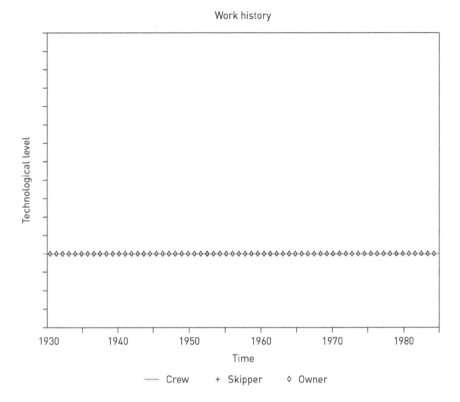

Figure 30 A reactionary traditionalist?

When his father fell ill during the war, he took over the responsibility for his craft as well as his family, thus starting his career as skipper (at least in the name), aboard a sailing craft, aged only 12. For five years he had that job; he then became one of the first villagers who got work aboard a purse seiner. He worked there for 10 years, until the boat was wrecked. Then he turned to a sailing craft again, this time as ordinary crewman. Again fate, disguised as a monsoon storm, struck: This craft, too, was wrecked. Later the same season, he got work aboard a trawler, staying there for only a year. He then felt that his income was insufficient, so he accepted an offer to work as a skipper aboard a *perahu* with an outboard engine. Three years thereafter, again he changed job, this time he was, in his own words, promoted to skipper aboard a purse seiner of the old type, and two years afterwards aboard the more modern type. In the late 1970s, however, he decided to move downwards in terms of technology. He applied for a subsidy and bought his own *perahu* with an outboard engine. Thus, he ended up, 56 years old, close to where he started.

Work history

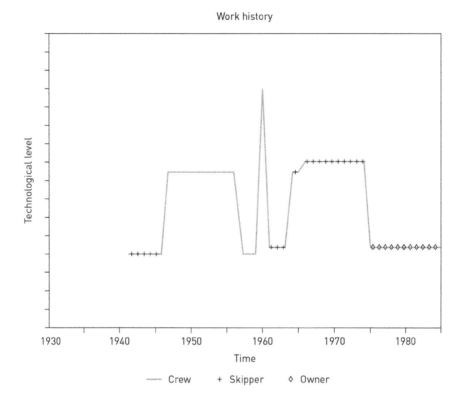

Figure 31 An aimlessly wavering man?

In terms of technology, this fisherman has tried almost everything; he has been but a year at the top level. Except when the craft was wrecked, he changed his job 'to earn more'. The last time as well, when he retrogressed from a responsible position as foreman for a crew of 22 men, to work aboard a tiny craft, he gave this as a reason for change. He has had steady periods, but has moved on to the boats aboard which he expected to earn more money.

When asked whether he was satisfied with his present job, he maintained that he had no other choice: there were no other opportunities in the village. Earlier he had discussed with his wife if they should leave, but now they both are too old. Besides, they have all their relatives here; and a small, but nice, home. Most of his eight children now have homes of their own, only the three youngest live with their parents. The oldest sons did not finish school but started early as fishermen.

Work history

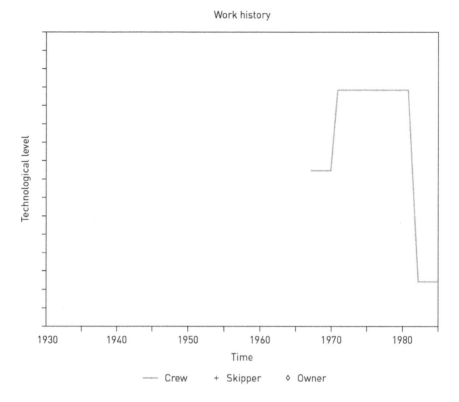

Figure 32 A complete failure?

This fisherman plans a new future; he wants to invest in a small inboard boat and work with his sons. This, he claims, is to secure their future. The sons have no qualifications, and it is getting more and more difficult to earn enough as a crewman. But in his opinion, there is little reason to worry about the resources: Some species have become extinct, but 'still there are fish in the sea'.

A complete failure?

The fisherman whose career path is presented in Figure 32 now uses a type of technology which could be termed rather primitive. He began his career at 17: an optimistic crewman aboard a purse seiner, which at that time was a very modern boat. After five years he got the chance to try even more advanced technology, a big trawler aboard which floating trawl was used. But then, after 11 years, still a relatively young man of 33, he decided to retrograde. Equipped with only a heavy box which he pushes in front of him, he gathers clams on the beach during low tide.

What made him, who had experience with advanced technology only, to turn to the lowest form of technology available in the village? A development planner in the Ministry of Fisheries claimed that 'We must expect that some of them don't make it, they are just not used to the tempo in modern fisheries' (Interview, Ministry of Fisheries). Is this fisherman one of the failures? Perhaps, but I do not think so. He has shown considerable initiative by creating his own job when he was dissatisfied with his masters. Paradoxically, he claims that he can earn more by producing less – if he works harder. When he was a trawler crewman, he changed boat five times. Every time he changed technology, he claimed he did it because he was dissatisfied with what he earned. He claimed that the owners' share of the value of the catch was unreasonably large: 'It was the usual thing, the *towkays* always cheated.' Gathering clams is heavy work, and the working hours long, but he is his own master, he can even make his own gear, and even more important: He does not have to share the catch with anyone. In terms of market, his business is, however, vulnerable, depending largely on tourism.

His youngest son is now 5 years old, therefore his wife sometimes works together with him. When he fell ill for a month, she had to support the family by selling food at the market. The couple does not have their own house but live in a small shack annexed to her parents' house. They have only four children.

This fisherman considers the prospects of fisheries in the area to be poor. The purse seiners now go less frequently to sea. He insists that the decrease in catches should be considered the fault of the trawlers. Nevertheless, he encourages his son to go into fisheries, since this is the only type of work available in the village. He has earlier applied for a subsidy to buy a boat, but this far he has not been 'on the list'. If he can save enough money, he will invest in a *perahu* with an outboard engine.

Standard of living

The four fishermen, whose different career paths are presented above, have one thing in common: a low standard of living. Nothing can, of course, be inferred from this observation before a thorough analysis of all possible parameters related to the fisherfolk's standard of living. Based on the standard of their houses and ownership of furniture and consumer durables,

I have grouped the households according to their standard of living.[11] In the analysis, the households are usually classified into three groups, in which case 37 households are classified as rich, 119 households are in the middle group, while 47 households are considered poor.[12] What kind of living conditions do they have, the fishermen who are classified as poor? To put it somewhat different: Some of the households which are classified as rich would, if they were placed in a Norwegian setting, probably qualify for welfare. The poorest have only their clothes and a shack to live in.

It is not unreasonable to assume that the fishing households' living standard is correlated with the size of their families, since household expenditures probably increase the more dependents the fisherman has. However, based on the analysis of living standard in relation to household size in both Kuala Kedah and in the Sri Lankan villages, this hypothesis is falsified. In view of the way in which standard of living is measured in this study (standard of house, possession of consumer durables), *time* should be expected to increase wealth. But the fisherman's age (which is linked to the length of his career used here) is not correlated with living standard. Next, the fisherman's education is not correlated with standard of living, which means that his incomes are not affected by his education. This is less surprising than the lack of correspondence between age and standard of living, since other factors, such as physical strength and kinship, are more important selection criteria than formal education. Neither is the hypothesis that additional incomes improve standard of living supported. In most cases, the wives try to supplement the fishermen's incomes by selling cookies at the market. A few of the women also work in agriculture. Some of the children work as extra hands now and then, earning a little by helping the fishermen or the fish merchants. Twelve fishermen have odd jobs, such as maintaining boats or paddy farming during peak seasons.

Although the extra incomes are minute, one cannot conclude that they are of no significance to the household which earns them. Without them, some poor households would be even worse off. But it reveals the household's dependence on fisheries and lack of other opportunities in the village. This was also supported by other researchers who concluded that the total

---

[11] The method of calculation is described in Endresen (1994, Appendix 4).

[12] Two hundred and three households are included in the standard of living analysis, since I do not have controllable information on standard of living in 13 cases (nine fishermen's families lived in their parents' or in-laws' house, while four fishermen's work histories were recorded while they were visiting another family's house).

income structure reflected the lack of alternative employment opportunities (Fredericks et al. 1985).

Security nets

When incomes from fisheries for various reasons are insufficient the fisherfolk need security nets. Relatives are the most important security net in Kuala Kedah, followed by savings, the pawnshop and boat owners' advance payments. It is difficult to measure how important security nets are to the fishing households. I found that asking the question 'what would you do if you had no income from fisheries for a period?' generally resulted in the answer 'manage the best we can'. Therefore, I asked all fishermen if they had a long period (a month or more) without any income. If they had, they were asked how they survived during this period. In most cases, illness caused the reduction in income.

Both rich and poor fell ill. But their means of survival differ. Rich fishing households can survive on savings unless the period of illness is prolonged. If they are crewmen, they can also get payment advances from the boat owner. The pawnshop is often considered the place where the poor go in times of need. But what can they give as security? The poorer the household is, the more important the security net represented by their relatives is. However, the conditions of the social stratum which may be termed 'destitute' suggests a weakening rather than a strengthening of security nets. The process of differentiation (which started as a result of the demand for efficient labour on the modern boats) may have been accompanied by a weakening of the moral obligation of the more fortunate to take care of the less productive of the community, whether their conditions are a result of illness, weakness, drunkenness or unlucky circumstances. Many of these fishermen are hired only as extra hands during peak seasons, resulting in uncertain incomes and unstable careers. In most fishing communities, only men are active in fishing operations, which limits the size of a reserve which can be mobilized during peak seasons. This may explain why some of the worse-off fishermen have got jobs at all. In periods of labour surplus, the position of the destitute becomes worse. At the time of the study, unemployed youth constitute the largest part of this reserve.

It is interesting to note that the type of security net used also varies with share of high form of technology in the fisherman's career: The higher the share, the more dependent he is on the goodwill of the boat owner. Industrial fishermen earn more, so they can save. But their savings are sometimes insufficient: The boat owner has taken over the security which the relatives used to represent. When the crewmen are free of one type of dependency another takes over. The degree to which industrial fishermen are free labour can thus be discussed.

To move forward in the understanding of living standard, the relationship with both ownership of means of production and the fishermen's technological past must be clarified. The latter analysis implies the formation of career path type variables, which means that this operation must first be undertaken.

Hidden variation within individual career paths

Intermediate technology

According to the hypotheses regarding the career paths of the fishermen who today use intermediate technology, we expect these paths to conform to Figures 19 and 20. This means that fishermen are expected to either have advanced from lower to intermediate technological level or to have always been in the intermediate level. However, through the work history method we discovered two additional categories: those who earlier have tried both low and high technology, and those who earlier worked aboard trawlers.

The majority of the 40 fishermen who are included in intermediate form of technology have career paths which correspond to the expected types. Seventy per cent of these fishermen have more than 20 years of experience from fisheries. Fourteen of the 17 fishermen who had experience from artisanal fisheries before they got jobs aboard purse seiners have careers longer than the group average, indicating that many pioneers have stayed aboard the purse seiners. As expected, after some time, many fishermen were recruited without any previous experience; most of them have average career lengths. However, 19 per cent of fishermen within the intermediate form of technology have unexpected career paths. Three previous experience from both artisanal fisheries and trawlers. Five fishermen have moved from the high form of technology to intermediate. Their careers are shorter than the group average.

Advanced high technology

My sample contains 96 trawler fishermen. The career paths of the trawler fishermen correspond to the expectations illustrated by Figures 21 and 22 to a great extent. Of the 96 fishermen, only 45 per cent have careers longer than 20 years. Forty-three of the trawler fishermen had experience from purse seiners before they got jobs aboard the trawlers; their career lengths equal the average. Some had experience from artisanal fisheries as well as purse seiners; most of them became modern step by step (15 of the 18 moved from low via intermediate to the high form of technology). They have careers much longer than the group average; this is also the case with the 10 fishermen who came aboard the trawlers directly from artisanal fisheries. Twenty-two of the trawler fishermen got their jobs without any previous experience; all of them have career lengths shorter than the group average, which was expected. Three fishermen have such confusing paths that they must be considered exceptions. This overall picture does, however, hide variations which are treated below: In periods, three of the trawler fishermen combined technologies, and as many as 14 of them had tried to get jobs outside the fisheries industry. Ten fishermen had for a period moved down in technological level but returned to the trawlers.

Low technology

The career paths of the fishermen who today use artisanal technology do not at all correspond to the expectations described above. Most artisanal fishermen were expected to stick till their end unable or unwilling to adapt, and a few were expected to try and fail in modern fisheries. However, my findings present quite another picture. The typical career path of an artisanal fisherman is not that of the traditionalist, but a technologically mobile person trying other technology levels before (currently) landing in artisanal fisheries. Only 18 per cent had never tried industrial technology, the rest had earlier worked aboard modern boats, not as short episodes, but most of them for longer periods. Does this village contain an improbable magnitude of complete failures? Are all exceptional fishermen pushed down to the low form of technology?

Contrary to expectations, the fishermen who are included in Always Low have careers shorter than the group average, and the four fishermen with career paths Earlier High are young as well. The fishermen with careers longer than the group average are those who have the career paths Earlier Intermediate, and Earlier Intermediate and High. This indicates that those who turn or return to artisanal fisheries from higher forms of technology are older fishermen – *but only if they were old when they (re)turned to low technology*. Their age at the time of the retrogression is presented below. It should also be mentioned that six fishermen earlier combined low form of technology with intermediate or high forms of technology, and that three fishermen had tried other occupations.

Combination

In total, 22 fishermen have combined technologies at different productivity levels. Twelve of them still did at the time of the study; the others have combined by season or weekly in earlier periods of their careers. Nine fishermen combined low and intermediate forms of technology, and seven combined low and high. Three fishermen combined high and intermediate forms of technology, whereas two combined two intermediate technologies, and one fisherman combined two low technologies. Combinations occur from 1940 onwards. The hypothesis that combination of low and higher levels of technology should occur *because of uncertainty in the early phase of modernization* is thus not supported. When the last job before combination is investigated, it appears that 11 of the fishermen moved from a higher level to a combination with low form of technology. The length of the period of combination varies from 1 to 31 years; the average is 14 years. There are many types of combination, but all who combined technologies at different levels claimed that they had to do so *to earn enough*. They are poorer than the rest of the fishermen. In conclusion: in Kuala Kedah, as well as in the Sri Lankan villages studied, combination of technologies at different levels should *not* be considered a means of the uncertain technological laggard for trying out new technology, while safely keeping one leg in artisanal fisheries. I rather consider it to be a way for the poorer to survive, as cases of multiactivity within the fishing industry.

Interrupted careers

In Kuala Kedah, 19 fishermen have tried other occupations for one year or longer and one fisherman has been ill for five years. Three of them are now artisanal fishermen, three work on purse seiners, and 14 of them are trawler fishermen. Before the interruption, however, nine of them worked as purse seiner fishermen. Most of the fishermen who tried other jobs were young. Ten had worked less than five years, and only two more than 10 years when they stopped fishing. On average, they stopped fishing for 4.2 years. The shortest period registered was a little less than a year, the longest period was 21 years. Many different occupations were tried out: small fish vendors, construction workers, sailors, in the police force, security guards and workers in agriculture.

The interruptions occur during the whole period of investigation, which indicates that there were always a few fishermen dissatisfied with the work – or were they rather dissatisfied with the living standard they obtained in the fishing industry?

There are reasons why one should expect sample fishermen who have left the village to work elsewhere for a period, to appear well off as compared to their neighbours. The things which people normally buy when they are away are consumer durables (such as radios), which influence the measurement of living standard. However, my findings showed that the fishermen who have had interrupted careers are poorer than those who have had no interruptions. This indicates that their earnings while they had other occupations were to a large extent used for food and clothing. Except for the very exceptional fisherman whose career path is shown in Figure 28, none of them owned boats before the interruption. Three fishermen, however, bought an artisanal craft after they returned; they were target workers.

Technology and standard of living

The hypothesis which structures my argument is that a high form of technology corresponds to good living conditions. My findings showed that there is a good correlation between the fishermen's present technology and their households' standard of living. Almost 88 per cent of those working within low form of technology were among the lower middle and the poor stratum of society. From those engaged in the intermediate form of technology, 67 per cent were among the lower and poor stratum, while 33 per cent among the upper middle and rich stratum. Within the high form of technology 15 per cent could be qualified as rich, 29 per cent upper middle class, while the rest 56 per cent were among the lower middle level and the poor.

Under other circumstances, that is, if all individuals classified for instance in the intermediate category had been working aboard purse seiners all the time, we would probably accept the above result without any reservations. But career paths differ. There are three ways to check this. One is to correlate the variable career *path – intermediate (or low or high) form of technology* and standard of living. Because of the sample size, this is not feasible. The second way is to figure out how many years each fisherman has worked aboard trawlers, purse seiners and/or *sampans/perahus*, and to correlate this with standard of living. The third way is to figure out how long a part of his career the fisherman has worked in modern fisheries. These ways have been tried out.

I investigated the significance of ownership of the means of production to the living standard. The result is quite clear; compared to the fishermen who never have owned a craft, the trawler owners are richer. Ownership of the means of production does, as expected, explain differences in standard of living among the fisherfolk. However, *the difference between owners of industrial boats and their crewmen is much greater than the difference between the owners of artisanal crafts and their crewmen.* This is not a manifestation of differences in technology level but reflects a change towards a less egalitarian society. Although the standard of living of artisanal fishermen is generally low, the variation which exists is not necessarily explained by ownership of the means of production alone. It may depend for instance on how great a part of the fisherman's career has been spent aboard the artisanal crafts. However, my findings show that neither the sheer number of years nor the share of career length spent in artisanal fisheries explains their household's standard of living.

In the intermediate form of technology, fishermen's chance to improve their standard of living increased very little with the absolute number of years they have spent in these fisheries, while the share of career length spent in intermediate form of technology did not correlate to an improvement of the standard of living. What concerns fishermen working with high form of technology, the results of the analysis have shown a correlation between share of career length and living standard. *The greater the share of advanced technology in the fisherman's technological past, the better his household's standard of living.* And the longer he has been aboard the trawler, the better off he is. The fact that fishermen who have spent less than 11 years in modern fisheries score low on the standard of living variable may be explained by the resource crisis. In the 1960s, it was easier for a fisherman to earn a lot in a short time and invest in a good house.

In conclusion, technological modernization has led to the betterment of many fishing households' standard of living. But there has been an increase in socio-economic polarization in the village society: Economic growth and economic inequality go hand in hand. The difference between rich and poor today, as seen with the villagers' eyes, has increased *immensely*.

Technological retrogression

In total, 86 fishermen have moved from a higher to a lower level of technology in terms of labour productivity, which is 40 per cent of the sample.[13] To 14 fishermen, the retrogression experience was but an episode, that is, they returned to the more advanced technology. As earlier shown, the fishermen mainly retrograded to inshore fisheries, and since most of them stayed there, they are to be found in the category of less advanced technology. It

---

[13] To sum up the information in the previous section: of the 86 fishermen who have experienced technological retrogression, 56 are artisanal fishermen pushed down from high or intermediate, 12 are purse seiner fishermen who earlier worked on trawlers (eight), or experienced episodes of technological retrogression (four). Ten are trawler fishermen who experienced similar episodes, and eight are combination fishermen who, while working on trawlers or purse seiners, started to combine with artisanal fisheries.

is also important to note that the fishermen who experience technological retrogression are crewmen, not boat owners. There are only three target workers, fishermen who worked aboard trawlers until they had earned enough to buy an artisanal craft.

The variables I have analysed in search of an explanation of retrogressive mobility of labour are whether they have any previous experience in artisanal fisheries when they retrograde, these fishermen's age, their households' standard of living and at what time retrogression occurs. The latter is related to the resource situation. Finally, the results of the investigation are summed up in a discussion of the rationality of behaviour of retrogression fishermen.

Turn or return?

Almost all fishermen interviewed (fishermen who have and who have not experienced technological retrogression) explained that they changed technology because their earnings were insufficient for survival. Only two fishermen said that they had to get a new job because the boat owner was dissatisfied with their work. Although there are sociocultural constraints which contribute to a limitation of the number of fishermen who lose their jobs, the real number may be higher, especially in cases of absentee ownership of the boats. Such causes may be hidden in the answer 'quarrels with the owner of the boat' when they were asked why they changed technology. This was the most frequent reason stated for moving down in technology level (57 per cent). The background of these quarrels was disagreements on the share system (six did not want to state the reason why). Three fishermen stated that they gave up the job on the trawler because of old age, and the rest said that they thought they would earn more. A few said that they turned to artisanal fisheries 'when the purse seiner closed business'.

According to the modernization view, retrogression fishermen should be conservatives *returning* to the safety of artisanal fisheries. The *work histories* enable me to analyse *how many* of the fishermen who have experienced a technological retrogression had previously had such experience. If they have, they *return*, if they do not have, they *turn* to low form of technology. My findings showed that *slightly more fishermen (53 per cent) who experience technological retrogression have no experience with the technology they move to.*

I searched for evidence that retrogression fishermen have more *negative attitudes* towards modern technology compared to those who had not experienced technological retrogression. No such differences could be traced. My observations are in perfect agreement with those of Gibbons (1977), who undertook research in Penang and Kedah fisheries in the 1970s, on the attitudes of traditional fishermen. He concluded that the

Malay fishermen, contrary to the view of their being tradition-bound and reluctant to innovate, seemed willing to change fishing methods, location of fishing, residence or even abandon fishing to raise their income and standard of living.

Those who have experienced and those who have not experienced technological retrogression have identical views on the resource situation as well as the future of the fisheries. What is even more important in terms of economic rationality is that there is hardly any difference in investment wishes between these groups. Those who have moved down are nearly as interested in investing in industrial technology as are the others (43 per cent of them wished to invest in trawlers). This also indicates that many would return to industrial fisheries – if prospects improve. Fishermen who have experienced technological retrogression were, however, more interested in investments in artisanal crafts than the others (24 per cent as compared to 10 per cent). In both groups, about 30 per cent had no investment wishes.

Old and tired?

Why is *age* an interesting variable when retrogressive mobility of labour is analysed? In the old days, when stability of careers was the rule and not the exception, it would have been unthinkable to push out older people who could not keep up with the speed aboard the craft. Gradually, the young and strong would take over the heaviest operations and dwindling physical strength among the old would be made up by knowledge of resource location and techniques of fishing. To me, it seems normal that older people are pushed out of modern fisheries, probably because capitalism to me is the normal system, and devaluation of the less productive of the society seems the normal thing. The old fisherman who told me that he had to stop working aboard a trawler 'because the others seemed reluctant to work with me any longer' judged it differently. He has experienced the time when respect for old people was inherent in culture. To him, the effects of the formation of free labour seem inhuman, and he feels that he now is living in hard times. The age of this retrogression fisherman is exceptional. Still, I think, tradition to some extent inhibits free mobility of labour. If cultural constraints were not there, more old fishermen will be pushed 'down'.

The fishermen who retrograde are not old. Seventy-four per cent of the fishermen who have experienced technological retrogression are under 41 years, and 84 per cent are under 46 years of age. The average age of the sample is 44 years (standard deviation 11). Testing of the representativity is not possible since accurate figures of the universe are unavailable. The older a fisherman gets, the more difficult it becomes to change technology. The young should be expected to be more technologically mobile. But even older fishermen change technology. If an older fisherman has experience from purse seiners or trawlers only, then the ancient technologies in the village are, in fact, new to him. The knowledge of techniques, fish behaviour and fishing grounds accumulated by artisanal fishermen should not be underestimated.

Rich or poor?

The fishermen who experience technological retrogression are poor. Ninety per cent of the fishermen who have experienced technological retrogression score below the middle standard of living value. It is thus highly probable that *retrogressive mobility is a strategy of the poor to improve their living standard.* In view of the present fish resource situation, it is equally probable that they try to prevent their standard of living from deteriorating. The reason why I consider the process rather dramatic is that the crewmen aboard artisanal crafts are the poorest group in the village: Most fishermen who move down join them. To me, it is a crux of thought that faced with similar fish resource situations, fishermen of industrial countries move *upwards* in terms of technology or leave the industry.

Time of occurrence

There are instances of technological retrogression during the whole period of investigation. The instances of technological retrogression increase in the early 1970s and reach a peak around 1975. In the period 1981–85, the number is still not down to the pre-1970 value. In the Sri Lankan case technological retrogression also occurred mainly during this period. The increase in oil prices is the major factor of explanation. As earlier explained, the increased expenses of inputs were deducted before the catches were shared. Thus, the effects of the crisis were turned over to the crewmen. When catches decrease, fuel costs (which account for a considerable proportion of the expenses) weigh more heavily on the owners' balance sheets.[14] This is felt by owners of outboard engines as well.

Trawlers and purse seiners where retrogression fishermen earlier worked still go fishing from Kuala Kedah: *The labour they lost was replaced with new.* In a community with a high unemployment level, this is not surprising. A large labour reserve also contributes to a lowering of the wage rate. In theory, the wage rate may decrease to the amount which will be accepted by the most

---

[14] Fredericks and Nair (1985, 125) found, both in the West and East coast villages studied, that 'Fuel turned out to be the most significant explanatory variable across gears and locations, and as such it can be considered as the limiting factor constraining catch.'

desperate of fishermen. The debut age of the fishermen has increased, which contributes to unemployment among the youth. On average, the fishermen who now are below 31 years got their first job when they were 17.2 years old, whereas the old fishermen (over 60 years) started when they were 15.3 years old. It was not uncommon that they started to work with their fathers before they were 13 years old. Few of the boys continue their education after secondary school. A heightening of the debut age contributes to an almost unlimited supply of labour.

Decreasing resources

Trial fishing has shown dramatically decreasing resources off the Kedah coast during the period 1966 to 1984, off the coast from Penang to Lankawi (the fishing grounds of the industrial fleet of Kuala Kedah). The decrease in resources normally exploited by trawlers represented a huge challenge for the few Malaysian patrol vessels. Violation of the zone regulation act was a severe resource management problem. As an artisanal fisherman smilingly put it, when asked about the resource situation in *inshore* fisheries, 'Everybody goes inshore these days. Even the trawlers.' An old artisanal fisherman told me the names of about 20 demersal species which had become extinct or had become rare.[15] This occurred during my pilot study when I discussed with the fishermen in a cafeteria. None of the many fishermen present contested his assertion. A probable hypothesis is that *decrease in inshore resources causes the slowing down of the retrogression trend in the 1980s.*

A question of 'culture'?

Of the relationships analysed, I found that the fishermen's age could not explain the retrogression process. The analysis of living standard brought me closer to an explanation; retrogressive mobility is a strategy of the poor to improve their living conditions – or rather, to prevent deterioration. Technological mobility is a strategy of crewmen, not of owners. Finally, the analysis of *when* technological retrogression occurred, combined with data showing resource situation, led me to the conclusion that a major cause of technological retrogression in Malaysian fisheries is decreasing resources.

---

[15] The species he listed were *temerik, ikan merah, ikan belanak, ikan selumbu, ikan senangen, ikan kekeh, ikan mengkeruh, ikan jerubuk, ikan pari, ikan nandung, ikan yu, ikan otek, ikan pelata, ikan tamban, ikan malong* and *ikan buki ayaur.* He also claimed that the last four years, the catch value was reduced from MR 30 to MR 10 a day. The purse seiner fishermen claimed that *mengkeroi, terubuk* and *selumbu* had become rare.

The reason why technological retrogression was considered a solution and not for instance further technological modernization is discussed in the final chapter: When explaining the process of technological retrogression, I find the concept of *structural constraint* too weak a characterization. Perhaps Galtung's (1974) concept of *structural violence* better describes causes of restrictions in freedom of choice which most fisherfolk now face.

Although half of the fishermen who experience technological retrogression had no earlier experience from artisanal fisheries, the question whether retrogressive mobility is a return to a traditional way of life still remains: Should I put more emphasis on the cultural dimension of the choice of technology? I have met with a *culture argument* when presenting my empirical findings to various audiences. My opponents insist that choice of less productive technology should be linked to cultural value systems; I may have failed to grasp how the fishermen themselves *conceptualize* their choices. I do not claim that retrogressive mobility of labour is *not* linked to culture. It is – since what partly explains the process is the reproduction of a relation which originates in a more egalitarian society, enabling the reproduction of a more egalitarian share system aboard the crafts to which fishermen (re)turn. The opponents did not, however, generalize at the societal level, but *at the individual*. Their arguments were somewhat more sophisticated than the modernization theorists', since they did not argue that the fishermen have 'traditional attitudes'. Rather, they claim, fishermen possess a *special kind of rationality* of behaviour which I fail to grasp: Because of their culture, fishermen do not necessarily choose the most productive technology, but for instance the one securing a special *way of life* aboard the craft. There is, however, no empirical evidence in support of such *non-income optimizing* rationality producing technological retrogression. I do realize that all data collected are already (pre-)conceptualized, and that there *are* special difficulties involved in cross-cultural research. I do not expect to have overcome all problems of communication. I find no reason, however, to believe that when the fishermen say 'income' they really mean 'better comradeship aboard *sampans*'.

One opponent who claimed that the fishermen chose social organization rather than technique, by consequence, questioned my operationalization: He argued that technology cannot be defined in terms of technique (type of craft) only. If I had not chosen labour productivity and capital intensity as criteria (both to a great extent determined by properties of technique), but for instance degree of 'independence', 'self-determination' or 'control over one's situation', then, what I term *retrogression* would appear as *progress*.

I believe that *perceived income-generating capacity is decisive when technology is chosen*, which implies that I think *technique* (boat and gear) is actively chosen, social organization they get into the bargain: One social organization of production may be preferable to another (irrespective of technique), and one position within the crew may be preferable to another. But one cannot choose freely: like having the social organization common on *sampans* transferred to trawlers. Technical constraints, established practices linked to profitability, prevent this. How the crew is organized of course influences productivity. But no matter how well fishermen cooperate and how well they know where resources are, their production capacity is linked closely to type of boat and gear. If I thought it necessary, I would suggest an investigation of social organization of production as a possible explanation factor of technological retrogression. But I do not. It would, however, be interesting from the point of view of examining technical versus socio-organizational constraints.

Furthermore, there are logical difficulties in considering retrogressive mobility of labour a function of rationality changes. If *non-income optimizing rationality* is considered a cultural heritage, *two* changes must have occurred: Firstly, when modern technology was accepted, its advantages must have been considered beneficial enough for them to shift from non-income-optimizing to income-optimizing rationality. Next, the fisherman finds out that he should not so easily have given up his previous way of life (he never quite liked modern technology, no matter how productive): He returns to non-income-optimizing rationality and thereby causes technological retrogression. Rationality, however, is not a turncoat. Such changes should be expected to be more lasting. Furthermore, there is no correlation between household life-cycle position and technological retrogression, which is an argument against a Chayanovian peasant rationality.

My arguments against a special rationality, whether culturally inherited or new, explaining technological retrogression, is *firstly* that I find it hard to attribute relatively sudden and simultaneous actions of many fishermen to cultural change, especially when it occurs simultaneously with changes in economic conditions: Technological retrogression in Sri Lankan fisheries came after an increase in cost of input factors due to the oil crisis. In the Malaysian case, resource depletion due to overexploitation increases simultaneously with the return to low-productive technologies. In the same period, disagreements on the share system became more frequent. Did the fishermen become more quarrelsome during this period (a cultural change) or was there less fish to share and thus more to quarrel about? The share system was the same during the whole period, ensuring that the boat owners got their expenses covered firstly. On some trips, the crewmen earned nothing.

Secondly, I find it hard to dispute the reasons stated by *the fishermen themselves* as to why they changed technology. When they claim it was to try to get a better income, I did not attempt to convince them that the real cause was another. I did try to capture underlying reasons when their statements were of a kind not instantly understandable. For instance, when they attributed the change to 'quarrels with the owners', I had to find out what caused the conflicts, leading me to the share system and dissatisfaction with their shares.

Thirdly, I am convinced that these fisherfolk's rationality does not differ much from my own capitalist one. Observations on consumer behaviour and preferences during the collection of information on living standard, as well as the more diffuse knowledge gained when getting acquainted with people, taught me that basically, we share visions of a good life in the material sense.[16] But fulfilling their aspirations now requires *much higher incomes* than what were common in the village a few decades ago. The rich already have some of the attractive items, and their aspirations on material consumption are continuously rising. The model is the consumption patterns typical of the urban areas. The poor have the same material aspirations – but no buying power. I do *not* attribute differences in level of consumption to differences in consumer preferences.

Fourthly, I could not detect any trace of an 'ecological' rationality resulting in changed behaviour. Although admitting that the rate of resource exploitation perhaps was wiser in the past, many fishermen, irrespective of the technology they use, would like to invest in trawlers – if they get the chance. Kurien (1978) claims that fishermen everywhere have *always* tried to obtain *maximum yield* of their operations. Such an indigenous income-optimal rationality might be explained by fishing communities' long history of market integration. Early in fishing communities a market economy developed together with specialization: It is possible for a farming community to be self-sufficient, but fisherfolk cannot live solely on animal proteins. There is no such category as a *subsistence fisherman* in the narrow sense.

The Kuala Jerlun hypothesis

According to local informers, Kuala Jerlun is typical of the small fishing villages on the Kedah coast. It is situated about 20 km north of Kuala Kedah in an important agricultural area. There are about 146 fishermen in this village (LKIM 1985). The information was collected with the objective of formulating new hypotheses; therefore, only 18 fishermen were interviewed.

---

[16] What is observed by Sang-Bok (1977, 125) as regards South Korean fishermen is valid in my cases too:

Although frequently the islanders' lack of motivation to accept innovation is cited by government officials as the reason for lack of progress, in reality the islanders are ready to accept new ideas and technology. They are discontent with present conditions and try to improve them, anticipating future rewards.

The data collection procedure described above was followed. Here I include a short summary of the findings only.

I thought that in this community, technological retrogression would not occur, since the fisherfolk perhaps would get work in agriculture (which might reduce possible lock-in effect). Additional income sources are more important here, 11 of the 18 households had additional incomes. Two of the wives worked in rice agriculture during peak season, and nine of the fishermen had irregular jobs as labourers, mainly in agriculture. But a retrogressive mobility of labour was found here too; six fishermen of the total of 18 had experienced it, which equals the frequency in Kuala Kedah. In fact, when technological change is analysed based on this tiny sample, this little village appears to be a miniature Kuala Kedah. The hypothesis that the processes at work in the larger community of Kuala Kedah would not reach the remote small community of Kuala Jerlun is falsified. The findings from Kuala Jerlun demonstrate that resources depletion is felt in the Northern part of the Kedah coastline as well and inspires to further investigation of the process. The serious fish resource situation in the Malacca Strait makes the whole industry more vulnerable to world market fluctuations of oil prices. A probable hypothesis is that the process of technological retrogression as described in the case of Kuala Kedah and Kuala Jerlun has occurred in many of the hundreds of fishing villages from Thailand to Singapore.

Perceptions on the villages' future

At the time of the study, most fishermen in Kuala Kedah perceived the future of fisheries to be very bleak. Only 6 per cent encouraged boys to go into fisheries, 18 per cent felt that they should become fishermen only if they had no other qualifications whereas 66 per cent discouraged the youth. Many who considered the future of fisheries to be dark had no investment wishes. However, even *more* of them still wished to invest in fisheries. When their future investment wishes are correlated with their view of the future of fisheries, this inconsistency in opinion becomes visible. Do they, perhaps, wish to invest in other types of boats to be able to exploit other species? The cause of the widespread pessimism as regards the future is the resource situation: About 70 per cent of the fishermen think that fish resources are decreasing. The same inconsistency in opinion appears when investment wishes are correlated with their perception of the fish resource situation. When they obviously see that fish resources are dramatically reduced, an observation which marine biologists agree with, why do they stubbornly wish to invest in fisheries?

When facing decreasing resources threatening standard of living, fishermen look to the better off in the community. They are the owners of trawlers: The future may be dark, fish resources are decreasing, but this does not necessarily affect *me*. There is still some fish left. I may be among the lucky ones – if only I can get a boat. The observations of Munro and Chee support this interpretation:

> Although the average return is low, and the failure rate high, the industry continues to expand. Essentially it is a matter of the new entrants expecting to be among the fortunate who still enjoy high returns. (Munro and Chee 1978, 38)

As shown, the fishermen have good reasons to relate high standard of living to high form of technology, since the prospects of prosperity with technological modernization were good for a long period of time. Hence, I do not question the *economic rationality* steering the inclinations or actions of the individual. Another matter is the game theory argument that the outcome of a series of such rational actions, undertaken separately by individual actors, may be irrational for all of them in the long run. Most fishermen who wish to invest do not have the capital to do so. But these results show that if they are provided with capital, they probably will invest in fisheries, no matter how they evaluate the resource situation. On the horizon of change, there is a potential for further overexploitation.

A typical way of getting out of a *resource squeeze* in the fisheries of industrial countries is to invest in *ultra-modern* technology, that is, deep sea fishing in remote waters. This is way beyond the capability of the (very) petty capitalists of Kuala Kedah. The boats they wish they could afford are not equipped for deep sea fishing: 56 per cent of the fishermen who wished to invest in a new modern boat would invest in a small trawler, 28 per cent wished to invest in a big trawler, whereas 14 per cent would like to invest in any trawler. Only 2 per cent wished to buy purse seiners. As regards investments in ultra-modern technology, the only chance is to mobilize non-local capital owners. In a situation with decreasing resources, the price of fish will increase. This will prolong the period of interest for investment in fisheries by the absentee owners. But if the prospect of profits decreases radically, will they be interested in investments in fisheries at all?

The reconstruction of technological change shows that the process of technological modernization has become retarded, even stagnated. And when the process of technological retrogression is at work, artisanal fisheries are not going to die with the old users. But *the artisanal fishery to which they turn or return is not the fishery many left*: Firstly, artisanal fishermen consider inshore resources to be decreasing, and any inflow of labour into these fisheries will increase overexploitation. Secondly, technological polarization can be observed within artisanal fisheries: On the one hand, artisanal fishermen who can afford it have put outboard engines aboard their crafts. This minor technological modernization has led to increased dependence upon price fluctuations of oil. On the other hand, the artisanal fishermen who cannot afford to buy outboard engines turn to rowing crafts. This change implies a retrogression of tools, quite like the process found within Sri Lankan fisheries: When the motors came in, the sails went out. When fishermen now turn or return to artisanal fisheries, the skilled artisanal fishermen who know sailing techniques work on trawlers or are dead.

Most Kuala Kedah fishermen are now modern in terms of technology, but will they remain so? They probably will; but only if the absentee owners do not experience severe losses and alternative job opportunities are few. Although the fishermen's chance to improve or uphold their standard of living within industrial fisheries is reduced, decreasing inshore resources may make technological retrogression an unprofitable alternative. However, if *one sacrifices labour productivity within artisanal fisheries*, the threat represented by increased prices of inputs may diminish: If the outboard engines are removed, artisanal crafts may be even more competitive for labour than they are today. There is also a potential for further retrogression of tools: Gathering of clams and the use of primitive crab traps by formerly industrial fishermen are cases in point.

If more and more industrial fishermen turn or return and young inexperienced fishermen are also attracted to artisanal fisheries, this does not necessarily affect the absolute number of industrial boats in the village. Labour will be recruited when unemployment prevails. But the already high turnover of labour aboard these boats may well increase. The number of technology choices of industrial fishermen decreases; and they are dilemmas rather than choices. The fishermen are between the devil and the deep blue sea; that is, between retrogressive technological mobility and the utopia of ultra-modern deep-sea fishing technology. In addition to vast amounts of capital, the village fishermen lack adequate training to man such boats.

The strategies of the poor fishermen are manifold. They try other occupations, they, or their wives and children, try laborious extra jobs, they rely on relatives in times of distress, they fight in vain with boat owners to increase the share of the catch, they combine technologies, they want to move up but must move down in technological level. What do they achieve? In terms of living standard, a few may have moved up from poor to lower middle; the rest struggle in vain. Faced with steadily decreasing fish resources, they must increase their efforts to prevent their living conditions from deteriorating. Like the Red Queen told Alice,

> It takes all the running *you* can do, to keep in the same place. If you want to get somewhere else, you must run at least twice as fast as that! (Carroll 1872, 216, emphasis in the original)

Chapter 6

A THEORY OF TECHNOLOGICAL RETROGRESSION

It is time to assemble the building blocks and present a theory of technological retrogression. Lessons learned from the empirical studies are presented first, forming the basis of a discussion on economic structures, the nature of capitalism manifested. I conclude that the transition to capitalism is *frozen*, supporting the dependency theory stance of peripheral capitalism: Lacking diversification of the economy at large partly explains the lock-in found in the cases analysed and thus reproduction of ancient production system relations. These insights are used to confront the evolutionism of both classical and Marxist modernization theory: Modernization may reverse, irreversibility is an empirical question, not a dogma. The process of technological retrogression is finally sought interpreted in Schumpeterian terms: Retrogressive economic dynamics are at work simultaneously with the progressive dynamics described in Schumpeter's theory. While the progressive dynamics result in technological progress and ultimately prosperity, retrogressive dynamics pushes producers into deepening poverty. The result is economic and social polarization.

Changes and continuity in the fishing villages

The fishing villages witnessed an immense technological polarization, which was reinforced by technological retrogression. The accompanying socio-economic polarization, increased by the opening of the village society through market expansion, led to sociocultural changes which should be studied with better tools than mine. The changes, however, have been fundamental. It can be argued that the price of economic growth was the breakdown of ancient social values: The share systems now promote social inequality, and absentee ownership has been introduced, reducing local control over production. The fisherfolk are now part of larger and even more complex systems: larger external markets and increasing scale of the fishing operations.

Before the inflow of modern Western technologies, the fishing communities were characterized by low level of productivity and a relatively equal surplus distribution, resulting in limited capital formation. Even if the total surplus were reinvested in productive activities, technological modernization based on locally accumulated capital would have been slow. Increased demand spurred non-local investors' interest in the exploitation of the fish resources. In Malaysia this resulted in a massive investment in modern technology. These industrial technologies have, however, not eradicated the artisanal; to the contrary, technological heterogeneity continued and deepened and were reinforced by the processes which reproduce artisanal technology. There was a high degree of heterogeneity in the villages studied. The production systems now encompass some new, some unaltered and some transformed relations of an ancient production system resembling the ideal type artisanal production system sketched above. Of the introduced new technologies, few seem to be modified in contact with the traditional environment, although during the early phase of technological modernization, some artisanal elements were adapted aboard industrial boats. Artisanal fishermen have, however, adapted many elements of modern technologies. But it will require more thorough technical, historical and anthropological studies to find exactly when the production systems got their present shapes.

The introduction of modern technology increased the rate of resource exploitation immensely. Production increase and market expansion led to reduced local control of resources. Fish marketing was no longer controlled by local middlemen but by city merchants. New technology was accompanied by share systems with low returns to labour, and a new principle of labour recruitment (from the preference of family labour to the preference of the best skilled) now operates in the villages. This was most evident as regards the recruitment to industrial boats. It is not possible, based on this investigation, to judge to what extent labour has become a commodity. The shift from family labour to free labour is under way, a change which is a prerequisite for capitalist production. In the present situation, labour supply is ample. And the process of the formation of free labour has been incomplete. This does not represent a serious limitation to capital accumulation.

At the time of the studies some share systems with high returns to labour had survived capitalist penetration. However, the price squeeze felt by artisanal fishermen may well lead to an undermining of their recruitment and catch share custom in future. Another survivor is the extraction of free labour for the maintenance of crafts – both artisanal and industrial. Still, artisanal as well as industrial fishermen depend upon various types of traditional security nets: In times of crisis, they lend money from their relatives, boat owners, middlemen or moneylenders, a characteristic of an artisanal production system. Some sources are not open to all, whereas artisanal fishermen rely mostly on their relatives, the industrial fishermen's major source of credit became the boat owners. It has thus been substantiated that security nets manifest themselves in new forms but have kept their basic function. I also underline that when studying technological change, it is essential to understand that technology is but *one* dimension of a production system; technological change may be conditioned by characteristics of other relations.

Technological heterogeneity is pronounced, but artisanal fishermen do not exist in splendid isolation from the modern world as part of a traditional sector. Artisanal fishermen, as well as industrial, work within *one* production system, which, lacking a better word, I have termed *a mixed production system*. The survived relations identified cannot be analytically arranged to form a totality which can be reproduced. Hence, they neither form a coherent production system, a sector, nor a form or mode of production. My investigation supports an *interconnected relations* stance. The technological mobility of the fishermen (making industrial fishermen dependent on a continuation of artisanal fisheries), the world market integration of artisanal fisheries, their dependence on non-local and imported inputs, the reproduction of ancient security nets, the actual and potential danger of overexploitation of the resources as the ultimate consequence of technological modernization – all these processes undermine any notion of separate, coherent economic spheres.

The modern technology introduced did not bring with it a separate economic sphere. This contests the conception of structural features of technologically heterogeneous fishing societies inspired by modernization theory (the dual society with a traditional and a modern sector), as well as the orthodox Marxist dualist contention of coexisting coherent modes of production. Whether the understanding of the *articulationists* meets with a similar destiny is a matter of judgement. I do consider the social formations in question *capitalist*, but will a more comprehensive analysis reveal the articulation of modes of production, where capitalism articulates to one or several modes (or forms) of production? It clearly depends on how mode or form is defined, and how the concept of articulation is understood. I conclude that *singular relations* of a previous production system are being reproduced, and that their reproduction is enabling in two senses; firstly, the reproduction of artisanal technology and security nets enables capital accumulation of owners of industrial boats (by lowering the wage rate); and secondly, the reproduction of artisanal technology enables the survival of marginalized producers through retrogressive mobility of labour. The (re)turners experience a reduction of exploitation (due to the more egalitarian artisanal share system), but their modernization vanished and with it the prospects of an improved standard of living. The articulation discourse on causes of reproduction of non-capitalist relations, as well as the notion of capitalist dominance found in dependency theory aided this understanding: My conclusion is very close to the notion of reproduction of labour in the pre-capitalist sector, found in dependency theory.

To position these results into an articulation discourse, the relationship between the Marxist concept of mode of production and the ideal type production systems should be sorted out. I must admit, however, that I consider this a futile exercise, since Marxist theory is here used as an aid to expose mechanisms, not to 'prove' a theory. The concept of *articulation*, that the reproduction of non-capitalist relations may be functional for the reproduction of capitalism, is worth discussing, but the concept of *coherence* (whether non-capitalist relations form systems able at reproduction as such or whether only singular relations of dissolved systems are being reproduced) is of importance only if one wishes to take part in an evolutionist discourse. Furthermore, the question of coherence is not only one of conceptual (un?) clarity but an *empirical* question: Suppose a researcher of the articulating coherent modes position and myself studied the same production system. We were in the village at the same point in time, asking the same questions, using the same method. The researcher of the other position concluded 'Eureka! We are faced with three articulating forms of production: A Chinese, an artisanal and a capitalist, making manifest the articulation of the capitalist and the petty commodity mode of production!' If (for the sake of the argument) I agreed that modes of production can be empirically reconstructed, I would perhaps conclude that I failed to identify more than one. We would have to clarify the concepts. My best bet is that the discrepancies can be traced to at what level of abstraction the concept of mode of production is sought conceptualized. But if our studies were undertaken in different contexts, I would not be able to refute his conclusions that easily. The point is that in some situations, analyses may uncover that capitalism articulates coherent systems, in other situations singular relations of dissolved systems – I do suspect, however, that this discourse is primarily a question of – words.

Causes and triggers of technological retrogression

The events that triggered the process of technological retrogression in the cases described are used to 'label' the conclusions. The Malaysian is the case of overexploitation of resources; the Sri Lankan is referred to as the case of oil price vulnerability; historical parallels referred to are termed the case of capital shortage, and the case of increased international competition/capital shortage. Firstly, however, it should be mentioned that when analysing the outcomes of technological modernization, I have met with the problem that it is very difficult to separate the effects of technological change from that of changed scale of production. This is of special relevance here; but I have not made any attempts at differentiating between them in the models. Stigler claims that

> the effects of scale economics are virtually inseparable from the effect of technical change [...] the two factors are so completely intertwined that any attempt to separate the one from the other is only hypothetical. (Stigler 1961 in Reinert 1980, 94)

The concept of technological change here refers to *modernization*, but the argument is valid in the case of retrogression as well. For instance, both reduced scale of operation and retrogression of tools may lead to a lower rate of resource exploitation. If these occur simultaneously, it is difficult to decide which factor produces the effect.

Furthermore, there are in the models pointed at strategies of owners and crewmen which are *not* empirically investigated. Since these are included, the models should be interpreted as possible outcomes of technological change and increased scale of production. Secondly, it may be useful to recall the contents of the concepts: Retrogressive mobility of labour denotes the outcome of the crewman's choice when he chooses to join a craft where labour productivity is lower. Retrogression of tools denotes changes of boat and/or gear which result in reduced labour productivity. There is thus a retrogressive mobility of labour involved although there may be no change of crew. The crewmen's reduced productivity is then the consequence of the owner's strategy.

Overexploitation

The results of the investigation of the Malaysian case are sketched in Figure 33. When modern technology entered the scene, skilled labour was recruited to the new boats, which presented a dilemma to the owners of artisanal crafts. Some of them invested in outboard engines and continued to exploit the same resources (technological advance), whereas others retrogressed from sails to oars. This contributed to an increased pressure on inshore resources, the crowding in inshore fisheries. If artisanal fishermen's statements are to be trusted, there is reason to believe that industrial boats, especially the small trawlers, have contributed to this.

The time of occurrence of technological retrogression in Malaysia shows that increased price of input during the oil crises triggered the process, but severe overfishing is the single most important factor of explanation of technological retrogression here. This led to income reductions, presenting

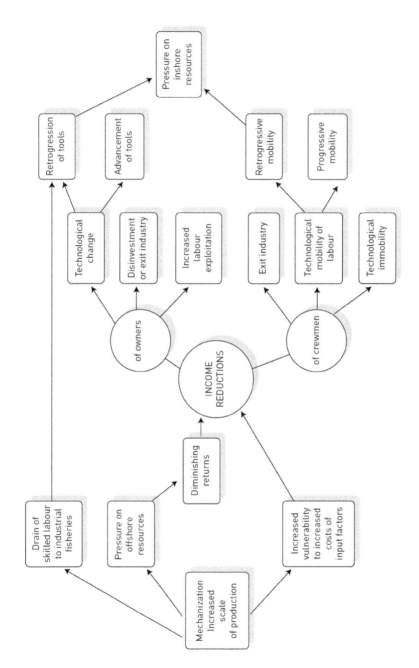

Figure 33 The Malaysian case: Overexploitation.

the boat owners with the options presented in the model; among owners of industrial boats, however, increased labour exploitation by turning over the effects of the crises to the crewmen was the preferred solution.

A justification for the argument that the crewmen were hit the harder by the increased price of inputs and the decrease in resources is the fact that many crewmen chose technological retrogression, the retrogressive mobility of labour option of the model. To exit the industry was not considered a viable option; many fishermen stayed aboard the industrial boats (technological immobility). To search for work aboard ultra-modern boats (progressive mobility of labour) was a theoretical possibility only for these Malaysian fishermen, but the (re) turn to artisanal fisheries has for many been a practical and preferred solution. This technological mobility of labour is not necessarily positive in the long run. Firstly, the chance of improving their standard of living is low, due to the low labour productivity of artisanal technology. Secondly, a continued expansion of inshore fisheries will ultimately lead to diminishing returns – and perhaps, to *further* technological retrogression.

In fisheries, like in manufacturing industry, capital owners' profits may decrease when prices of inputs increase. But in fisheries, share systems secure the spread, and in some cases even the turning over of the negative effects to the crew. In fact, the crew may carry the whole burden, since expenses are deducted before they get their share. Industrial fishermen are severely exploited. This is how decreasing resources combined with increased fuel prices put pressure on the wage rate in modern fisheries and result in technological mobility of labour. Since there is no scarcity of labour, those who leave the modern boats are instantly replaced by unemployed fishermen and youngsters.

Based on my investigation it is not possible to discern whether the fisherfolk now face the *extensive* or the *intensive margin diminishing returns*. It will be recalled that the former denotes the resource quality depletion situation which may result from a prolonged use of resources which are gradually depleted, or when new and inferior resources are exploited. The other factors of production are constant, there is no increase in scale of operation or in technology. In contrast, the intensive margin is the labour/capital pressure situation where more technology and labour are added to a fixed amount of resources. To substantiate which type of diminishing returns is found requires more studies; my first hypothesis would be that the Malaysian case should be termed a case of combined extensive and intensive margin diminishing returns. Increased amounts of capital (more technology) and labour (more fishermen) are applied to a decreasing physical quantity and deteriorating quality of a factor of production (the resources). Ultimately, whether the situation facing the fisherfolk resulted from one or the other type of diminishing returns, the outcome may be identical. Overexploiting a biological resource, the producers endanger their natural capital.

I started out with the statement that technological modernization led to a pronounced technological polarization. When faced with the problem of diminishing returns, this hypothesis should perhaps be contrasted to the converse hypothesis, namely that a more thorough investigation would reveal that there has been a *convergence* of the productivity levels of industrial and artisanal technologies. No doubt, labour productivity is reduced – but can it be reduced to a point lower than that of artisanal technology? Can mobility of labour from artisanal to industrial boats be a progressive mobility in terms of labour productivity? I do not think that it is *possible* to operate industrial boats if labour productivity is reduced to that of artisanal crafts. They would be unable to pay for the fuel needed. Productivity was probably still higher aboard industrial boats, but due to a more egalitarian share system aboard artisanal boats there is a higher return to labour. The returners, however, do not come back to the fisheries they once left. In the meantime, the rate of exploitation of inshore resources has increased.

Oil price vulnerability

While it is true that primary production is vulnerable to diminishing returns, fisheries do not *continuously* experience diminishing returns. Producers are driven into diminishing returns unless measures are taken *not* to exhaust the limitations of nature, the carrying capacity. This means that producers that move out of areas that are endangered will avoid diminishing returns. But a rise in the prices of inputs may make this option, for example, investing in boats that go further out, untenable. If they must turn to less modern boats, they increase the exploitation of inshore resources and drive *these* fisheries into diminishing returns. So, when producers start to exploit other resources, returns will increase until the 'danger level' is reached.

The model sketched in Figure 34 shows the results from the Sri Lankan case. Here, the tendency of inshore crowding is pronounced; there was thus a potential for overexploiting the resources here as well. Like in the Malaysian case, part of the explanation was a drain of the skilled fishermen to industrial fisheries.

An important factor of explanation of technological *stagnation* in the Sri Lankan case is shortage of capital, but the single most important factor of explanation of technological retrogression is the increased price of oil. Some of the owners of industrial boats tried to mitigate this effect by attaching sails, which reduced oil costs. The crewmen, however, faced the same situation as

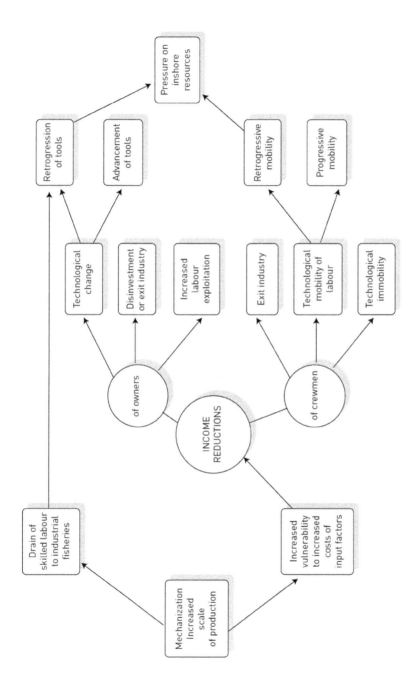

Figure 34 The Sri Lankan case: Oil price vulnerability.

described in the Malaysian case; the effect of the crisis was turned over from boat owners to crewmen.

To struggle with oars and destitution: Historical parallels

Although overlooked by theorists of technological change, historians have documented that the fisherfolk of Norway experienced a reversal of technological modernization twice, in both cases during severe economic crises. Historians term this process *primitivization*. In the mid-eighteenth century, evidence suggests that

> fishermen left the more advanced methods of nets and lines and turned to handlining, thereby giving up the equipment which they hoped would give bigger catches per man. The cause of this paradoxical setback is presumably that the fish merchants were reluctant to supply credit. The fishermen were therefore forced to use the cheapest and most simple equipment. (Dyrvik 1988, 117, my translation)

To meet the crisis of capital shortage, the fishermen practised a cost reduction strategy. They kept the boats, but to reduce the cost of maintaining and renewing the modern equipment, they turned to retrogression of tools (Figure 35).

Again, this time during the Great Depression of the 1930s, a reversal could be witnessed. Since the turn of the century, technological advancement had been significant; the most important change was that mechanized boats to a great extent replaced open rowing and sailing crafts. This continued during the Depression, but at the same time,

> the opposite, a 'primitivization' occurred. In Lofoten, handlining had almost disappeared in the beginning of the century. In the 1930s, nearly half of the fishermen used the simplest of all fishing methods during the Lofoten seasonal cod fisheries. (Bull 1988, 160, my translation)

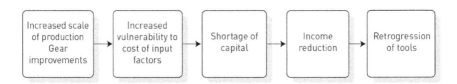

Figure 35 The first Norwegian case: Capital shortage.

The extent of the process described was sizeable in the cod fisheries. The number of participants in the Lofoten seasonal cod fisheries increased by a third from the 1920s to the 1930s, but this was not reflected in production volumes. Historians take this as an indicator of a lowering of labour productivity:

> This is how primitivization appears, in spite of the simultaneous technological progress in those years. (Bull 1988, 164, my translation)

The progress referred to is the echo sounder and stronger inboard motors, which the richer owners could invest in. Echo sounders were installed in state research vessels, and information on the location of fish was broadcasted (Bull 1988). In this manner, the positive effects of this invention were spread even before it got a 'democratic price'.

In herring fisheries, the answer to the crisis was technological modernization and increased production. But a similar process, yet even more dramatic, was observed in the small community of Veidholmen on the north-western coast. In 1920, there were nine rather big herring boats; in 1932–33, only two of them were used. During years of low demand and lacking investments maintaining and running of the modern boats became too costly. In this case, the fishermen went from big boats to rowing crafts, where they had to 'struggle with oars and destitution' (Bull 1988, 163, my translation).

Historians point at capital shortages and increased international competition when explaining the phenomenon. The cost of maintenance of the equipment had become too high, and the cost reduction strategy again resulted in retrogression of tools. What the historians observe was a technological polarization, a situation with increased differences between low and high productive technologies. It was a solution which secured the spread of the most limited good of all during the Depression, namely workplaces (Figure 36).

In the literature I build on it is not possible to make certain whether the process described implies that the fishermen from one season to the other shifted from more to less advanced methods, which is my interpretation. There may be an additional explanation factor. They observed that the cod fisheries had become less advanced, but this may result from fleet expansion, which is possible where there is open access to resources: there may have been an inflow of labour from other industries, which had to make use of the cheapest gear.

The crises leading to retrogression of tools in the Norwegian cases seem to have *hit owners and crewmen alike*. The process was mainly the result of owners' cost reduction strategies, whereas in the Asian case studies are mainly cases of

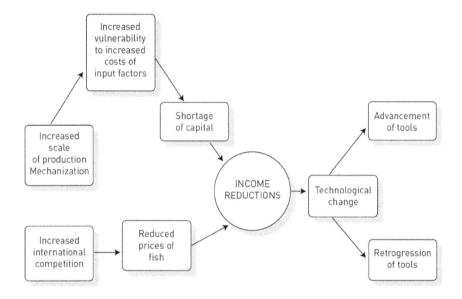

Figure 36 The second Norwegian case: Increased international competition and shortage of capital.

retrogressive mobility of labour, the result of strategies of crewmen to obtain a better share. The triggers of technological retrogression identified by the historians in the Norwegian cases are also dissimilar; diminishing returns due to overexploitation of resources resulting from technological progress are not mentioned as a factor of explanation in the Norwegian cases; but in all cases identified, technological modernization made the industry more vulnerable to increased costs of input factors.

A difficulty of drawing a historical parallel is that we know the end of the story in the one case, but not in the other. The problems causing technological retrogression in Norwegian fisheries found their solution a long time ago. In the example from the mid-eighteenth century, there was a gradual return to more modern methods in the decades after the plight. In the case of the 1930s, the return to advanced technologies came in the years following the Second World War, simultaneously with the exit of labour from the industry. The formation of huge labour reserves, fishermen willing to accept any wage, is not a characteristic of the Norwegian case. In fact, small-scale Norwegian fishermen were anxious that they would face such a situation. This is evident in their struggle to preserve the small-scale character of their fishing operations. In the 1930s, they feared that the entry of big business and the subsequent technological modernization would make a substantial portion of the fishing population 'superfluous'. Where would they go, in a time where both manufacturing industries and agriculture were overpopulated? (Bull 1988, 170, my translation)

According to Bull (1988, 170), in contrast to small-scale fisheries, 'organization of the trawler operations was capitalist'; the means of production were owned by shipping companies which also invested in manufacturing industry: The trawler fishermen were employed wage workers. But the small-scale fishermen's fight against 'rationalization' resulted in extensive organization building and political victories; a law limiting trawling came as early as 1936. When the *trawler question* was debated in Parliament in 1938, a member from Vesterålen argued that

> the fishermen do not want to become a wage proletariat, and lose even their freedom. (Bull 1988, 170, my translation)

There are still productivity differences between different types of fishing technologies in Norway, but extreme technological heterogeneity and dramatic retrogression processes are history. Technological retrogression in the Norwegian cases was temporary setbacks, the lock-in situations did not last long; since then, fisheries have modernized at a steady pace. Political organization of fishermen has secured the continuation of an increasingly more advanced small-scale coastal fleet, in addition to the capital-intensive one. The size of the fishing population has diminished; labour made superfluous in the process of technological modernization exited the fishing villages. They were to a large extent absorbed during the expansion of manufacturing after the Second World War.

Capitalism: pure, perverted, or peripheral?

Returning to the Asian fishing villages, the capitalism prevailing in these societies cannot be *pure*, since so many old relations are being reproduced. Being an ideal type with negligible empirical contents, capitalism is found in a pure state nowhere and never. What justifies this part of the above headline question is, however, my crux of thought, witnessing the extreme socio-economic polarization: *Is this the true face of capitalism if allowed to develop unchecked?* The factors mitigating the effects of labour exploitation in most industrialized countries are political. Trade unions struggle to increase returns to labour and to curb what they perceive are the negative effects of technological modernization. In addition, there may be systems of redistribution of the surplus of production; state welfare schemes are the result of more than a century of workers' struggles. Efficient resource management, however, is to some extent lacking both in industrialized and developing countries. Technological modernization in primary production occurred simultaneously with population growth in industrialized countries; spatial mobility was normally the strategy of producers made superfluous. Many historians consider a labour surplus in primary production a prerequisite for industrial growth, whereby the primary production revolution becomes necessary for the growth of manufacturing industries and the diversification of the economy. In developing countries, the industrialization process is extremely uneven.

To establish what kind of capitalism was found in the Asian fishing villages one must not solely study phenomena and processes which are manifest. Equally relevant is the counterfactual question on which relations *could have been there* if an industrial production system had been adopted in its totality. It was not; there was a *selective adoption*; technology and share systems with low returns to labour, and a non-adoption of relations which might mitigate exploitation: No effective state redistribution systems were introduced, and the line of division in labour organization follows divisions of technology rather than the capital/labour division. With the resource situation, what would Malaysian crewmen gain by fighting for a larger share of the catch? They probably felt that they had more to gain by supporting the owners in their fight against politicians who want to ban the trawlers. Lacking maintenance of boats bears witness of an increased rate of value extraction without compensation to the villagers: What profits there may be, are not reinvested in fisheries, boats are run down. The profits were not reinvested in more advanced technology, to go further out where and while there are resources.

To understand the politico-economic system, it is essential to establish which relations of old production systems vanish and which survive. Repeating my conclusion, *I found a selective reproduction of artisanal relations which were functional for the short-run capital accumulation of the owners of industrial boats, as well as for the survival of marginalized producers.* Labour is being reproduced through the reproduction of relations originating in the old production system, such as surplus distribution mechanisms and low-productive technology. Their reproduction is functional for the survival of the fisherfolk in the short run. But is their reproduction functional for the betterment of their living conditions in the long run? Would not the disappearance of artisanal technology and the vanishing of old security nets lead to an increase in the wage rate? For most fisherfolk, this is a futile question. When you live in poverty, wondering whether your family will have enough to survive the next month, you must live your life in the short run only. It may well be that I have studied the villagers' standard of living at the stage before starvation or migration to urban slums.

Or, optimistically, before a massive growth of manufacturing industries which absorbs the reserve army of labour.

There is an immediate objection to the above contention of 'functional for' capital accumulation; the connotations of the concept lead us to some strands of Marxist theory, where the outcomes of societal processes seem planned by evil capitalists. The notion of injustice inherent in structures, *structural violence* (Galtung 1974), is closer to my understanding of the limitation in the freedom of choice which the fisherfolk now face. He recommends 'the equation of structural violence with social injustice' (Galtung 1974, 37, my translation). As opposed to the concept of *exploitation*, structural violence turns the connotations away from the notion of a personal oppressor and towards the structural character of the social injustice: 'If people starve where it objectively can be avoided, violence is committed, whether there is a clear subject-action-object relationship [...] or not' (Galtung 1974, 36, my translation).

Recalling the orthodox Marxist position, the hypotheses derived on the causes of technological retrogression were active political resistance to capitalist penetration, and a strategy of capital owners to extract more surplus value. Both hypotheses are falsified. Where I have studied technological retrogression, it cannot be understood in terms of traditional resistance to change, neither in a culturally determined rationality version nor in a political resistance to the capitalism version. Although often occurring simultaneously, no collective political decision is behind the fishermen's actions. In many cases, the fishermen would have preferred to stay aboard the industrial boats – if they could. It is therefore a question of structural coercion rather than free choice or conscious political action. The continued existence of low-productive technology and ancient security nets probably has a restraining effect on the development of labour movements. In effect, they make starvation wages possible and are thus a major explanation of technological retrogression. The latter argument may lead to the conclusion that 'there has not been enough capitalism', traditional relations must be completely eradicated before the growth potential of capitalism can be evaluated. What is implied by 'more capitalism'? Increased scale of production? Will the introduction of more advanced technology by necessity lead to a more equal distribution of the economic surpluses produced? No. There is no automatic spread of riches and little trickle down to the poorest.

Rejecting the notion of *pure* capitalism, could the cases from the fishing villages in Sri Lanka and Malaysia be considered cases of *perverted* capitalism, exceptional in the history of capitalist expansion? Alternatively, are they cases of *peripheral* capitalism; are the phenomena observed typical of capitalist expansion in the Third World? According to its proponents, what capitalism at least should accomplish is the formation of a prosperous middle class, an expanding market for more and more goods. There is no shortage of commodities; in the towns and increasingly in the villages, all your heart's material desires can be bought. But buying power is diminishing among fisherfolk – and frustration increasing. Something went wrong in the process of capitalist penetration: The fisherfolk seem to be labour to be exploited rather than a market to be captured. It is difficult to substantiate the modernization hypothesis that the increased production resulting from technological modernization leads to welfare and growth, thus making superfluous security nets like the reliance on family networks and usury loans. Instead, old systems of social security are reproduced, but they are undermined and insufficient. A new security net has been invented, that of technological retrogression. In view of the consumption pressure which the villagers experience, the struggle to uphold their standard of living is harsh. The fisherfolk are exposed to Western mass consumption culture, glossy magazines and television advertisements fuel ever-growing expectations of increased consumption and comfortable lives. The rich trawler owners' wives now dream of Italian furniture; while aboard their boats, the crewmen's wages are decreasing in real terms to what only the most desperate of men can accept.

A frozen transition

Notwithstanding the above, it may be argued that the fishing villages studied experience *a period of transition*, it is just a matter of time, and they have all become modern: Relations of an industrial production system have gradually increased in importance during the past 50 years. But artisanal relations are continuously being reproduced: As regards technology, the relative strength of artisanal versus industrial technology in terms of employment has been stable for a long period of time, and a backwards movement is identified. The latter is not necessarily an argument against the ultimate argument of the modernization hypothesis; that all non-capitalist relations eventually die. Although the period of stagnation is more than a decade long, it can be interpreted as a temporary setback of modernization. However, to me it seems that the process of technological modernization has come to a dead end, where its lack of momentum cannot be explained by lack of capital or unwillingness among the producers to adopt. If not blocked, the transition seems frozen, and thawing up requires more than just time. It depends mainly on factors external to the villages: the world market price of oil, state resource management and ultimately the pace of industrialization, which increasingly depends on global markets.

Mechanisms of marginalization are, according to Amin (1976), the manifestation of the peripheral capitalist nature of Third World economies: Positive effects of technological modernization are way out of reach of many producers; their living conditions may even deteriorate as a result of the modernization. Technological retrogression has the characteristics of a marginalization process; my contribution to the furthering of development theory is thus that technological heterogeneity enables technological retrogression when labour exploitation deepens, resources are exhausted and when weak economies are hit by increased world market prices of essential raw materials. How far may retrogression processes go? Hypothetically, if the producers withdraw completely from the market, will this be a reversal of capitalism? This will be the case only if the resulting society becomes a non-integrated non-capitalist island. But future economic growth – if they are few and primary producers only – would depend upon a reopening of relations with the capitalist surroundings for supply of input factors and to market goods produced.

When modern technologies are chosen, the capacity to absorb labour is less than it would have been if increased production were achieved through a gradual expansion of artisanal fisheries. The introduction of high-productive boats may generate a labour surplus which would not be there if a lower rate of resource exploitation had been chosen. In both cases studied, the choice of more productive technologies made parts of the labour force superfluous. Retrogressive mobility of labour did not lead to a situation of undersupply: New labour immediately replaced those who exited industrial boats. If women are excluded, the labour reserve consists of unemployed experienced fishermen and young sons of fishermen who are unable to get work outside fisheries. Also, fishermen start their working career much later, which results in an increase in the number of unemployed young men. Technological mobility can thus be considered a consequence of low spatial mobility: Few have left the village; some have tried but returned. Instead of leaving to seek work in other places, they stay on and must retrograde technologically. The alternatives are considered unpromising or non-existent: the causes of which must be searched for in the insufficient differentiation and growth of national economies. The capacity to absorb labour within manufacturing industries and services was inadequate. Marginalized people, made superfluous in the industrialization process, must nevertheless make a living. Some of them turn to technologies which are inferior in terms of labour productivity. The reproduction of artisanal fisheries secures a labour reserve which may seize any chance for even a slight betterment of the prospects of income. Unemployment and underemployment in these fishing villages should therefore be analysed in terms of lacking outlets of labour and technological unemployment, since a major cause is lacking alternative employment and technology choice, rather than population increase. My results thus support Amin's (1976) theory of the formation of a reserve army of labour where producers, following Reinert's (1980) argument, are victims of lock-in. One may recommend more appropriate technologies and argue that the level of technology should have been chosen according to the job needs of the people. Regulating population growth is far more controversial. Fleet expansion may also be a dubious solution. Where the reproduction capacity of nature for decades is exceeded, the producers' problems can only be solved either by creating jobs outside fisheries or by a continued reduction of productivity levels within fisheries to absorb more labour. If a reasonable standard of living of the fisherfolk is to be achieved and upheld where resources are threatened, resource management systems must be developed which are accepted and respected by the fishermen. But equally important is that the society at large accepts a high level of subsidies. Fish resources, like land, is a limited and exhaustible source of wealth and thereby vulnerable to the process of diminishing returns.

According to Amin (1976), a large reserve army is functional for further capital accumulation, since it lowers the wage rate. Therefore, the unlimited supply of labour (Lewis 1954) partly explains why the wages in industrial fisheries may *remain* low. The fishermen who accept these wages have no other choices; they are willing to work for almost any wage: An iron law of wages is at work. But, as I have shown, there is a threshold which is reached when labour starts to flow from industrial to artisanal fisheries. The (re)turners believe that they, at least in the short run, will gain by doing so. Given the low standard of living of artisanal fishermen, I doubt that they consider the long-term prospects very promising. There is, however, an additional explanation of the pressure on the wage rate: industrial fishermen can accept a low wage because the security nets are being reproduced – and they are being reproduced because the wages are low:

> If the capitalist system does not provide adequately for old-age pensions, sick-leave and unemployment compensations, they have to rely on another comprehensive socio-economic organization to fulfil these vital needs. Consequently, preservation of the relations with the village and the familial community is an absolute requirement for the wage-earners, and so is the maintenance of the traditional mode of production as the only one capable of ensuring survival. (Meillassoux 1980, 198)

The continuation of redistribution mechanisms typical of an artisanal production system was insufficient for the upkeep of an egalitarian society. The contrast in living conditions of the privileged and the needy is immense.

The argument that an ample labour supply puts strain on security nets may mislead the readers to believe that overpopulation in the absolute sense has caused the poverty observed. To regard poverty as a population problem, indicates, firstly, that the villagers' misery is their own fault, and, secondly, that the solution is population control. It is neither: The technologies introduced were not democratically chosen by the fisherfolk. In many cases modernization was dictated by strong, mainly non-local economic interests. If poverty in fishing villages of Third World fish-exporting countries is considered a population problem, this would probably imply that we should recommend a regulation of their population according to the level of demand in the fish market in Tokyo. But what population control measures should we recommend to coastal communities which get their resources destroyed by foreign fishing vessels? A regulation according to the long-term prospects for the tuna and prawn population?

Amin (1976) argues that with technological modernization, the producers do not necessarily benefit: Unlike in the core economies, there is a non-correspondence between productivity improvements and the wage rate. The low wages benefit consumers in the First World as well as capital owners. I have, however, found that not only consumers and the elites benefitted from technological modernization. There is ample evidence that for some time, technological modernization improved the material living conditions of the producers. For a long time therefore, technological retrogression appeared as a paradox to me (who supports the notion of '*economic man*'). The hypothesis of a non-correspondence between the wage rate and productivity improvements cannot be substantiated. On the other hand, socioeconomic inequality, even polarization, is well documented, which supports Amin's theory; the owners of the means of production got the lion's share of the surplus resulting from technological modernization. Furthermore, that so many fishermen stay on the crafts while incomes reduce demonstrates that real wages are reversible in lock-in situations (Reinert 1980), affecting the shares of owners as well as those of crewmen.

Beyond doubt, the introduction of modern technologies has profoundly changed the character of the fishing societies. It cannot be held that these technologies brought with them their own, separate economic sphere, but it must be concluded that social relations of a capitalist character *associated with their introduction* have gained in importance. This does not imply, however, that the technologies introduced *by necessity* were carriers of capitalist relations of production and therefore should be characterized as capitalist technologies. In a sense, the introduction of modern Western technology brought with it capitalism – but here we must beware of technological determinism (unless, of course, you wish to argue that the Soviet agricultural producers in fact were using capitalist tractors for 70 years, and that this explains why private property was reintroduced in the former communist state). If you consider modern boats *by force of their origin* capitalist implements of labour, you must show me where aboard the boat capitalism is attached: There is no such thing as a capitalist tool. If you consider tools capitalist, you confuse the sphere of technology with the sphere of power. This may create an atmosphere of *inevitability* as regards social change: If you choose these tools, then you *must accept* private accumulation of wealth, changed redistributive mechanisms, destruction of nature and so on. This atmosphere of inevitability may, however, be convenient – for the actor who has the power to decide.

When modern technology is introduced, what is changed by necessity and what by choice? There are technical constraints to social organization of production – but there may be social constraints to the choice of tools. If we wish for a specific kind of society, we cannot choose all sorts of technologies: Labour absorption capacity in production is a case in point, exhaustion of natural resources another. Then, if we select an efficient tool – there comes capitalism? No. People can decide what kind of society they wish to have. The first problem with this contention is of course that this is not necessarily a democratic decision. It is not necessarily your choice as a crewman or petty capitalist boat owner. Those who wish for quick capital accumulation may have the power to choose – and the choice is accepted by someone who did not realize the vast potential for increased exploitation, of his labour power as well as the natural resources he depends upon. Not at the time when the choice was made, at least. The second problem is linked to the latter dimension; we may not understand the consequences of our actions. Perhaps most of the time, we do not. The devastation of natural resources is a case in point, in which my findings could be used as an argument.

Confronting evolutionism

When I contend that tools *an sich* (which are molecular clusters only) cannot be capitalist (socialist, social democratic, communist or whatever), I contest Marx's definition of the capitalist mode of production: The level of development of the productive forces (which include technology) should be high for capitalism to exist. In contrast, I claim that societies may be capitalist *although* they are technologically heterogeneous, and *although* the subsumption of labour by capital is incomplete. What is left of Marx in the concept of peripheral capitalism is thus that these processes have begun, and that the law of motion of the capitalist mode of production (the necessity of capital accumulation), may shape the direction of societal change. What should be added to this recipe is the concept of *super-exploitation*, and the dependency pie is cooked.

Marx needed the concept of the level of the productive forces in the theory of historical materialism; the antagonistic character of the relationship between the level of the productive forces and the relations of production produces the qualitative changes of societies, the ascent from a lower to a higher stage. This is central in his evolutionist scheme – which I can very well do without.

My research problem is not special in economic geography. We often study time–space edges, situations when new meets old. In studies by early development geographers, at the peak of the spatial analysis period, such interface situations were analysed in terms of modernization surfaces. To me, human geography represents a valuable scientific tradition in which one may search for ways to describe and analyse such situations. However, tradition never provides full answers, neither as to which problems we should investigate nor how they should be studied. And when searching for inspiration in tradition, I hope to have demonstrated that it is essential to distinguish between sophistication of social theory and sophistication of method. Then even modernization surfaces of diffusionists may have something to contribute.

I set out with conventional conceptions on how technological innovations diffuse in a population; my understanding is considerably shaken. I now find the causes of non-adoption of modern technology far more interesting than the causes of its adoption. At the heart of theories of diffusion of technology are modernization theories, based on empirical generalizations of historical experiences of industrial countries. These theories lack explanations of technological retrogression, which in simple words means that they offer no concepts which may characterize the process. Maybe those who reject modern technology have always been ignored? When sought to be explained in terms of modernization theory, knowers but non-adopters are either considered *Luddites* or simply stubborn traditionalists. It is often explicitly assumed that they are future adopters: it is only a matter of time, and we all will be modern.

Analysing why, when pushed out of modern production, producers turn to artisanal technology rather than to more advanced modern technology, or leave the industry, one is faced with a counterfactual inquiry to which an ideal type approach is particularly suited. When figuring out why only specific, not all, features of the industrial production system are found, fundamental differences between courses of technological change in industrial and developing countries appear. One such difference is that in the former countries, the building of manufacturing industry came simultaneously with labour displacements due to the mechanization in primary production. In developing countries today, there are fewer outlets of labour made superfluous. This approach also has the advantage that neither the eradication of old relations nor the non-adoption of new is overlooked.

The application of the old diffusionist modernization model on the course of technological change in the fishing societies studied was successful: Although its explanatory power is limited, it is useful when demonstrating consequences of dissimilarities in context when modern technology is introduced. To find such differences, modernization theories must be taken seriously. Modernization theories are more vital than some of us tend to assume. They should be dead, but 'they won't lie down': They provide the basis of most government planning, and to state the obvious, they provide the dominant ideology of international organizations such as Western aid agencies and the World Bank. Furthermore, development geographers originating in industrial countries must continuously confront the basic assumptions of modernization theories since they are an integral part of our cultural heritage: The ideology of progress is ingrained in our minds, especially the minds of students of technological change.

The technological changes I have described cannot be explained without theories which explicitly address Third World development. The processes of technological stagnation and retrogression found are inexplicable without them. Moreover, the phenomenon of technological retrogression cannot even be *discovered* without theories of Third World development. It would have been very easy *not* to observe the process: When you see a fisherman using a very low productive cast net on the shore day after day, do you consider it a matter of course that he earlier worked aboard a trawler? And if you try to reconstruct the process of technological change by means of boat statistics, you will *not* observe retrogression at all: it is an *intra-industry mobility of labour*, which only will become visible when many modern boats lie permanently idle. But why should they, in societies with, to paraphrase Lewis, an almost unlimited demand for workplaces? The fact that the process of technological retrogression becomes manifest in intra-industry mobility of labour, and therefore is variation hidden unless especially focused upon, has made me forever suspicious of aggregate figures.

When starting research in Third World countries, one must at the outset expect and understand that the production systems of these societies may be fundamentally different; diverging not only from contemporary production systems here, but in particular from our production systems of the *past*: There are other processes at work, resulting in dissimilar outcomes of similar interventions, for instance introduction of high technology. The differences may have been shaped in a colonial past but are being reinforced during the integration in a world economy which places developing countries in a subordinate position in the international division of labour. We have not yet succeeded in de-learning evolutionism. Problems of developing countries may remind us of our problems of the past, but the processes shaping them and ultimately their solutions may differ. This is of special significance now, when neoliberals rule the world: Theories based on empirical generalizations of Western experiences provide insufficient explanations as well as starting points.

Schumpeterian dynamics in reverse

Cascading fragilities, a metaphor cast by Erik S. Reinert, captures retrogressive economic dynamics.[1] Cascading fragilities are economic mechanisms, often induced by external shocks, that may precipitate chains of events producing retrogression, measured as falling real wages, increased mortality, use of less capital-intensive technologies, environmental degradation and energy shortages. Economies may move from financial fragility (Hyman Minsky's term) to wage fragility, livelihood fragility and, lastly, into a state of technological fragility. Understanding the last state of fragility is the core of this book. According to Schumpeter, the economy turns from decline to development during the downswing of a cycle, when entrepreneurs start adopting new technology. As demonstrated, Schumpeterian dynamics have an evil twin, retrogressive dynamics that are set in motion where (un) favourable contextual preconditions prevail. Myrdal's (1957) term *cumulative causation* can fruitfully be applied, depicting spiralling effects, positive and negative, of economic upturns and downturns. The twin theories are similar in that the cyclicality of capitalist economies is of major importance. Whereas Schumpeter discusses technological changes that result in increasing returns and economic progress, my theory points at changes resulting in diminishing returns and economic decline. The theory of technological retrogression is at odds with the conceptual frameworks that seek to capture technological change in classical (including Marxist), neo-classical as well as Schumpeterian economic thought.

Schumpeter's main contribution to theories of development is his analysis of the cyclicality of technological progress that results in economic and social development. The roles of inventors, entrepreneurs and foresighted capitalists that make the right choices are crucial. Cast in Schumpeterian terms, technological retrogression may be considered the *resurrection* of technologies and production systems previously swept away by gales of creative destruction. The concept of resurrection may have positive connotations; however, in my book there is no nostalgia: the phenomenon of technological retrogression is considered detrimental to economic growth, social and regional development.

---

[1] Erik S. Reinert, unpublished research proposal. The Other Canon, Cascading Fragilities. Conference, Voksenåsen, Oslo, June 2009.

There is thus a major difference between turning to the low-tech solutions of the past by choice and when their result is from structural coercion. In the contexts analysed, turning to production technologies and social organizations of the past are desperate remedies, other options are (or are perceived to be) non-existent. The producers are trapped in activities characterized by low returns. Therefore, technological retrogression presupposes lock-in of the producers either because mobility may be restricted or the producers may believe that they have nothing to gain by moving out.

Thus, I consider lock-in a structural precondition of technological retrogression. Situations where there are no outlets of labour which is made superfluous by technological modernization are in this thesis considered produced by a lock-in effect as described by Reinert (1980). In such situations, a retrogressive mobility of labour may occur – especially where the iron law of wages operates. Also, owners who have no other options may in lock-in situations resort to retrogression of tools. The lock-in period may be short, such as in the Norwegian cases described, or long, such as in the cases from the developing countries described. As regards other structural preconditions for technological retrogression, I am more reluctant to conclude. The phenomenon should not be linked to specific economic, political or social systems; I think that it may occur wherever technological heterogeneity is present – or where it can be recreated. The latter requires that knowledge of less labour productive technologies can be found. Then where should we look for technological retrogression? Technological retrogression results from individual action: by necessity, by choice or by profit opportunity. Technological heterogeneity should be present, or it should be possible to recreate technologies of the past. The precondition of lock-in, that technological retrogression occurs where outlet of labour to other industries to other industries are lacking, needs a qualification. Where producers retrograde by lifestyle choice and could easily have chosen otherwise, they may be said to have *locked themselves in*. Such cases are not described in this book. We are then left with necessity and profit opportunity.

Where the exploitation of natural resources has driven the economies into areas of diminishing returns, retrogression of tools as well as retrogressive mobility of labour may occur. Sectors subject to diminishing returns are typically agriculture, fisheries and mining where biological or other natural resources are exploited. As we have seen in the cases of fisheries, there is an important factor in addition to diminishing returns and increased price of input that spurs technological retrogression, namely the system of surplus distribution. If the effects of reduced profitability can be turned over to the workers, this may lead to retrogressive mobility of labour. The workers who (re) turn to less productive technology and thus to more equal systems of surplus distribution paradoxically earn more by producing less. With capitalism comes also the ruthlessly sorting of labour according to productivity, pushing some workers out of modern production.

Within manufacturing, some producers may be forced into diminishing returns. Technological modernization in other subsectors may lead to a drain of skilled labour from artisan production. This may lead marginalized producers to retrogression of tools. Increased competition may force technologically inferior producers to survive by technological retrogression and the poverty market.

The example of technological retrogression from Russia discussed in the introduction to this book, occurred because of a sudden and severe scarcity of input factors (including capital). The preconditions of technological retrogression should thus be present in post-Soviet economies.

The actual and hypothetical situations mentioned are technological retrogression by necessity. Then what about the third category, technological retrogression by profit opportunity? This concept should be reserved to capital owners in charge of the technology choice of the production unit. In later years, I have read with interest accounts of changes in European agriculture. Producers have access to migrant labour that are willing to work for a fraction of the 'normal' wage of European countries, and Schengen secures free movement of labour. If you add the fact that mechanization may be difficult and costly in agricultural production, increased labour intensity may be considered a viable solution. In addition, there is the workings of Say's law, that supply may create its own demand: Access to a vast pool of poor workers, willing to accept any wage and living conditions, may tempt farmers into technological retrogression by profit opportunity. Where unions are absent or weak and wages remain low, profits may increase. But they do not escape diminishing returns. Who is locked-in in such situations is an empirical question: Workers may judge that moving on geographically will not improve their lot, in which case their immobility is a result of the levelling out of the wage rate in Europe. But also, with the flow of cheap labour, prices of agricultural produce may reduce and competition increase. Reduced capital accumulation and therefore reduced mechanization may thus be a necessity rather than choice; owners as well as workers are 'stuck'.

To conclude on the *generality* of the process of technological retrogression is impossible. To investigate whether such processes have earlier been at work, as well as identifying them in contemporary settings, implies an inquiry into structural and contextual preconditions. Although I conclude on the *peripheral capitalist* nature of the societies in which I found the phenomenon, I am reluctant to claim that technological retrogression now may occur in developing countries only. The example from Norwegian fisheries shows that this can be found in the history of industrial countries, but here retrogression of tools was episodic. A substantial amount of research is needed to find out if technological retrogression is part of the anatomy of economic decline and thus found in many industries during economic crises. There may well be situations in centre capitalist societies in which an iron law of wages operates due to economic hardship. Changes from factory to manufacture production could be analysed in these terms: While at the same time labour productivity reduces, the owner's profits could increase. I believe, however, that technological retrogression will be more frequently found in developing countries. The justification is that technological heterogeneity, lock-in and the presence of an iron law of wages are prominent features of these societies. Furthermore, many developing countries are heavily dependent on export earnings from production based on the exploitation of natural resources and may therefore be more easily tempted into areas of diminishing returns than highly diversified, industrial economies.

Should evidence of technological retrogression be considered dystopian omens? Yes and no. Yes, because it signifies a reversal of modernization that historically has been the way out of poverty for billions of people. Going for low-tech, labour-intensive production runs counter to what has created wealth since the agricultural and industrial revolutions began. However, negative effects for long-term growth are probably the least of the producers' worries when they make the decision to reduce labour productivity or move from urban to rural occupations: It is positive for immediate survival: a means to a higher end, a changed lifestyle or an accumulation strategy of capital owners. And these categories may overlap – losing the job during a recession may spur lifestyle changes, as when the unemployed computer engineer turns to his grandfather's farm to survive.

This ambiguity regarding the effects of technological retrogression is not a product of *conceptual* shortcomings – there is no need for a concept of technological change which carries both progressive and retrogressive outcomes, but the development dilemma involved should be discussed: De-industrialization may lead to reindustrialization at a lower technological level, and technological retrogression may therefore be seen as expressions of *resilience*. However, this solution comes with a 'catch': low labour productivity limits opportunities for capital accumulation. Throughout the history of economic prosperity, we find technological modernization at the core. Capital strong production units innovate their way out of recessions through technological progress, adopting more advanced production equipment that improves productivity, forming virtuous spirals of growth. When producers resort to technologies which secure survival, but which result in low labour productivity, the possibility of capital accumulation diminishes and thus modernization that could form an escape from poverty: Vicious spirals of decline are formed. Therefore, reversal of technological modernization is closely related to marginalization of producers on the one hand, and increased inequality on the other; leading to social and economic decline.

Modernization in reverse

What, then, is the significance of the experiences of a few Sri Lankan and Malaysian fishermen, living in remote villages, far from any centre of power, who chose less productive technology than what I expected? What have I learned from studying their careers? I have described and analysed the living conditions of a negligible part of Asia's millions of fisherfolk. They are seen with Western eyes – with one general exception: I see nothing exotic or picturesque, neither in human, architectural nor technological manifestations of poverty, no matter how much sunshine is added. My eyes are, however, the only ones I have got. Besides, if making explicit Western prejudices as regards courses of technological change may contribute to killing the delusion of the poor but smiling villagers, happy with their primitive tools, then I have not worked in vain.

I do believe that differences in physical strength, intelligence, personality, preferences and skills *are* of importance. There are also social and cultural constraints to individual action. But the economic context decides whether such differences play prominent parts: A fisherman may be as skilled and needy for achievement as can be, but unless provided with an amount of capital, he will remain in his *sampan* with but a vision of his 50-ton trawler. The fishermen whose careers I have studied are very mobile in terms of technology, and they are eager to improve their lot. They are not culturally dependent traditionalists; they wish for a better life. Uncontrolled investments in modern technology may lead to increased dependence on fluctuating world market prices and the overexploitation and even destruction of resources. Economic growth may result, but also accelerating socio-economic inequality. My studies show that the penetration of capitalism has helped some producers out of poverty; but for how long will their riches last? And other producers are worse off than before. Being victims of a marginalization process, some producers have experienced a reversal of technological modernization. These fishermen are too few for a statistical proof. They are, however, too many for the technology choices they have made to be classified as whims of indecisive persons. Technological retrogression is part of a process of technological polarization, which is linked to socio-economic polarization. Therefore, I do not hesitate to take the examples of technological retrogression in

Sri Lankan and Malaysian fisheries as starting points for a reappraisal of the concepts of technological change and diffusion:

> On principle, it is quite wrong to try founding a theory on observable magnitudes alone. In reality the very opposite happens. It is the theory which decides what we can observe. (Albert Einstein in a conversation with Heisenberg, in Heisenberg 1971, 63)

REFERENCES

Abeydeera, W. P. P. 1980. Small-Scale Fisheries, Sri Lanka. Some facts pertaining to the Marketing of Marine Fish. *Marga Institute, Res/71–1.* Colombo.

Abramovitz, Moses. 1982. 'The Retreat from Economic Advance: Changing Ideas About Economic Progress'. In Gabriel A. Almond, Marvin Chodorow and Ray Harvey Pearce. *Progress and Its Discontents.* Berkeley: University of California Press, 253–80.

———. 1986. 'Catching Up, Forging Ahead, and Falling Behind'. *Journal of Economic History* 46 (2): 385–407.

Acheson, James. 1981. 'Anthropology of Fishing'. *Annual Review of Anthropology* 10: 275–316.

Alavi, Hamza. 1975. *India and the Colonial Mode of Production.* London: Merlin Press.

Alexander, Paul. 1975a. 'Innovation in a Cultural Vacuum: The Mechanization of Sri Lankan Fisheries'. *Human Organization* 34 (3): 333–44.

———. 1975b. 'Do Fisheries' Experts Aid Fisheries Development? The Case of Sri Lankan Fisheries'. *Maritime Studies and Management* 3(1): 5–11.

Amin, Samir. 1976. *Unequal Development.* Sussex: Hassocks.

———. 1984. 'Self-Reliance and the New International Economic Order'. In Herb Addo (ed.), *Transforming the World Economy: Nine Critical Essays on the New International Economic Order.* London: Hodder & Stoughton, 204–19.

Anand, Sudhir. 1983. *Inequality and Poverty in Malaysia: Measurement and Decomposition.* Kuala Lumpur: Oxford University Press.

Arrighi, Giovanni. 1970. 'Labor Supplies in Historical Perspective: A Study of the Proletarianization of the African Peasantry in Rhodesia'. *Journal of Development Studies* 6 (3): 197–234.

Asheim, Bjørn T. 1985. 'Capital Accumulation, Technological Development and the Spatial Division of Labour: A Framework for Analysis'. *Norsk Geografisk Tidsskrift* 39: 87–97.

Avinieri, Shlomo. 1969. *Karl Marx on Colonialism and Modernization.* New York: Anchor Books.

Bailey, Conner. 1983. *The Sociology of Production in Rural Malay Society.* Kuala Lumpur: Oxford University Press.

Balibar, Etienne. 1970. 'The Basic Concepts of Historical Materialism'. In Louis Althusser and Etienne Balibar (eds), *Reading Capital.* London: New Left Books, 199–208.

Banaji, Jairus. 1977. 'Modes of Production in a Materialist Conception of History'. *Capital and Class* 1 (3): 1–44.

Baran, Paul A. 1957. *The Political Economy of Growth.* New York: Modern Reader.

Bartra, Roger. 1979. 'Modes of Production and Agrarian Imbalances'. *International Social Science Journal* 31 (2): 226–36.

Bernard, H. Russell, Peter Killworth, David Kronenfeld and Lee Sailer. 1984. 'The Problem of Informant Accuracy: The Validity of Retrospective Data'. *Annual Review of Anthropology* 13: 495–517.

Bettelheim, Charles. 1972. 'Theoretical Comments'. In Arghiri Emmanuel (ed.), *Unequal Exchange: A Study of the Imperialism of Trade (Appendix I)*. New York: Monthly Review Press, xlii, 453.

Bjøru, Kirsten. 1982. *Share Systems in Fishing*. M.Phil. diss., University of Cambridge.

Bradby, Barbara. 1980. 'The Destruction of Natural Economy'. In Harold Wolpe (ed.), *The Articulation of Modes of Production*. London: Routledge & Kegan Paul, 93–127.

Braverman, Harry. 1974. *Labour and Monopoly Capital: The Degradation of Work in the Twentieth Century*. New York: Monthly Review Press.

Brenner, Robert. 1977. 'The Origins of Capitalist Development: A Critique of Neo-Smithian Marxism'. *New Left Review* I/104 (July/Aug.): 25–92.

Brenner, Yehojachin S. 1966. *Theories of Economic Development and Growth*. London: George Allen & Unwin.

Brue, Stanley L. 1994. *The Evolution of Economic Thought*, 5th edn. Fort Worth, TX: Dryden Press.

Bucksimir, A. H. 1982. Fishermen's Associations. *Dossier, No. 85. Centre for Society and Religion*. Colombo.

Bull, Edvard. 1988. 'Klassekamp og fellesskap 1920–1945.' In Knut Mykland (ed.). *Norges Historie* 13. Oslo: JW Cappelens forlag.

Cardoso, Ciro F. S. 1975. 'On the Colonial Modes of Production of the Americas'. *Critique of Anthropology* 2 (4–5): 1–37.

Carroll, Lewis. 1872. *Through the Looking Glass*. London: Puffin books, Penguin, 1981.

Christensen, James B. 1977. 'Motor Power and Women Power: Technological and Economic Change among the Fanti Fishermen of Ghana'. In M. Estellie Smith (ed.). *Those Who Live from the Sea. A Study in Maritime Anthropology*. The American Ethnological Society, Monograph 62. St. Paul, MN: West Publishing, 71–85.

Coquery-Vidrovitch, Catherine. 1975. 'Research on an African Mode of Production'. *Critique of Anthropology* 2 (4–5): 38–71.

Deere, Carmen D., and Alain de Janvry. 1979. 'A Conceptual Framework for the Empirical Analysis of Peasants'. *American Journal of Agricultural Economics* 61 (4): 601–11.

Dillard, Dudley, Lennart Jörberg and Synnöve Olsson. 1977. *Västeuropas och Förenta Staternas ekonomiska historia*. Lund: Liber Läromedel.

Dupré, Georges, and Pierre-Philippe Rey. 1980. 'Reflections on the Pertinence of a Theory of the History of Exchange'. In Harold Wolpe (ed.), *The Articulation of Modes of Production*. London: Routledge & Kegan Paul, 128–60.

Dyrvik, Ståle. 1988. 'Den lange fredstiden 1720–1784'. In Knut Mykland (ed.). *Norges Historie*. Vol. 8. Oslo: Cappelen.

Eisenstadt, Shmuel N. 1973. *Tradition, Change, and Modernity*. New York: John Wiley.

Elliston, George R. 1967. 'The Role of the Middleman in the Fishing Industry of West Malaysia'. *Review of Agricultural Economics Malaysia* 1: 16–33.

Emmerson, Donald K. 1980. 'Rethinking Artisanal Fisheries Development: Western Concepts, Asian Experiences'. *World Bank Staff Working Paper* No. 423.

Endresen, Sylvi B. 1983. 'Teknologisk endring og levekår. En studie av to fiskerlandsbyer på Sri Lanka'. *Hovedfagsoppgave i kulturgeografi. Geografisk institutt, Universitetet i Oslo*.

———. 1985. 'Technological Change and Level of Living. A Study of Two Fishing Villages in Southern Sri Lanka'. *Meddelelser fra Geografisk institutt, Universitetet i Oslo*.

———. 1987. Technological Retardation, a Neglected Field of Study? *Norsk geogr. Tidsskr* 41: 1–10.

————. 1988. 'Reconstruction of "Technological Pasts": An Appraisal of the "Work History Method"'. *Norsk geogr. Tidsskr* 42: 93–101.

————. 1994. 'Modernization Reversed? Technological Change in Four Asian Fishing Villages'. Dr. Philos. diss., University of Oslo.

Epple, George M. 1977. 'Technological Change in Grenada, W.I. Fishery, 1950–1970'. In Estellie M. Smith (ed.), *Those Who Live from the Sea. A Study in Maritime Anthropology*. The American Ethnological Society, Monograph 62. St. Paul, MN: West Publishing, 173–93.

Eriksen, Thomas H. 1991. 'Den paradoksale fremskrittstroen'. In Kristin Clemet, Martin Eide, Trond Berg Eriksen, Thomas Hylland Eriksen, Anders Johansen, and Sissel Myklebust (eds), *Tror vi fortsatt på fremskrittet? En antologi*. Oslo: Aschehoug Argument, 66–99.

Fernando, U. F. N., and W. P. P. Abeydeera. 1980. 'An Introduction to the Trade Sector Operations in the Small-Scale Fishery of Sri Lanka'. *Marga Institute, SEM/100/80(6)*. Colombo.

Firth, Raymond. 1939. *Primitive Polynesian Economy*. London: Routledge.

————. 1966. *Malay Fishermen. Their Peasant Economy*. London: Routledge & Kegan Paul.

————. 1981. 'Asian Fisheries'. *Royal Anthropological Institute News* 47: 3–4.

Fisheries Department. 1984. *Annual Fisheries Statistics 1983*. Ministry of Agriculture, Kuala Lumpur.

Foster-Carter, Aidan. 1978. 'The Modes of Production Controversy'. *New Left Review* I/107 (Jan./Feb.): 47–77.

Frank, Andre Gunder. 1969. *Capitalism and Underdevelopment in Latin America*. New York: Monthly Review Press.

Fredericks, Leo J., and Raymond J. G. Wells. 1980. 'Marine Fisheries Policy Planning in West Malaysia'. *Journal of Development Areas* 15 (1): 3–20.

Fredericks, Leo J., Sulochana Nair and Jahara Yahaya.1985. 'Small-Scale Fisheries in Peninsular Malaysia: Socioeconomic Profile and Income Distribution'. In Theodore Panayotou (ed.), *Small-Scale Fisheries in Asia. Socioeconomic Analysis and Policy*. Ottawa: International Development Research Centre.

Fredericks, Leo J., and Sulochana Nair. 1985. 'Production Technology of Small-Scale Fisheries in Peninsular Malaysia'. In Theodore Panayotou (ed.). *Small-Scale Fisheries in Asia. Socioeconomic Analysis and Policy*. Ottawa: International Development Research Centre, 121–27.

Galtung, Johan. 1974. 'En strukturell teori om imperialisme'. In Johan Galtung. *Fred, vold og imperialisme. 6 essays i fredsforskning*. Oslo: Dreyer: 122–61.

————. 1980. 'Development from Above and the Blue Revolution: The Indo–Norwegian Project in Kerala'. *Peace Problems: Some Case Studies*. Oslo: PRIO Publication No. 2–12, 343–60.

Gibbons, David S. 1977. 'Public Policy towards Fisheries Development in Peninsular Malaysia. A Critical Review Emphasising Penang and Kedah'. Paper presented at the Malaysian Economic Association's Seminar on the Development of the Fisheries Industry, Universiti Kebangsaan Malaysia, Kuala Lumpur, January 10–13.

Giddens, Anthony. 1984. *The Constitution of Society: Outline of the Theory of Structuration*. Cambridge, MA: Polity Press.

Gill, N. S. 2020. '*Who Was the Ancient Roman God Janus?*' ThoughtCo, Feb. 11. thoughtco. com/ancient-roman-god-janus-112605.

Godelier, Maurice. 1977. *Perspectives in Marxist Anthropology.* Cambridge: Cambridge University Press.

Goonewardena, T. P. 1980. A Survey of some of Sri Lanka's State-Aided Development Programmes in the Fisheries Sector. Marga Institute, SEM/100/80(4). Colombo.

Goulet, Denis. 1971. *The Cruel Choice: A New Concept in the Theory of Development.* New York: Atheneum.

Hardin, Garrett. 1968. 'The Tragedy of the Commons'. *Science* 162 (3859): 1243–48.

Harrison, David. 1988. *The Sociology of Modernization and Development.* London: Unwin Hyman.

Hassan, Sharifah Z. 1977. 'Institution vs. Technology in the Fishing Industry: A Case Study'. Paper presented at the Malaysian Economic Association's seminar on the Development of the Fisheries Industry, Universiti Kebangsaan Malaysia, Kuala Lumpur, January 10–13.

Heisenberg, Werner. 1971. *Physics and Beyond.* New York: Harper & Row.

Hesselberg, Jan. 1986. 'Myten om avhengighetsperspektivets død'. *Internasjonal Politikk* 4–5: 119–39.

Hindess, Barry, and Paul Hirst. 1975. *Pre-Capitalist Modes of Production.* London: Routledge & Kegan Paul.

Hirschman, Albert O. 1958. *The Strategy of Economic Development.* New Haven, CT: Yale University Press.

Hodne, Fritz. 1979. 'Dualøkonomimodellen og langtidslinjene i økonomisk utvikling'. *Historisk Tidsskrift, Nr. 4.*

Høst, Iens L. 1980. 'Teknologisk involusjon. Teknologiske, praktiske og sosiologiske perspektiver i analysen av arbeid på tråler'. In Iens L. Høst and Cato Wadel (eds), *Fiske og lokalsamfunn.* Oslo: Universitetsforlaget, 43–75.

Janvry, Alain de, and Carlos Garramón. 1977. 'Laws of Motion of Capital in the Center-Periphery Structure'. *Review of Radical Political Economics* 9 (2): 29–38.

Jensen, Inge. 1988. *Marxistisk utviklingsteori og analyse av empiriske data.* Geografisk Institutt, Universitetet i Oslo.

Jomo, Kwame S.1991. 'Fishing for Trouble. Malaysian Fisheries, Sustainable Development and Inequality'. Occasional Papers and Reports: KLB. No. 3. Institute for Advanced Studies, University of Malaya.

Kalugina, Z. I. 2014. Agricultural Policy in Russia: Global Challenges and the Viability of Rural Communities. *The International Journal of Sociology of Agriculture and Food* 21 (1): 115–31.

Karunaratne, W. D. M. 1979. Catamaran's Dramatic Come-back. *Ceylon Daily News,* 28th of August.

Kurien, John. 1978. 'Entry of Big Business into Fishing. Its impact on Fish Economy'. *Economic and Political Weekly* 13 (36): 1557–76.

Laclau, Ernesto. 1971. 'Feudalism and Capitalism in Latin America'. *New Left Review* I/67 (May–June): 19–38.

Leeson, Phil F. 1982. 'The Lewis Model and Development Theory'. In T. E. Barker, A. S. Downes and J. A. Sackey (eds), *Perspectives on Economic Development. Essays in the Honour of W. Arthur Lewis.* Lanham, MD: University Press of America, 1–20.

Lerner, Daniel. 1958. *The Passing of Traditional Society.* New York: Free Press.

Levy, Marion. Jr. 1966. *Modernization and the Structure of Societies.* Princeton, NJ: Princeton University Press.

Lewis, W. Arthur. 1954. *Economic Development with Unlimited Supplies of Labour.* Manchester: Manchester School of Economic and Social Studies.

Ling, Yap C. 1976. 'Fishery Policies and Development with Special Reference to the West Coast of Peninsular Malaysia from the Early 1900's'. *Kajian Ekonomi Malaysia* 13 (1–2): 9–14.

———. 1978a. 'The Diseconomy of Technological Progress: A Note on Fishery Regulations'. Paper presented at the Regional Conference on Technology for Rural Development, Kuala Lumpur, April 24–29.

———. 1978b. 'Employment in the Fishing Industry: Some Preliminary Findings on Fishermen's Mobility'. *The Developing Economies* 16 (3), September. Tokyo. LKIM. 1985. *Rancangan Perspektif Bagi KPN Kuala Kedah*. Bahagian Perancang, Majuikan, Kuala Lumpur.

Lloyd, Peter E., and Peter Dicken. 1972. *Location in Space: A Theoretical Approach to Economic Geography*. New York: Harper & Row.

———. 1977. *Location in Space: A Theoretical Approach to Economic Geography*. 2nd edn. New York: Harper & Row.

Löfgren, O. 1972. 'Resource Management and Family Firms: Swedish West Coast Fishermen'. In R. Andersen and C. Wadel (eds), *North Atlantic Fishermen: Anthropological Essays on Modern Fishing*. Toronto: University of Toronto Press, 82–103.

Luxemburg, Rosa. 1913. 'Reproduksjonen av Kapitalen og dens omgivelser. Utdrag fra kapitalens akkumulasjon'. *Skrifter i utvalg* Vol 2. Oslo: Pax, 1973.

Majuikan. 1983. *Perspective Plan for Pekan Fishermen Development Area*. Kuala Lumpur: Majuikan.

Marshall, Alfred. 1890. *Principles of Economics*. Amherst, NY: Great Minds Series, 1997.

Marx, Karl. 1867a. *Forord til første utgave av Kapitalen, Første Bok*. Oslo: Fram Forlag, 1932.

———. 1867b. *Capital Vol. I*. Moscow: Foreign Languages Publishing House, 1961.

———. 1885. *Capital Vol. II*. Moscow: Foreign Language Publishing House, 1961.

———. 1894. *Capital Vol. III*. Moscow: Foreign Language Publishing House, 1962.

Marx, Karl, and Friedrich Engels. 1848. 'The Manifesto of the Communist Party'. *Selected Works*. Vol. 1. Moscow: Foreign Languages Publishing House, 1962.

McClelland, David C. 1961. *The Achieving Society*. New York: Free Press.

Meillassoux, Claude. 1980. 'From Reproduction to Production: A Marxist Approach to Economic Anthropology'. In Harold Wolpe (ed.), *The Articulation of Modes of Production*. London: Routledge & Kegan Paul, 189–201.

Mel, B. de. 1976. The Present and Future Role of Fish Satisfying Nutritional Needs in Sri Lanka. *Country Monograph Series, No. 4*. Colombo.

Merlijn, Alexander G. 1989. 'The Role of Middlemen in Small-scale Fisheries: A Case Study of Sarawak, Malaysia'. *Development and Change* 20 (4): 683–700.

Meynen, W. 1989. 'Fisheries Development, Resources Depletion and Political Mobilization in Kerala: The Problem of Alternatives'. *Development and Change* 20 (4): 735–70.

Ministry of Agriculture and Co-operatives. 1970. *The Proposed Objectives and Plans of the Division of Fisheries for the Second Malaysia Plan (1971–75)*. Kuala Lumpur: Ministry of Agriculture and Co-operatives.

Ministry of Fisheries. 1972a. *Socio-economic Conditions of the Fishing Population. Report on the Census of Fisheries. Part III*. Colombo: Ministry of Fisheries.

———. 1972b. *Survey of the Capacity Utilization in Fishing Industry. Beruwala and Mirissa*. Colombo: Ministry of Fisheries.

———. 1977. *Fisheries Development Project. 1977: Hambantota District Statistics. District Fisheries Committee*. Hambantota. Colombo: Ministry of Fisheries.

———. 1980. *Master Plan for the Development of Fisheries in Sri Lanka. 1979–1983*. Colombo: Ministry of Fisheries.

Ministry of Plan Implementation. 1982. *Labour Force and Socio-Economic Survey 1980/ 81. Preliminary Report. Department of Census and Statistics*. Colombo: Ministry of Plan Implementation.

Munasinghe, H., H. P. Karunagoda, W. Gamage and S. Fernando. 1980. 'Socio-Economic Conditions of Small-Scale Fishermen in Sri Lanka'. *Marga Institute, SEM/100/80(3)*. Colombo.

Munro, Gordon R. and Kim L. Chee. 1978. *The Economics of Fishing and the Developing World. A Malaysian Case Study*. The School of Comparative Social Sciences, Penang.

Myrdal, Gunnar. 1957. *Economic Theory and Under-developed Regions*. London: Gerald Duckworth.

Nabseth, Lars and George F. Ray (eds). 1974. *The Diffusion of New Industrial Processes: An International Study*. Cambridge: Cambridge University Press.

Nieuwenhuys, Olga. 1989. 'Invisible Nets: Women and Children in Kerala's Fishing'. *MAST Maritime Anthropological Studies* 2 (2): 174–93.

Nisbet, Robert. 2009. *History of the Idea of Progress*. New Brunswick: Transaction.

Nowak, Stefan. 1990. 'Models of Directional Change and Human Values: The Theory of Progress as an Applied Social Science'. In Jeffrey Alexander and Piotr Sztompka (eds), *Rethinking Progress. Movements, forces, and ideas at the end of the 20th Century*. London: Unwin Hyman, 229–46.

Ooi, San K. 1970. *A Study of the Fishing Industry in Penang*. E. Econ. diss., University of Malaya.

Palmer, Craig T. 1989. 'The Ritual Taboos of Fisherman: An Alternative Explanation'. *MAST. Maritime Anthropological Studies* 2 (1): 15–28.

Papalexiou, Olga. 2015. 'The Persistence of Poverty in Rural Russia. A Critical Discourse Analysis of the Consequences of the Agrarian Reforms and the Causes of Poverty Among the Agrarian Population in Russia, period 1992–2014'. MA Thesis, University of Oslo.

Parsons, Talcott. 1951. *The Social System*. Glencoe, IL: Free Press.

People's Bank. 1977. *Survey of Sri Lankan Fisheries*. People's Bank Research Department. Colombo: People's Bank.

Perez, Carlota. 1985. 'Microelectronics, Long Waves and World Structural Change: New Perspectives for Developing Countries?' *World Development* 13 (3): 441–63.

Platteau, Jean-Philippe. 1989. 'The Dynamics of Fisheries Development in Developing Countries: A General Overview'. *Development and Change* 20 (4): 565–98.

Raychaudhuri, Bikash. 1980. *The Moon and the Net: Study of a Transient Community of fishermen at Jambudwip*. Anthropological Survey of India, Calcutta.

Reinert, Erik S. 1980. *International Trade and the Economic Mechanisms of Underdevelopment*. Ann Arbor, MI: University Microfilms.

———. 2004. 'Globalisation in the Periphery as a Morgenthau Plan: The Underdevelopment of Mongolia in the 1990s'. In Erik S. Reinert (ed.), *Globalization, Economic Development, and Inequality*. An Alternative Perspective. Cheltenham: Edward Elgar, 157–214.

———. 2007. *How Rich Countries Get Rich ... and Why Poor Countries Stay Poor*. London: Constable.

Reinert, Erik S., Sylvi B. Endresen, Ioan Ianos and Andrea Saltelli (2016). 'The Future of Economic Development between Utopias and Dystopias'. In Erik S. Reinert, Jayati Gosh and Rainer Kattel (eds), *Elgar Handbook of Alternative Theories of Economic Development*. Cheltenham: Edward Elgar, 738–86.

Ricardo, David. 1817. *Principles of Political Economy and Taxation*. London: Everyman's Library.

Rostow, Walt W. 1971. 'The Take-off into Self-sustained Growth'. In Alan B. Mountjoy (ed.), *Developing the Underdeveloped Countries*. London: Macmillan, 86–114.

Ruccio, David F., and Lawrence H. Simon. 1986. 'Methodological Aspects of a Marxian Approach to Development: An Analysis of the Modes of Production School'. *World Development* 14 (2): 211–22.

Sahlins, Marshall D., and Elman R. Service. 1960. *Evolution and Culture*. Ann Arbor: University of Michigan Press.

Sang-Bok, Han. 1977. *Korean Fishermen. Ecological Adaptation in Three Communities*. Seoul: Seoul National University Press.

Schumacher, Ernst F. 1973. *Small Is Beautiful*. London: Blond & Briggs.

Schumpeter, Joseph. 1934. *The Theory of Economic Development. An inquiry into Profits, Capital, Credit, Interest, and the Business Cycle*. London: Routledge, 2017.

Scott, Christopher D. 1976. 'Peasants, Proletarianization and the Articulation of Modes of Production: The Case of Sugar Cane Cutters in Northern Peru, 1940–69'. *Journal of Peasant Studies* 3 (3): 321–41.

Sejersted, Francis. 1979. 'Norsk økonomi etter krigen med særlig vekt på strukturendringene i industrien'. Seminar paper. Historisk Institutt, Universitetet i Oslo.

Silva, M.W. Amarasiri de. 1977. 'Structural Change in a Coastal Fishing Village in Southern Sri Lanka'. *Marga Quarterly Journal* 4 (2): 13–27.

Singer, Hans and Javed Ansari. 1978. *Rich and Poor Countries*. 2nd edn. London: George Allen & Unwin.

Snodgrass, Donald R. 1980. *Inequality and Economic Development in Malaysia*. Kuala Lumpur: Oxford University Press.

Soete, Luc. 1985. 'International Diffusion of Technology, Industrial Development and Technological Leapfrogging'. *World Development* 13 (3): 409–22.

Spengen, Wim van. 1992. 'Tibetan Border Worlds. A Geo-Historical Analysis of Trade and Traders'. PhD diss., Universiteit van Amsterdam.

Standing, Guy. 1984. 'The Notion of Technological Unemployment'. *International Labour Review* 123 (2): 127–47.

Stigler, George J. 1961. 'Economic Problems in Measuring Changes in Productivity'. In John W. Kendrick (ed.), *Output, Input, and Productivity Measurement. Studies in Income and Wealth. The Conference on Research in Income and Wealth. Vol. 25*: 47–78. New York: National Bureau of Economic Research.

Stirrat, Roderick. L. 1974. 'Fish to Market: Traders in Rural Sri Lanka'. *South Asian Review: Journal of the Royal Society for India, Pakistan and Ceylon* 7 (3), 189–207.

———. 1977. 'The Social Organization of Fishing in a Sinhalese Village'. *Ethnos* 42 (3–4): 122–48.

Sudman, Seymour, and Norman M. Bradburn. 1973. 'Effects of Time and Memory Factors on Response in Surveys'. *Journal of the American Statistical Association* 68 (344): 805–15.

Sutinen, Jon G. 1979. 'Fishermen's Remuneration Systems and Implications for Fisheries Development'. *Scottish Journal of Political Economy* 26 (2): 147–62.

Sztompka, Piotr. 1990. 'Agency and Progress: The Idea of Progress and Changing Theories of Change'. In Jeffrey Alexander and Piotr Sztompka (eds), *Rethinking Progress: Movements, Forces, and Ideas at the End of the 20th Century*. London: Unwin Hyman, 247–64.

Sætersdal, G. S., and G. H. P. de Bruin. 1978. Report on a Survey of the Coastal Fish Resources of Sri Lanka. *Reports on Surveys with the R/V 'Dr Fridtjof Nansen'. Fisheries Research Station, Colombo / Institute of Marine Research, Bergen*.

Taylor, John G. 1979. *From Modernization to Modes of Production: A Critique of the Sociologies of Development and Underdevelopment*. London: Macmillan.

Taylor, Peter J. 1992. 'Understanding Global Inequalities: A World-System Approach'. *Geography* 77: 10–21.

Terray, Emmanuel. 1972. *Marxism and 'Primitive Societies'*. New York: Monthly Review Press.

Tregenna, Fiona. 2016. 'De-industrialisation and Premature De-industrialisation'. In Erik Reinert, Jayati Ghosh and Rainer Kattel (eds), *Elgar Handbook of Alternative Theories of Economic Development*. Cheltenham: Edward Elgar, 710–28.

Vercruijsse, Emile. 1984. *The Penetration of Capitalism: A West African Case Study*. London: Zed Books.

Warren, Bill and John Sender. 1980. *Imperialism, Pioneer of Capitalism*. London: Verso.

Weber, Max 1971. *Makt og byråkrati. Essays om politikk og klasse, samfunnsforskning og verdier*. Oslo: Gyldendal.

White, Leslie A. 1959. *The Evolution of Culture*. New York: McGraw-Hill.

Wolpe, Harold (Ed.). 1980. *The Articulation of Modes of Production: Essays from Economy and Society*. London: Routledge &Kegan Paul.

Yahaya, Jahara. 1976. 'The Socio-Economic Impact of the Trawler Fishing Industry in Malaysia'. *Occasional Papers on Malaysian Socio-Economic Affairs* No. 5. Faculty of Economics and Administration, University of Malaya.

———. 1978. 'Technology and the Fishing Labour Force. Scarcity or Surplus?' Paper presented at the Regional Conference on Technology for Rural Development, Kuala Lumpur, April 24–29.

———. 1981. 'Capture Fisheries in Peninsular Malaysia. Lessons from Majuikan's Experience'. *Marine Policy*, October.

Yahaya, Jahara, and Raymond J. G. Wells. 1982. 'A Case Study of Costs and Earnings of Three Gears in the Trengganu Fishery, Malaysia'. *Developing Economies* 20 (I): 73–99.

Yusuf, Z. 1988. 'Coastal Fishermen's Hardships Worsen'. *Suara Sam* 5 (2).

INDEX

Lightning Source UK Ltd.
Milton Keynes UK
UKHW012159250521
384369UK00001B/59